CELEBRATING THE SAINTS

CELEBRATING THE SAINTS

Readings and Prayers
in Honor of the Saints and the Solemnities
of Our Lord and Our Lady

Adapted from the Liturgy of the Hours

PUEBLO PUBLISHING COMPANY

New York

Nihil Obstat:
Daniel V. Flynn, J.C.D.
Censor Librorum

Imprimatur:
Joseph T. O'Keefe
Vicar General, Archdiocese of New York
June 12, 1978

Design: Frank Kacmarcik, D.F.A.

Excerpts from the English translation of the Roman Missal
© 1973, International Committee on English in the
Liturgy, Inc. (ICEL); excerpts from the English translation
of the Liturgy of the Hours © 1974, ICEL. All rights
reserved.

ISBN: 0-916134-30-X

Copyright © 1978 Pueblo Publishing Company, Inc.
1860 Broadway, New York, N.Y. 10023. All rights reserved.

Printed in the United States of America

TABLE OF CONTENTS

PREFACE

Devotion to the saints, the heroes of the Christian life, dates from the earliest ages of the Church, and has been a source of inspiration and help for the people of God; thus the celebration of the saints acts "as a source of devotion and nourishment for personal prayer" (Second Vatican Council, Constitution on the Sacred Liturgy, no. 90).

This book follows the structure of the Proper of the Saints in the Liturgy of the Hours as set forth in the Roman Calendar: there is first a brief sketch of the life of the saint; then a reading from the Fathers, traditional church writers, or the saint himself; a responsory type of reflection; and finally, the prayer of the Mass of the day. In some cases only portions of the readings are given to insure a more direct appeal to a modern community unaccustomed to the sometimes complex style of writers from other cultures and ages. Also included are celebrations in honor of the major mysteries in the life of our Lord and the Blessed Virgin.

The code of rubrics divides the above celebrations into three classes, plus a fourth for saints of lesser importance, namely, a commemoration in the office of the day.

The three main classes of celebration are as follows: "solemnity," "feast," and "memorial," with the latter being either "obligatory" or "optional." Solemnities are and should be truly festive days, whereas a memorial is a single remembrance of a saint on his spiritual birthday. Solemnities and feasts are held by way of exception; memorials are part of daily liturgical life.

As regards the saints themselves, they have various titles:

1. Traditional titles — apostle, evangelist, martyr, virgin.
2. Titles of hierarchical rank — bishop (pope), presbyter (priest), deacon. The title "doctor of the Church" is also given to various saints who were great writers or teachers.

3. Titles of rank within an order — abbot (monk, hermit), religious. The term "religious" refers to those who were not presbyters and to women who were married before entering an order; otherwise women religious are known by the title "virgin."

We have edited this book as a source of texts not only for public reading, but for private devotion as well. Although the biographical details of many of the saints are limited, the readings and prayers from the official liturgical texts will serve as an enrichment for any gathering of the faithful.

January 1

OCTAVE OF CHRISTMAS

MARY, MOTHER OF GOD
Solemnity

Today the Church celebrates the great part the Virgin Mary played in the events which we recalled on Christmas. She is the mother of God. As Saint Paul says: "God sent forth his Son, born of woman" so that we might become adopted sons and daughters of the Father. And so today we honor Mary: not only as God's mother, but our mother too.

READING

A reading from a letter by Saint Athanasius, bishop.

Our Savior truly became man, and from this has followed the salvation of man as a whole. Our salvation is in no way fictitious, nor does it apply only to the body. The salvation of the whole man, that is, of soul and body, has really been achieved in the Word himself.

What was born of Mary was therefore human by nature, and the body of the Lord was a true body: It was a true body because it was the same as ours. Mary, you see, is our sister, for we are all born from Adam.

Man's body has acquired something great through its communion and union with the Word. From being mortal it has been made immortal; though it was a living body it has become a spiritual one; though it was made from the earth it has passed through the gates of heaven.

RESPONSORY

O pure and holy Virgin,
how can I find words to praise your beauty?

1

The highest heavens cannot contain God whom you carried
in your womb.

Blessed are you among women,
and blessed is the fruit of your womb.

The highest heavens cannot contain God whom you carried
in your womb.

PRAYER

God our Father,
may we always profit by the prayers
of the Virgin Mother Mary,
for you bring us life and salvation
through Jesus Christ her Son
who lives and reigns with you and the Holy Spirit,
one God, for ever and ever.

Our Father . . .

January 2

BASIL THE GREAT AND GREGORY NAZIANZEN,
BISHOPS AND DOCTORS
Memorial

Basil was born of a Christian family at Caesarea in Asia Minor in
330. He was outstanding for his learning and virtue. For a time
he led the life of a hermit but in 370 was made bishop of
Caesarea. He fought against the Arians and wrote many fine
works, especially his monastic rule which many Eastern monks
still follow. Saint Basil died on January 1, 379.

Gregory Nazianzen was also born in 330. Traveling as a youth in
the pursuit of learning, he first joined his friend Basil as a hermit
and was later ordained priest and bishop. In the year 381 he was
elected bishop of Constantinople; however, because of factions

dividing the Church, he returned to Nazianzen where he died on January 25, 389 or 390.

A reading from a sermon by Saint Gregory Nazianzen, bishop.

Basil and I, were both in Athens. We had come, like streams of a river, from the same source in our native land, had separated from each other in pursuit of learning, and were now united again as if by plan, for God so arranged it.

When, in the course of time, we acknowledged our friendship and recognized that our ambition was a life of true wisdom, we became everything to each other: we shared the same lodging, the same table, the same desires, the same goal. Our love for each other grew daily warmer and deeper.

The same hope inspired us: the pursuit of learning. We seemed to be two bodies with a single spirit. Our single object and ambition was virtue, and a life of hope in the blessings that are to come.

We followed the guidance of God's law and spurred each other on to virtue. If it is not too boastful to say, we found in each other a standard and rule for discerning right from wrong.

Different men have different names, which they owe to their parents or to themselves, that is, to their own pursuits and achievements. But our great pursuit, the great name we wanted, was to be Christians, to be called Christians.

The Lord gives wisdom to the wise
and knowledge to those who have understanding.

He reveals what is deep and hidden;
all light has its source in him.

One and the same Spirit is at work in all,
and he gives to each as he wills.

He reveals what is deep and hidden;
all light has its source in him.
Daniel 2:21-22, 1 Corinthians 12:11

PRAYER

God our Father,
you inspired the Church
with the example and teaching of your saints Basil and Gregory.
In humility may we come to know your truth
and put it into action with faith and love.

Grant this through our Lord Jesus Christ, your Son,
who lives and reigns with you and the Holy Spirit,
one God, for ever and ever.

Our Father . . .

The Sunday between January 2 and January 8

EPIPHANY
Solemnity

On this day we call to mind the story in Saint Matthew's gospel
of how the wise men from the East came to worship the child
Jesus. They were led by a star, Saint Matthew tells us. We may
look upon this story as telling us that God was leading the
peoples of the world to discover Jesus, who would be their
savior.

READING

A reading from a sermon by Saint Leo the Great, pope.

[God] decreed that all nations should be saved in Christ.

Dear friends, now that we have received instruction in this revelation of God's grace, let us celebrate with spiritual joy the day of our first harvesting, of the first calling of the Gentiles. Let us give thanks to the merciful God, "who has made us worthy," in the words of the Apostle, "to share the position of the saints in light; who has rescued us from the power of darkness, and brought us into the kingdom of his beloved Son."

This came to be fulfilled, as we know, from the time when the star beckoned the three wise men out of their distant country and led them to recognize and adore the King of heaven and earth. The obedience of the star calls us to imitate its humble service: to be servants, as best we can, of the grace that invites all men to find Christ.

RESPONSORY

This is the glorious day on which Christ himself, the savior of
    the world, appeared;
the prophets foretold him, the angels worshiped him;

the Magi saw his star and rejoiced to lay their treasures at his feet.

God's holy day has dawned for us at last;
come, all you peoples, and adore the Lord.

The Magi saw his star and rejoiced to lay their treasures at his feet.

PRAYER

Father,
you revealed your Son to the nations
by the guidance of a star.
Lead us to your glory in heaven
by the light of faith.

We ask this through our Lord Jesus Christ, your Son,
who lives and reigns with you and the Holy Spirit,
one God, for ever and ever.

Our Father . . .

January 4

ELIZABETH ANN SETON
Memorial

Elizabeth Seton was born on August 28, 1774, of a wealthy and
distinguished Episcopalian family. She was baptized in the
Episcopalian faith and was a faithful adherent of the Episcopal
Church until her conversion to Catholicism. In 1794, Elizabeth
married William Seton and they reared five children amid suffering and sickness. Elizabeth and her sick husband traveled to
Leghorn, Italy, and there William died. While in Italy Elizabeth
became acquainted with Catholicism and in 1805 she made her
profession of faith in the Catholic Church. She established her
first Catholic school in Baltimore in 1808; in 1809, she established a religious community in Emmitsburg, Maryland. After
seeing the expansion of her small community of teaching sisters
to New York and as far as St. Louis, she died on January 4, 1821
and was declared a saint by Pope Paul VI on September 14, 1975.

READING

A reading from the writings of Elizabeth Ann Seton.

What was the first rule of our dear Savior's life? You know it was
to do his Father's will. Well, then, the first purpose of our daily
work is to do the will of God; secondly, to do it in the manner he
wills; and thirdly, to do it because it is his will.

We know certainly that our God calls us to a holy life. We know
that he gives us every grace, every abundant grace; and though
we are so weak of ourselves, this grace is able to carry us

6

through every obstacle and difficulty.

RESPONSORY

The time is growing short,
so we must rejoice as though we were not rejoicing;
we must work in the world yet without becoming immersed in
    it,
for the world as we know it is passing away.

We have not adopted the spirit of the world.
For the world as we know it is passing away.
1 *Corinthians 7:29, 30, 31; 2:12*

PRAYER

Lord God,
you blessed Elizabeth Seton with gifts of grace
as wife and mother, educator and foundress,
so that she might spend her life in service to your people.
Through her example and prayers
may we learn to express our love for you
in love for our fellow men and women.

We ask this through our Lord Jesus Christ, your Son,
who lives and reigns with you and the Holy Spirit,
one God, for ever and ever.

Our Father . . .

January 5
JOHN NEUMANN, BISHOP
Memorial

John Neumann was born in Bohemia on March 20, 1811. Since
he had a great desire to dedicate himself to the American mis-

7

sions, he came to the United States as a cleric and was ordained in New York in 1836 by Bishop Dubois. In 1840, he entered the Congregation of the Most Holy Redeemer (Redemptorists). He labored in Ohio, Pennsylvania and Maryland. In 1852, he was consecrated bishop of Philadelphia. There he worked hard for the establishment of parish schools and for the erection of many parishes for the numerous immigrants. Bishop Neumann died on January 5, 1860. He was beatified in 1963, and canonized in 1977.

The following reading sums up the spirit that guided Saint Paul, just as it guided Bishop John Neumann.

READING

A reading from the Acts of the Apostles.

Paul called together certain pastors of the Church, and said to them:
"You know how I lived among you; how I served the Lord in humility through the sorrows and trials that came my way. Never did I shrink from telling you what was for your own good, or from teaching you in public or in private. I insisted on repentance before God and on faith in our Lord Jesus."

"I put no value on my life if only I can finish my race and complete the service to which I have been assigned by the Lord Jesus, bearing witness to God's grace."
Acts 20:17ff.

RESPONSORY

Well done, my good and faithful servant;
you have been faithful in the little tasks I gave you;
now I will entrust you with greater ones.
Come and share my joy.

Lord, you gave me five coins,

and see, I bring you back double.

Come and share my joy.

Matthew 25:21, 20

PRAYER

Father,
you called Bishop John Neumann to labor for the gospel
among the people of the new world.
His ministry strengthened many others in the Christian faith:
through his prayers may faith grow strong in this land.

Grant this through our Lord Jesus Christ, your Son,
who lives and reigns with you and the Holy Spirit,
one God, for ever and ever.

Our Father . . .

January 7

RAYMOND OF PENYAFORT, PRIEST

Raymond of Penyafort was born near Barcelona around 1175. He
became an official of the diocese of Barcelona and afterward
joined the Order of Preachers. At the command of Pope Gregory
IX, he produced a collection of canon law. He was elected general of his order and directed it wisely. His most important work
is a book about the sacrament of penance. He died in 1275.

READING

A reading from a letter by Saint Raymond, priest.

Look then on Jesus, the author and preserver of faith: in complete sinlessness he suffered, and at the hands of those who
were his own, and was numbered among the wicked. As you
drink the cup of the Lord Jesus (how glorious it is!), give thanks
to the Lord, the giver of all blessings.

9

May the God of love and peace set your hearts at rest and speed you on your journey; may he meanwhile shelter you from disturbance by others in the hidden recesses of his love, until he brings you at last into that place of complete plenitude where you will repose for ever in the vision of peace, in the security of trust and in the restful enjoyment of his riches.

RESPONSORY

The light of his teaching has shone on those who dwelt in darkness.

By the strength of his love he has delivered the poor and freed captives from their chains.

He led out those who wandered in the paths of sin, and freed the poor man from the grasp of his oppressors.

By the strength of his love he has delivered the poor and freed captives from their chains.

PRAYER

Lord,
you gave Saint Raymond the gift of compassion
in his ministry to sinners.
May his prayers free us from the slavery of sin
and help us to love and serve you in liberty.

We ask this through our Lord Jesus Christ, your Son,
who lives and reigns with you and the Holy Spirit,
one God, for ever and ever.

Our Father . . .

The Sunday after January 6

BAPTISM OF THE LORD
Feast

This feast celebrates the baptism of the Lord by John. Saint Matthew tells us that after John had baptized Jesus the sky opened and "he saw the Spirit of God descend like a dove and hover over him" (Matthew 3:16). This was a sign the Father was making Jesus the one who would bring salvation to all men through baptism into his Church.

READING

A reading from a sermon by Saint Gregory of Nazianzus, bishop.

Today let us do honor to Christ's baptism and celebrate this feast in holiness. Be cleansed entirely and continue to be cleansed. Nothing gives such pleasure to God as the conversion and salvation of men, for whom his every word and every revelation exist. He wants you to become a living force for all mankind, lights shining in the world. You are to be radiant lights as you stand beside Christ, the great light, bathed in the glory of him who is the light of heaven. You are to enjoy more and more the pure and dazzling light of the Trinity, as now you have received—though not in its fullness—a ray of its splendor, proceeding from the one God, in Christ Jesus our Lord, to whom be glory and power for ever and ever. Amen.

RESPONSORY

Today in the Jordan as the Lord was baptized,
the heavens opened and the Spirit in the form of a dove rested
    upon him;
the voice of the Father was heard;

This is my beloved Son in whom I am well pleased.

The Spirit descended in visible form as a dove,

and a voice from heaven was heard:

This is my beloved Son in whom I am well pleased.
Matthew 3:16, 17; Luke 3:22

PRAYER

Almighty, eternal God,
when the Spirit descended upon Jesus
at his baptism in the Jordan,
you revealed him as your own beloved Son.
Keep us, your children born of water and the Spirit,
faithful to our calling.

We ask this through our Lord Jesus Christ, your Son,
who lives and reigns with you and the Holy Spirit,
one God, for ever and ever.

Our Father . . .

January 13

HILARY, BISHOP AND DOCTOR

Saint Hilary was born early in the year 300, at Poitiers, a city in France. When he was about thirty-five years old he was chosen bishop of that city. He fought vigorously against the Arians, who taught that Jesus Christ was not truly God. He spoke out so forcefully against this false teaching that the Emperor Constantine sent him into exile. To strengthen the Catholic faith and to help people understand the Scriptures better, he wrote many works of wisdom and learning.

READING

A reading from a sermon on the Trinity by Saint Hilary

We have been promised, and he who made the promise is

12

trustworthy: "Ask, and it will be given to you; seek, and you will find; knock, and it will be opened to you."

Yes, in our poverty we will pray for our needs. We will study the sayings of your prophets and apostles with unflagging attention, and knock for admittance wherever the gift of understanding is safely kept. But yours it is, Lord, to grant our petitions, to be present when we seek you and to open when we knock.

Impart to us, then, the meaning of the words of Scripture and the light to understand it, with reverence for the doctrine and confidence in its truth. Grant that we may express what we believe. Through the prophets and apostles we know about you, the one God the Father, and the one Lord Jesus Christ. May we have the grace, in the face of heretics who deny you, to honor you as God, who is not alone, and to proclaim this as truth.

RESPONSORY

Everyone who acknowledges that Jesus Christ came as a man of
    flesh and blood is of God;
anyone who denies this of Jesus is not of God;

this is how you may know the spirit of truth from the spirit of falsehood.

He who proclaims that Jesus is the Son of God
lives in God and God in him.

This is how you may know the spirit of truth from the spirit of falsehood.

PRAYER

All-powerful God,
as Saint Hilary defended the divinity of Christ your Son,
give us a deeper understanding of this mystery
and help us to profess it in all truth.

13

Grant this through our Lord Jesus Christ, your Son,
who lives and reigns with you and the Holy Spirit,
one God, for ever and ever.

Our Father . . .

January 17

ANTHONY, ABBOT

Saint Anthony was born in Egypt around the year 250. After his
parents died, he gave everything he owned to the poor. He
went to live alone in the desert wilderness. There he spent his
time in prayer and fasting, giving up all pleasures and comforts
out of love for God.

Even though he remained quite alone, other people found out
about him and came to him to learn how to live like he did.
These people were called monks, and Saint Anthony is rightly
called the Father of Monks.

Saint Anthony's life of sacrifice and devotion to God inspired
the growing number of Christians in the Roman Empire to fight
against paganism and to stand up for the true Church.

Saint Anthony died when he was over a hundred years old.

READING

A reading from the Life of Saint Anthony by Saint Athanasius.

When Anthony was about eighteen or twenty years old, his
parents died. Not six months after his parents' death, as he was
on his way to church for his usual visit, he began to think of how
the apostles had left everything and followed the Savior, and
also of those mentioned in the book of Acts who had sold their
possessions and brought the apostles the money for distribution

to the needy. This was all in his mind when, entering the church just as the Gospel was being read, he heard the Lord's words to the rich man: "If you want to be perfect, go and sell all you have and give the money to the poor—you will have riches in heaven. Then come and follow me."

It seemed to Anthony that it was God who had brought the saints to his mind and that the words of the Gospel had been spoken directly to him. Immediately he left the church and gave away to the villagers all the property he inherited, about 200 acres of very beautiful and fertile land. He sold all his other possessions as well, giving to the poor the considerable sum of money he collected. However, to care for his sister he retained a few things.

He gave himself up to the ascetic life, not far from his own home. He did manual work because he had heard the words: "If anyone will not work, do not let him eat." He spent some of his earnings on bread and the rest he gave to the poor.

Seeing the kind of life he lived, the villagers and all the good men he knew called him the friend of God, and they loved him as a son and brother.

RESPONSORY

If you wish to be perfect,
go, sell what you have,
and give to the poor;
you will be rich in heaven.

Then come, follow me.

No one who will not renounce all his possessions can be my
    disciple.

Then come, follow me.

Matthew 19:21; Luke 14:33

Father,
you called Saint Anthony
to renounce the world
and serve you in the solitude of the desert.
By his prayers and example,
may we learn to deny ourselves
and love you above all things.

We ask this through our Lord Jesus Christ, your Son,
who lives and reigns with you and the Holy Spirit,
one God, for ever and ever.

Our Father . . .

January 20

FABIAN, POPE AND MARTYR

Saint Fabian was elected bishop of the Church of Rome in 236.
In 250, at the beginning of the persecution of Decius, he won the
crown of martyrdom. He was buried in one of the catacombs, or
underground cemeteries, near Rome.

READING

A reading from a letter about the death of Saint Fabian, pope, by
Saint Cyprian and the Roman Church.

Informed of the death of Pope Fabian, Saint Cyprian sent this
letter to the priests and deacons of Rome:

"My dear brothers, I received your letter in which I was most
fully informed of Fabian's glorious death. Through you we can
see quite clearly what an example of faith and courage [his
death] offers us. It is helpful and encouraging when a bishop
offers himself as a model for his brothers by the constancy of his
faith."

Apparently before Cyprian received this letter the Church of Rome had given the community at Carthage testimony of its loyalty in times of persecution.

"Our church stands firmly in the faith, although some have lapsed because they fear the loss of their outstanding positions or other personal sufferings. Although these have separated from us, we have not given them up. In the past we have urged them and now we continue to encourage them to do penance, in the hope that they may receive pardon from him who can give it; whereas, if they were abandoned by us, they might become worse. If any of those who have fallen should become ill and, after doing penance, should desire to receive communion, they should certainly be assisted.

"Your brothers who are in chains send you their greetings, and also the priests, and the entire Church which lies awake in great anxiety to pray for all those who invoke the name of the Lord."

RESPONSORY

I desire to leave this world and to be with Christ;
I consider all that this world offers worthless,
if only I can gain union with Christ.

Life for me means Christ;
death is as a prize to be won.

Even if I am to be poured out as a libation,
on the sacrificial offering of your faith,
I rejoice and wish to share my happiness with you.

Life for me means Christ;
death is as a prize to be won.
Philippians 1:23; 3:18; 1:21; 2:17

PRAYER

God our Father, glory of your priests,

may the prayers of your martyr Fabian
help us to share his faith
and offer you loving service.

Grant this through our Lord Jesus Christ, your Son,
who lives and reigns with you and the Holy Spirit,
one God, for ever and ever.

Our Father . . .

On the same day, January 20

SEBASTIAN, MARTYR

Saint Sebastian died a martyr at Rome early in the year 300.
From early times the faithful have honored his tomb on the
Appian Way near Rome.

READING

From an explanation of psalm 118 by Saint Ambrose, bishop.

"To enter the kingdom of God we must endure many sufferings."

Take the example of the martyr Sebastian, whose birthday in
glory we celebrate today. He was a native of Milan. He set out
for Rome, where bitter persecutions were raging because of the
fervor of the Christians. There he endured suffering; there he
gained his crown. He went to the city as a stranger and there
established a home of undying glory.

The persecutors who are visible are not the only ones. There are
also invisible persecutors, much greater in number. Of this kind
of persecution Scripture says: "All who wish to live a holy life in
Christ Jesus suffer persecution." "All" suffer persecution; there

is no exception. Who can claim exemption if the Lord himself endured the testing of persecution?

RESPONSORY

For the law of God this holy man engaged in combat even unto
   death.
He feared no wicked threats;
his faith was founded on solid rock.

He renounced earthly joys,
and so gained the kingdom of heaven.
His faith was founded on solid rock.

PRAYER

Lord, fill us with that spirit of courage
which gave your martyr Sebastian
strength to offer his life in faithful witness.
Help us to learn from him to cherish your law
and to obey you rather than men.

We ask this through our Lord Jesus Christ, your Son,
who lives and reigns with you and the Holy Spirit,
one God, for ever and ever.

Our Father . . .

January 21
AGNES, VIRGIN AND MARTYR
Memorial

Saint Agnes died a martyr at Rome. Many of the Fathers of the

Church, following Saint Ambrose, have honored her in their writings.

A reading from an essay On Virgins by Saint Ambrose, bishop

Today is the birthday of a virgin; let us imitate her purity. It is the birthday of a martyr; let us offer ourselves in sacrifice. It is the birthday of Saint Agnes, who is said to have suffered martyrdom at the age of twelve.

There was little or no room in that small body for a wound. Yet she shows no fear of the blood-stained hands of her executioners. She offers her whole body to be put to the sword by fierce soldiers. She is too young to know of death, yet is ready to face it. Dragged against her will to the altars, she stretches out her hands to the Lord in the midst of the flames, making the triumphant sign of Christ the victor on the altars of sacrilege. She puts her neck and hands in iron chains, but no chain can hold fast her tiny limbs.

In the midst of tears, she sheds no tears herself. She stood still, she prayed, she offered her neck.

You could see fear in the eyes of the executioner, as if he were the one condemned. His right hand trembled, his face grew pale as he saw the girl's peril, while she had no fear for herself. One victim, but a twin martyrdom, to modesty and religion; Agnes preserved her virginity and gained a martyr's crown.

Let us keep the feast of Saint Agnes
by recalling all that she suffered.

While still so young, she overcame death and found true life.

For the giver of life was her only love.

While still so young, she overcame death and found true life.

PRAYER

Almighty, eternal God,
you choose what the world considers weak
to put the worldly power to shame.
May we who celebrate the birth of Saint Agnes into eternal joy
be loyal to the faith she professed.

Grant this through our Lord Jesus Christ, your Son,
who lives and reigns with you and the Holy Spirit,
one God, for ever and ever.

Our Father . . .

January 22

VINCENT, DEACON AND MARTYR

Saint Vincent was a deacon. After suffering extreme tortures, he died as a martyr at Valencia in Spain. He was soon honored throughout the Church because he so willingly sacrificed his life for Christ.

READING

A reading from a sermon by Saint Augustine, bishop

"To you has been granted in Christ's behalf not only that you should believe in him but also that you should suffer for him."

Vincent had received both these gifts and held them as his own. For how could he have them if he had not received them? And he displayed his faith in what he said, his endurance in what he suffered.

No one ought to be confident in his own strength when he undergoes temptation. For whenever we endure evils courageously, our long-suffering comes from him [Christ].

He once said to his disciples: "In this world you will suffer persecution," and then, to allay their fears, he added, "but rest assured, I have conquered the world."

There is no need to wonder then, my dearly beloved brothers, that Vincent conquered in him who conquered the world. It offers temptation to lead us astray; it strikes terror into us to break our spirit.

Hence if our personal pleasures do not hold us captive, and if we are not frightened by brutality, then the world is overcome. At both of these approaches Christ rushes to our aid, and the Christian is not conquered.

RESPONSORY

The Lord has tried me as gold is assayed by fire;

I have walked in his way;
I have not wandered from his path.

I count all that this world offers as worthless,
if only I may know Christ,
and share in his sufferings.

I have walked in his way;
I have not wandered from his path.

Eternal Father,
you gave Saint Vincent
the courage to endure torture and death for the gospel:
fill us with your Spirit
and strengthen us in your love.

We ask this through our Lord Jesus Christ, your Son,
who lives and reigns with you and the Holy Spirit,
one God, for ever and ever.

Our Father . . .

January 24

FRANCIS DE SALES, BISHOP AND DOCTOR
Memorial

Saint Francis was born in 1567 in the southeastern section of
France, called Savoy. By this time many people all over Europe
had become Protestants. After having been ordained priest,
Francis labored diligently to restore Catholicism in his country.
Chosen bishop of Geneva, he was a firm but loving shepherd of
his clergy and his people. He strengthened their faith by his
writings, works and example. He died at Lyons on December
28, 1622, and was buried at Annecy on this day.

READING

A reading from The Introduction to the Devout Life by Saint
Francis de Sales, bishop

When God the Creator made all things, he commanded the
plants to bring forth fruit each according to its own kind. He has

likewise commanded Christians, who are the living plants of his Church, to bring forth the fruits of devotion, each one in accord with his character, his station, and his calling.

I say that devotion must be practiced in different ways by the nobleman and by the working man, by the servant and by the prince, by the widow, by the unmarried girl and by the married woman. But even this distinction is not sufficient; for the practice of devotion must be adapted to the strength, to the occupation and to the duties of each one in particular.

Moreover, just as every sort of gem, cast in honey, becomes brighter and more sparkling, each according to its color, so each person becomes more acceptable and fitting in his own vocation when he sets his vocation in the context of devotion. Through devotion your family cares become more peaceful, mutual love between husband and wife becomes more sincere, the service we owe to the prince becomes more faithful, and our work, no matter what is is, becomes more pleasant and agreeable.

RESPONSORY

Be kind and compassionate to one another;
forgive each other as God has forgiven you in Christ.
Be imitators of God the Father who loves you as his own dear children.

Take my yoke upon you, and learn of me,
for I am gentle and humble of heart.
Be imitators of God the Father who loves you as his own dear children.
Ephesians 4:32–5:1; Mt. 11:29

PRAYER

Father,
you gave Francis de Sales the spirit of compassion

to befriend all men on the way to salvation.
By his example, lead us to show your gentle love
in the service of our fellow men.

Grant this through our Lord Jesus Christ, your Son,
who lives and reigns with you and the Holy Spirit,
one God, for ever and ever.

Our Father . . .

January 25

CONVERSION OF PAUL, APOSTLE
Feast

This feast recalls the time when Saul, who had been persecuting
the Christians, was called by Christ to become one of his followers. After Saul's conversion he took the name Paul. He became
one of the bravest Christians who not only preached about
Christ, but suffered for him and his Church. Through Christ's
grace and Saint Paul's preaching thousands of people became
Christians. Today we honor him as one of the greatest Apostles.

READING

A reading from a letter of the apostle Paul to the Galatians

I assure you, brothers, the gospel I proclaimed to you is no mere
human invention. I did not receive it from any man, nor was I
schooled in it. It came by revelation from Jesus Christ.

You have heard, I know, the story of my former way of life in
Judaism. You know that I went to extremes in persecuting the
Church of God and tried to destroy it.

But the time came when he who had set me apart before I was
born and called me by his favor chose to reveal his Son to me,
that I might spread among the Gentiles the good tidings con-

cerning him. Immediately, without seeking human advisers or even going to Jerusalem to see those who were apostles before me, I went off to Arabia; later I returned to Damascus. Three years after that I went up to Jerusalem to get to know Cephas, with whom I stayed fifteen days. I did not meet any other apostles except James, the brother of the Lord.

The communities of Christ in Judea had no idea what I looked like; they had only heard that "he who was formerly persecuting us is now preaching the faith he tried to destroy," and they gave glory to God on my account.

RESPONSORY

The Gospel which I preached to you is not a human message.

I did not receive it through any man,
but from our Lord Jesus Christ who revealed it to me.

As surely as Christ's truth is in me,
I have preached the Gospel to you.

I did not receive it through any man,
but from our Lord Jesus Christ who revealed it to me.

Galatians 1:11-12; 2 Corinthians 11:10, 7

PRAYER

God our Father,
you taught the gospel to all the world
through the preaching of Paul your apostle.
May we who celebrate his conversion to the faith
follow him in bearing witness to your truth.

We ask this through our Lord Jesus Christ, your Son,
who lives and reigns with you and the Holy Spirit,
one God, for ever and ever.

Our Father . . .

January 26

TIMOTHY AND TITUS, BISHOPS
Memorial

Saints Timothy and Titus were disciples and assistants of the apostle Paul. Timothy had charge of the Church at Ephesus and Titus of the Church in Crete. The letters written to them are called the pastoral epistles, for they contain much good advice for the instruction of both pastors and the people of God. When we think of Saints Timothy and Titus, we also think of Saint Paul, who was their guide as he can still be our guide.

READING

A reading from a sermon by Saint John Chrysostom, bishop

In thinking of Paul we should not consider only his noble and lofty virtues or the strong and ready will that disposed him for such great graces. We should also realize that he shares our nature in every respect. If we do, then even what is very difficult will seem to us easy and light; we shall work hard during the short time we have on earth and someday we shall wear the incorruptible, immortal crown. This we shall do by the grace and mercy of our Lord Jesus Christ, to whom all glory and power belongs now and always through endless ages. Amen.

RESPONSORY

Man of God, you must strive for holiness, goodness, fidelity, love, patience and gentleness.
**Fight the good fight of faith,
and win the prize of eternal life.**

Preach nothing but sound doctrine.
**Fight the good fight of faith,
and win the prize of eternal life.**
Timothy 6:11-12; Titus 2:1

27

God our Father,
you gave your saints Timothy and Titus
the courage and wisdom of the apostles:
may their prayers help us to live holy lives
and lead us to heaven, our true home.

Grant this through our Lord Jesus Christ, your Son,
who lives and reigns with you and the Holy Spirit,
one God, for ever and ever.

Our Father . . .

January 27

ANGELA MERICI, VIRGIN

Saint Angela was born in 1470 in Italy. She took the habit of the Third Order of Saint Francis and called together girls whom she instructed in charitable works. In 1535, under the patronage of Saint Ursula, she founded a congregation of women who instructed poor girls in the Christian life. Saint Angela died in 1540.

READING

A reading from the Spiritual Testament by Saint Angela Merici, virgin

As our Savior says: "A good tree is not able to produce bad fruit."

He says: A good tree, that is, a good heart as well as a soul on fire with charity, can do nothing but good and holy works. For this reason Saint Augustine said: "Love, and do what you will," namely, possess love and charity and then do what you will.

It is as if he had said: Charity is not able to sin.

Mothers of children, even if they have a thousand, carry each and every one fixed in their hearts, and because of the strength of their love they do not forget any of them. In fact, it seems that the more children they have the more their love and care for each one is increased.

Be sincerely kind to every one according to the words of our Lord: "Learn of me, for I am meek and humble of heart." Thus you are imitating God, of whom it is said: "He has disposed all things pleasantly." And again Jesus said: "My yoke is easy and my burden light."

RESPONSORY

Now you are light in the Lord;
live as men native to the light.

Such light bears fruit in goodness, holiness and truth.

I have given you to the world as its light,
and you must shine for all to see.

Such light bears fruit in goodness, holiness and truth.
Ephesians 5:8-9; Matthew 5:14, 16

PRAYER

Lord,
may Saint Angela commend us to your mercy;
may her charity and wisdom help us
to be faithful to your teaching
and to follow it in our lives.

We ask this through our Lord Jesus Christ, your Son,
who lives and reigns with you and the Holy Spirit,
one God, for ever and ever.

Our Father . . .

January 28

THOMAS AQUINAS, PRIEST AND DOCTOR
Memorial

Thomas was born about the year 1225 into the family of the Count of Aquino. He first studied at the monastery of Monte Cassino and later at the University of Naples. Afterwards he joined the Friars Preachers and completed his studies at Paris and Cologne, his instructor being Saint Albert the Great. Becoming himself a teacher, he wrote many learned volumes and was especially renowned for his philosophical and theological studies. Saint Thomas died in Italy on March 7, 1274, but his memory is honored on January 28, the day his body was transferred to Toulouse in 1369.

READING

A reading from one of the works of Saint Thomas Aquinas, priest

If you seek the example of love: "Greater love than this no man has, than to lay down his life for his friends." Such a man was Christ on the cross. And if he gave his life for us, then it should not be difficult to bear whatever hardships arise for his sake.

If you seek patience, you will find no better example than the cross. Christ endured much on the cross, and did so patiently, because "when he suffered he did not threaten; he was led like a sheep to the slaughter and he did not open his mouth."

If you seek an example of obedience, follow him who became obedient to the Father even unto death. "For just as by the disobedience of one man," namely, Adam, "many were made sinners, so by the obedience of one man, many were made righteous."

If you seek an example of despising earthly things, follow him who is "the King of kings and the Lord of lords, in whom are hidden all the treasures of wisdom and knowledge." Upon the cross he was stripped, mocked, spat upon, struck, crowned with thorns, and given only vinegar and gall to drink.

Do not be attached, therefore, to clothing and riches, because "they divided my garments among themselves." Nor to honors, for he experienced harsh words and scourgings. Nor to greatness of rank, for "weaving a crown of thorns they placed it on my head." Nor to anything delightful, for "in my thirst they gave me vinegar to drink."

RESPONSORY

I prayed, and understanding was given me;
I entreated, and the spirit of wisdom came to me;

I esteemed wisdom more than scepter or throne;
compared with her, I held riches to be nothing.

Who will know your will, O Lord,
unless you bestow wisdom,
and send your Holy Spirit from above?

I esteemed wisdom more than scepter or throne;
compared with her, I held riches to be nothing.
Wisdom 7:7-8; 9:17

PRAYER

God our Father,
you made Thomas Aquinas known for his holiness and
    and learning.
Help us to grow in wisdom by his teaching,
and in holiness by imitating his faith.

Grant this through our Lord Jesus Christ, your Son,
who lives and reigns with you and the Holy Spirit,

one God, for ever and ever.

Our Father . .

January 31
JOHN BOSCO, PRIEST
Memorial

Saint John was born in Italy in 1815. His early life was very hard, and so, when he became a priest he dedicated himself to the education of the young. He founded schools to teach young people both how to make a living and how to be good Christians. He also composed pamphlets for the support and defense of religion. Saint John died in 1888.

In the following reading Saint John Bosco gives us a picture of what a Christian teacher ought to be. Students can also learn from this how they should behave toward such a teacher.

READING

A reading from a letter by Saint John Bosco, priest

My sons, in my long experience very often I had to be convinced of this great truth. It is easier to become angry than to restrain oneself, and to threaten a boy than to persuade him. Yes, indeed, it is more fitting to be persistent in punishing our own impatience and pride than to correct the boys. We must be firm but kind, and be patient with them.

See that no one finds you motivated by impetuosity or willfulness. It is difficult to keep calm when administering punishment, but this must be done if we are to keep ourselves from showing off our authority or spilling out our anger.

Let us regard those boys over whom we have some authority as our own sons. Let us place ourselves in their service. Let us be ashamed to assume an attitude of superiority. Let us not rule over them except for the pupose of serving them better.

This was the method that Jesus used with the apostles. He put up with their ignorance and roughness and even their infidelity. He treated sinners with a kindness and affection that caused some to be shocked, others to be scandalized, and still others to hope for God's mercy. And so he bade us to be gentle and humble of heart.

RESPONSORY

The people brought little children to Jesus that he might touch
    them,
but the disciples tried to discourage them.
Jesus saw this and said:

Let the little children come to me, and do not prevent them, for the kingdom of God belongs to such as these.

He that receives one such child in my name, receives me.

Let the little children come to me, and do not prevent them, for the kingdom of God belongs to such as these.
Mark 10:13-14; Matthew 18:5

PRAYER

Lord,
you called John Bosco
to be a teacher and father to the young.
Fill us with love like his:
may we give ourselves completely to your service
and to the salvation of mankind.

We ask this through our Lord Jesus Christ, your Son,
who lives and reigns with you and the Holy Spirit,
one God, for ever and ever.

Our Father . . .

February 2

PRESENTATION OF THE LORD
Feast

Today the Church recalls how Joseph and Mary brought Jesus to the temple in Jerusalem to present him to the Lord. They did this to obey the law which required that the first son born of Jewish parents should be dedicated to God. God made this law to remind his people how he brought them out of Egypt on the night of the Passover, when the angel of death passed over the homes of the Israelites and spared them from the punishment he inflicted on all the first-born of the Egyptians.

Today is also a feast of lights, for the Church honors Jesus as the light who came into the world to enlighten all men. And so, on this day the Church blesses candles whose light reminds us of Christ the true light.

READING

A reading from a sermon by Saint Sophronius, bishop

In honor of the divine mystery that we celebrate today, let us hasten to meet Christ. Everyone should be eager to join the procession and to carry a light.

Our lighted candles are a sign of the divine splendor of the one who comes to expel the dark shadows of evil and to make the whole universe radiant with the brilliance of his eternal light. Our candles also show how bright our souls should be when we go to meet Christ.

The Mother of God, the most pure Virgin, carried the true light in her arms and brought him to those who lay in darkness. We too should carry a light for all to see and reflect the radiance of the true light as we hasten to meet him.

34

The light has come and has shone upon a world enveloped in shadows; the Dayspring from on high has visited us and given light to those who lived in darkness. This, then, is our feast, and we join in procession with lighted candles to reveal the light that has shone upon us and the glory that is yet to come to us through him. So let us hasten all together to meet our God.

The true light has come, "the light that enlightens every man who is born into this world." Let all of us, my brethren, be enlightened and made radiant by this light. Let all of us share in its splendor, and be so filled with it that no one remains in the darkness.

RESPONSORY

The glory of the Lord entered the temple by the eastward gate,

and the house of God was filled with his splendor.

His parents took the child Jesus into the temple.

And the house of God was filled with his splendor.
Ezekiel 43:5; see Luke 2:22

PRAYER

All-powerful Father,
Christ your Son became man for us
and was presented in the temple.
May he free our hearts from sin
and bring us into your presence.

We ask this through our Lord Jesus Christ, your Son,
who lives and reigns with you and the Holy Spirit,
one God, for ever and ever.

Our Father . . .

February 3

BLASE, BISHOP AND MARTYR χ

Saint Blase was a bishop who lived in Armenia during the fourth century. During the Middle Ages, especially, people prayed to him that they might be cured of diseases and sicknesses of the throat, if God willed it.

In our reading for today Saint Augustine points out how our Lord suffered and died for us. This reading helps us to see how Christian martyrs like Saint Blase followed in Christ's footsteps by their sufferings and death.

READING

A reading from a sermon by Saint Augustine, bishop

"The Son of Man has come not to be served, but to serve, and to give his own life as a ransom for many." Consider how the Lord served, and see what kind of servants he bids us to be. He gave "his own life as a ransom for many;" he ransomed us.

But who of us is fit to ransom anyone? By his blood, by his death we were ransomed from death. And yet we, too, have a duty to contribute our meager offerings to his members, for we have become his members. He is the head; we are the body.

In his letter, the apostle John holds up the Lord as our model. Jesus said: "Whoever wishes to be the greater among you will be your servant, just as the Son of Man has come not to be served but to serve and to give his own life as a ransom for many." So in his exhortation to us to act likewise, John says: "Christ laid down his life for us; so we, too, ought to lay down our lives for our brothers."

RESPONSORY

Nothing can make me ashamed;

I have utter confidence in Christ that through my life or
through my death,
he will use my mortal body for his glory.

Contempt has broken my heart and all my strength has gone.

I have utter confidence in Christ that through my life or
through my death,
he will use my mortal body for his glory.
Philippians 1:20; Psalm 69:21

PRAYER

Lord,
hear the prayers of your martyr Blase.
Give us the joy of your peace in this life
and help us to gain the happiness that will never end.

Grant this through our Lord Jesus Christ, your Son,
who lives and reigns with you and the Holy Spirit,
one God, for ever and ever.

Our Father, . . .

On the same day, February 3

ANSGAR, BISHOP

Saint Ansgar was born in France at the beginning of the ninth
century and educated in the monastery of Corbie. In 826 he
preached the faith in Denmark with little success but later labored to greater effect in Sweden. Appointed bishop of
Hamburg by Pope Gregory IV, he was sent as the pope's representative to Denmark and Sweden. There he met with many
difficulties in his work as a missionary but bravely overcame
them. Saint Ansgar died in 865.

Let us think of Saint Ansgar, the missionary, as we learn from the following reading what it really means to be a missionary.

A reading from the decree on the missionary activity of the Church of the Second Vatican Council.

Every disciple of Christ is responsible in his own measure for the spread of the faith. But Christ the Lord is always calling from his followers those whom he wills, so that they may be with him and be sent by him to preach to the nations.

A special vocation marks out those priests, religious and lay people who are prepared to undertake the missionary task in their own country or abroad, and have the right natural disposition for it, with suitable gifts and talents.

Those whom God calls must answer his call in such a way that, without regard for purely human counsel, they may devote themselves wholly to the work of the Gospel. This response cannot be given except with the inspiration and strength of the Holy Spirit.

The person who is sent enters into the life and mission of him who "emptied himself, taking the nature of a slave." He must be ready therefore to be true to his vocation for life, to deny himself, renouncing all that he had before, and to become all things to all men.

He must follow in the footsteps of his Master, who was gentle and humble of heart, and reveal to others that his yoke is easy and his burden light.

By a life that is truly according to the Gospel, by much endurance, by forbearance, by kindness and sincere love, he must bear witness to his Lord, even if need be, by the shedding of his blood.

I do not boast of preaching the Gospel,
since it is a duty with which I am charged.

It would go hard with me indeed if I did not preach the Gospel.

I have been all things to all men
in the hope of saving some of them at the least.

It would go hard with me indeed if I did not preach the Gospel.
1 Corinthians 9:16, 22

PRAYER

Father,
you sent Saint Ansgar
to bring the light of Christ to many nations.
May his prayers help us
to walk in the light of your truth.

We ask this through our Lord Jesus Christ, your Son,
who lives and reigns with you and the Holy Spirit,
one God, for ever and ever.

Our Father . . .

February 5

AGATHA, VIRGIN AND MARTYR
Memorial

Agatha suffered martyrdom at Catania in Sicily, during the
reign of one of the Roman Emperors who feared and hated
Christianity. The fame of this Saint soon spread throughout the
Church and we still honor her bravery in suffering and dying for
Christ.

A reading from a homily on Saint Agatha by Saint Methodius of Sicily, bishop

My fellow Christians, our annual celebration of a martyr's feast has brought us together. Agatha achieved renown in the early Church for her noble victory.

For her, Christ's death was recent, his blood was still moist. Her robe is the mark of her faithful witness to Christ.

Agatha, the name of our saint, means "good." She was truly good, for she lived as a child of God.

Agatha, her goodness coincides with her name and her way of life. She won a good name by her noble deeds, and by her name she points to the nobility of those deeds. Agatha, her mere name wins all men over to her company. She teaches them by her example to hasten with her to the true Good, God alone.

RESPONSORY

But as for me, helped by the Lord,
I shall stand firm in proclaiming his praises.
He has become my salvation and my consoler.

In his mercy, the sinless Lord has consecrated his servant, for she remained pure in his sight.
He has become my salvation and my consoler.

PRAYER

Lord,
let your forgiveness be won for us

by the pleading of Saint Agatha,
who found favor with you by her chastity
and by her courage in suffering death for the gospel.

Grant this through our Lord Jesus Christ, your Son,
who lives and reigns with you and the Holy Spirit,
one God, for ever and ever.

Our Father . . .

February 6

PAUL MIKI AND COMPANIONS, MARTYRS
Memorial

Saint Paul was born in Japan between 1564 and 1566. Entering
the Society of Jesus, he preached the gospel to the people with
great success. But when persecution against Catholics became
oppressive, he was arrested along with twenty-five others. After
enduring torment and derision they were finally taken to
Nagasaki and there suffered death in 1597.

READING

A reading from an account of the martyrdom of Saint Paul Miki
and his companions

The crosses were set in place. Father Pasio and Father
Rodriguez took turns encouraging the victims. Their steadfast
behavior was wonderful to see. Father Bursar stood motionless,
his eyes turned heavenward. Brother Martin gave thanks to
God's goodness by singing psalms. Again and again he re-
peated: "Into your hands, Lord, I entrust my life." Brother Francis Branco also thanked God in a loud voice. Brother Gonsalvo
in a very loud voice kept saying the Our Father and Hail Mary.

Our brother, Paul Miki, saw himself standing now in the noblest pulpit he had ever filled. To his "congregation" he began by proclaiming himself a Japanese and a Jesuit. He was dying for the Gospel he preached. He gave thanks to God for this wonderful blessing and he ended his "sermon" with these words: "As I come to this supreme moment of my life, I am sure none of you would suppose I want to deceive you. And so I tell you plainly: there is no way to be saved except the Christian way. My religion teaches me to pardon my enemies and all who have offended me. I do gladly pardon the Emperor and all who have sought my death. I beg them to seek baptism and be Christians themselves."

Then he looked at his comrades and began to encourage them in their final struggle. Their faces were serene. Some of them even took to urging the people standing by to live worthy Christian lives. In these and other ways they showed their readiness to die.

Then, according to Japanese custom, the four executioners began to unsheathe their spears. At this dreadful sight, all the Christians cried out, "Jesus, Mary!" And the storm of anguished weeping then rose to batter the very skies. The executioners killed them one by one. One thrust of the spear, then a second blow. It was over in a very short time.

RESPONSORY

We must glory in the cross of our Lord Jesus Christ;
in him is our salvation, life and resurrection.
Through him we are saved and set free.

This grace has been given to you,
not only to believe in Christ, but also to suffer for his sake.
Through him we are saved and set free.
See Galatians 6:14; Philippians 1:29

God our Father,
source of strength for all your saints,
you led Paul Miki and his companions
through the suffering of the cross
to the joy of eternal life.
May their prayers give us the courage
to be loyal until death in professing our faith.

We ask this through our Lord Jesus Christ, your Son,
who lives and reigns with you and the Holy Spirit,
one God, for ever and ever.

Our Father . . .

February 8

JEROME EMILIANI

Jerome was born at Venice in 1486. He first embraced the military life but later dedicated himself to helping the poor, distributing to them his own possessions. He founded a religious Order, which supported orphan boys and the poor. Jerome died in Italy in 1537.

READING

A reading from a letter to his brothers by Saint Jerome Emiliani

I urge you to persevere in your love for Christ and your faithful observance of the law of Christ.

Our goal is God, the source of all good. As we say in our prayer, we are to place our trust in God and in no one else. In his kindness, our Lord wished to strengthen your faith, for without it, as the evangelist points out, Christ could not have performed many of his miracles. He also wished to listen to your prayer,

43

and so he ordained that you experience poverty, distress, abandonment, weariness and scorn.

God alone knows the reasons for all this, yet we can recognize three causes. In the first place, our blessed Lord is telling you that he desires to include you among his beloved sons, provided that you remain steadfast in his ways, for this is the way he treats his friends and makes them holy.

The second reason is that he is asking you to grow continually in your confidence in him alone and not in others.

Now there is a third reason. God wishes to test you like gold in the furnace. The dross is consumed by the fire, but the pure gold remains and its value increases. It is in this manner that God acts with his good servant, who puts his hope in him and remains unshaken in times of distress. God raises him up and, in return for the things he has left out of love for God, he repays him a hundredfold in this life and with eternal life hereafter.

If then you remain constant in faith in the face of trial, the Lord will give you peace and rest for a time in this world, and for ever in the next.

RESPONSORY

Be of one heart and soul, be sympathetic, and love the brothers; have compassion for all and be self-effacing.

**To this way of life you are called that you may inherit
a blessing.**

Love each other as true brothers should,
and always respect one another.
Serve the Lord and never grow tired;
keep your spirit alive and willing.

**To this way of life you are called that you may inherit
a blessing.**
1 Peter 3:7, 8; Romans 12:10-11

God of mercy,
you chose Jerome Emiliani
to be a father and friend of orphans.
May his prayers keep us faithful
to the Spirit we have received,
who makes us your children.

Grant this through our Lord Jesus Christ, your Son,
who lives and reigns with you and the Holy Spirit,
one God, for ever and ever.

Our Father . . .

February 10

SCHOLASTICA, VIRGIN
Memorial

Scholastica, a sister of Saint Benedict, was born in Italy about
the year 480. She vowed herself to God and followed her
brother to Monte Cassino, the monastery which he had
founded. She died there around the year 547.

READING

A reading from the books of Dialogues by Saint Gregory the
Great, pope

Scholastica, the sister of Saint Benedict, had been consecrated to
God from her earliest years. She was accustomed to visiting her
brother once a year. He would come down to meet her at a place
on the monastery property, not far outside the gate.

One day she came as usual and her saintly brother went with
some of his disciples; they spent the whole day praising God
and talking of sacred things. As night fell they had supper together.

Their spiritual conversation went on and the hour grew late. The holy nun said to her brother: "Please do not leave me tonight; let us go on until morning talking about the delights of the spiritual life." "Sister," he replied, "what are you saying? I simply cannot stay outside my cell."

When she heard her brother refuse her request, the holy woman joined her hands on the table, laid her head on them and began to pray. As she raised her head from the table, there were such brilliant flashes of lightning, such great peals of thunder and such a heavy downpour of rain that neither Benedict nor his brethren could stir across the threshold of the place where they had been seated. Sadly he began to complain: "May God forgive you, sister. What have you done?" "Well" she answered, "I asked you and you would not listen; so I asked my God and he did listen. So now go off, if you can, leave me and return to your monastery."

So it came about that they stayed awake the whole night, engrossed in their conversation about the spiritual life.

Three days later, Benedict was in his cell. Looking up to the sky, he saw his sister's soul leave her body in the form of a dove, and fly up to the secret places of heaven. Rejoicing in her great glory, he thanked almighty God with hymns and words of praise. He then sent his brethren to bring her body to the monastery and lay it in the tomb he had prepared for himself.

RESPONSORY

When the saintly nun begged the Lord that her brother might
    not leave her,

**she received more than her brother did from the Lord of her
    heart**
because she loved him so much.

How good, how delightful it is
for brothers and sisters to live in unity.

She received more than her brother did from the Lord of her
   heart
because she loved him so much.

Lord,
as we recall the memory of Saint Scholastica,
we ask that by her example
we may serve you with love and obtain perfect joy.

Grant this through our Lord Jesus Christ, your Son,
who lives and reigns with you and the Holy Spirit,
one God, for ever and ever.

Our Father . . .

✗ February 11

OUR LADY OF LOURDES

In 1858 the Virgin Mary Immaculate appeared to Bernadette
Soubirous near Lourdes in France. Through this humble girl,
Mary called sinners to conversion and enkindled within the
Church a great zeal for prayer and charity, especially service to
the sick and poor.

READING

A reading from a letter by Saint Marie Bernadette Soubirous,
virgin

I had gone down one day with two other girls to the bank of the
river Gave when suddenly I heard a kind of rustling sound. I
turned my head toward the field by the side of the river but the
trees seemed quite still and the noise was evidently not from
them. Then I looked up and caught sight of the cave where I saw

a lady wearing a lovely white dress with a bright belt. On top of each of her feet was a pale yellow rose, the same color as her rosary beads.

At this I rubbed my eyes, thinking I was seeing things, and I put my hands into the fold of my dress where my rosary was. I wanted to make the sign of the cross but for the life of me I couldn't manage it and my hand just fell down. Then the lady made the sign of the cross herself and at the second attempt I managed to do the same, though my hands were trembling. Then I began to say the rosary while the lady let her beads slip through her fingers, without moving her lips. When I stopped saying the Hail Mary, she immediately vanished.

I asked my two companions if they had noticed anything, but they said no. Of course they wanted to know what I was doing and I told them that I had seen a lady wearing a nice white dress, though I didn't know who she was. I told them not to say anything about it, and they said I was silly to have anything to do with it. I said they were wrong and I came back next Sunday, feeling myself drawn to the place . . .

The third time I went the lady spoke to me and asked me to come every day for fifteen days. I said I would and then she said that she wanted me to tell the priests to build a chapel there. She also told me to drink from the stream. I went to the Gave, the only stream I could see. Then she made me realize she was not speaking of the Gave and she indicated a little trickle of water close-by. When I got to it I could only find a few drops, mostly mud. I cupped my hands to catch some liquid without success and then I started to scrape the ground. I managed to find a few drops of water but only at the fourth attempt was there sufficient for any kind of drink. The lady then vanished and I went back home.

I went back each day for fifteen days and each time, except one Monday and one Friday, the lady appeared and told me to look for a stream and wash in it and to see that the priests build a chapel there. I must also pray, she said, for the conversion of sinners. I asked her many times what she meant by that, but she only smiled. Finally with outstretched arms and eyes looking up to heaven she told me she was the Immaculate Conception.

During the fifteen days she told me three secrets but I was not to speak about them to anyone and so far I have not.

RESPONSORY

My soul proclaims the greatness of the Lord.

The Almighty has done great things for me, and holy is his Name.

From this day all generations will call me blessed.

The Almighty has done great things for me, and holy is his Name.
Luke 1:46, 49, 48

PRAYER

God of mercy,
we celebrate the feast of Mary,
the sinless mother of God.
May her prayers help us
to rise above our human weakness.

We ask this through our Lord Jesus Christ, your Son,
who lives and reigns with you and the Holy Spirit,
one God, for ever and ever.

Our Father . . .

February 14

CYRIL, MONK, AND METHODIUS, BISHOP
Memorial

Saint Cyril was born in Thessalonica and educated in
Constantinople. He accompanied his brother Methodius to
Moravia to preach the faith. They both prepared Slavic liturgical
texts in what would come to be known as the Old Slavonic
language. Both were called to Rome, where Cyril died on February 14, 869, while Methodius was consecrated bishop and
went to lands around the Danube where he tirelessly preached
the Gospel. Methodius died on April 6, 885 in Czechoslovakia.

READING

A reading from an Old Slavonic Life of Cyril

When the time came for Cyril to set out from this world to the
peace of his heavenly homeland, he prayed to God with his
hands outstretched and his eyes filled with tears: "O Lord, my
God, you have created the choirs of angels and spiritual powers;
you have stretched forth the heavens and established the earth,
creating all that exists from nothing. You hear those who obey
your will and keep your commands in holy fear. Hear my prayer
and protect your faithful people, for you have established me as
their unsuitable and unworthy servant.

"Make your people known for the unity and profession of their
faith. Inspire the hearts of your people with your word and your
teaching. You called us to preach the Gospel of your Christ and
to encourage them to lives and works pleasing to you.

"I now return to you, your people, your gift to me. Direct them
with your powerful right hand, and protect them under the
shadow of your wings. May all praise and glorify your name,
the Father, Son and Holy Spirit. Amen."

You spoke to your saints and told them:
I have exalted one chosen from the people;
I have found David my servant.

With my holy oil I have anointed him;
the power of my hand will be with him.

I will give you shepherds after my own heart;
they will nourish you on knowledge and understanding.

With my holy oil I have anointed him;
the power of my hand will be with him.

Psalm 89:20, 21-22; Jeremiah 3:15

PRAYER

Father, you brought the light of the gospel to the Slavic nations
through Saint Cyril and his brother Saint Methodius.
Open our hearts to understand your teaching
and help us to become one in faith and praise.

Grant this through our Lord Jesus Christ, your Son,
who lives and reigns with you and the Holy Spirit,
one God, for ever and ever.

Our Father . . .

February 17

SEVEN FOUNDERS OF THE ORDER OF SERVITES

Seven men, born at Florence, began a life on Monte Senario
with a particular veneration of the Blessed Virgin Mary. Later
they preached throughout parts of Italy and founded the Order

of Servites (or Servants) of the Blessed Virgin Mary, approved by the Holy See in 1304. Alexis Falconieri, one of the seven, died on this day in 1310.

READING

A reading from an account of the origin of the Servite Order

There were seven men worthy of all our praise and veneration, whom our Lady brought into one community to form this order of hers and of her servants.

But where did these men stand before they formed their own community?

Some of them had never married, having vowed themselves to perpetual celibacy; some were married men at the time; some had lost their wives after marriage and now were widowers.

They belonged to the merchant class and engaged in buying and selling the goods of this world. But once they found the pearl of great price, our order, they not only gave all they had to the poor but cheerfully offered themselves to God and our Lady in true and loyal service.

They loved God above all things and dedicated their whole lives to him by honoring him in their every thought, word and deed.

But when by God's inspiration and the special urging of our Lady they had firmly resolved to form a community together, they set in order everything that concerned their homes and families, left to their families what they needed and gave all the rest to the poor.

They climbed the heights of Monte Senario and built on its summit a little house that would suit their purpose, and there they lived in common. As time passed, they began to realize that they were called not simply to sanctify themselves but to receive others into their community, and so increase the membership of this new order our Lady had inspired them to found. In the beginning our Lady was the chief architect of this new order which was founded on the humility of its members, built up by their mutual love, and preserved by their poverty.

RESPONSORY

The community of believers was of one heart, one mind.

No one claimed as his own anything he possessed; all things were held in common.

They took their food joyfully, in simplicity of heart; they praised God, and were respected by all.

No one claimed as his own anything he possessed; all things were held in common.
Acts 4:32; 2:46b-47a

PRAYER

Lord,
fill us with the love
which inspired the seven holy brothers
to honor the mother of God with special devotion
and to lead your people to you.

We ask this through our Lord Jesus Christ, your Son,
who lives and reigns with you and the Holy Spirit,
one God, for ever and ever.

Our Father . . .

February 21

PETER DAMIAN, BISHOP AND DOCTOR

Saint Peter Damian was born at Ravenna in Italy in 1007. After completing his studies he began to teach, but soon abandoned this and became a member of a community of hermits where, once elected prior, he promoted the religious life with great fervor. His holy life and work affected people throughout Italy. When the Church was attacked by her enemies, he defended her by his writings and went on about like a missionary, helping others to reform their lives. He was created bishop and cardinal by Pope Stephen IX. Peter Damian died in 1072 and soon afterward was venerated as a saint.

READING

A reading from a letter by Saint Peter Damian, bishop

When men suffer pain for the evil they have perpetrated in life, they should take some reassurance. They also know that for their good deeds undying rewards await them in the life to come.

Do not be depressed. Do not let your weakness make you impatient. Instead, let the serenity of your spirit shine through your face. Let the joy of your mind burst forth. Let words of thanks break from your lips.

The way that God deals with men can only be praised. He pins people down now; at a later time he will raise them up.

The Scriptures reassure us: let your understanding strengthen your patience. In serenity look forward to the joy that follows sadness.

RESPONSORY

Blessed is the man who is found without fault,

who does not make gold his life's object,
who does not put his trust in wealth.

His future will be secure in the Lord.

He was able to sin, but did not;
he was able to do wrong, but would not.

His future will be secure in the Lord.
Sirach 31:8, 11, 10

PRAYER

All-powerful God,
help us to follow the teachings and example of Peter Damian.
By making Christ and the service of his Church
the first love of our lives,
may we come to the joys of eternal light,
where he lives and reigns with you and the Holy Spirit,
one God, for ever and ever.

Our Father . . .

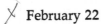 February 22

CHAIR OF PETER, APOSTLE
Feast

The feast of the Chair of Peter reflects the Church's belief that
Peter presided over the Church at Rome. Since the fourth century, this feast has been celebrated at Rome as a sign of the unity
of the Church founded upon that apostle.

READING

A reading from a sermon by Saint Leo the Great, pope

Out of the whole world one man, Peter, is chosen to preside at

55

the calling of all nations, and to be set over all the apostles and all the fathers of the Church. Though there are in God's people many bishops and many shepherds, Peter is thus appointed to rule in his own person those whom Christ also rules as the original ruler. Beloved, how great and wonderful is this sharing in his power that God in his goodness has given to this man. Whatever Christ has willed to be shared in common by Peter and the other leaders of the Church, it is only through Peter that he has given to others what he has not refused to bestow on them.

[Jesus said:] "Upon this rock I will build my Church, and the gates of hell shall not prevail against it." On this strong foundation, he says, I will build an everlasting temple. The great height of my Church, which is to penetrate the heavens, shall rise on the firm foundation of this faith.

Blessed Peter is therefore told: "To you I will give the keys of the kingdom of heaven. Whatever you bind on earth shall be bound also in heaven. Whatever you loose on earth shall be loosed also in heaven."

RESPONSORY

Before I called you from the boat, I knew you, Simon Peter, and I have appointed you leader of my people.
I have entrusted to you the keys of the kingdom of heaven.

Whatever you bind on earth
will be held bound in heaven.
Whatever you loose on earth
will be held loosed in heaven.
I have entrusted to you the keys of the kingdom of heaven.

All-powerful Father,
you have built your Church
on the rock of Saint Peter's confession of faith.
May nothing divide or weaken
our unity in faith and love.

Grant this through our Lord Jesus Christ, your Son,
who lives and reigns with you and the Holy Spirit,
one God, for ever and ever.

Our Father . . .

February 23

POLYCARP, BISHOP AND MARTYR
Memorial

Saint Polycarp, the bishop of Smyrna and a disciple of the apostles, accompanied Saint Ignatius of Antioch to Rome to confer with the Pope concerning the celebration of Easter. About the year 155 he suffered martyrdom by burning at the stake in the amphitheater at Smyrna.

READING

A reading from a letter by the Church of Smyrna on the martyrdom of Saint Polycarp

When the pyre was ready, Polycarp took off all his outer clothes and loosened his under-garment.

There and then he was surrounded by the material for the pyre. When they tried to fasten him also with nails, he said: "Leave me as I am. The one who gives me strength to endure the fire will also give me strength to stay quite still on the pyre, even

without the precaution of your nails." So they did not fix him to
the pyre with nails but only fastened him instead.

Looking up to heaven, he said: "Lord, almighty God, Father of
your beloved and blessed Son Jesus Christ, through whom we
have come to the knowledge of yourself, God of angels, of powers, of all creation, of all the race of saints who live in your sight,
I bless you for judging me worthy of this day, this hour, so that
in the company of the martyrs I may share the cup of Christ,
your anointed one, and so rise again to eternal life in soul and
body through the power of the Holy Spirit.

"I praise you for all things, I bless you, I glorify you through the
eternal priest of heaven, Jesus Christ, your beloved Son.
Through him be glory to you, together with him and the Holy
Spirit, now and for ever. Amen."

When he had said "Amen" and finished the prayer, the officials
at the pyre lit it. But, when a great flame burst out, those of us
privileged to see it witnessed a strange and wonderful thing.
Like a ship's sail swelling in the wind, the flame became as it
were a dome encircling the martyr's body. Surrounded by the
fire, his body was like bread that is baked, or gold and silver
white-hot in a furnace, not like flesh that has been burnt. So
sweet a fragrance came to us that it was like that of burning
incense or some other costly and sweet-smelling gum.

RESPONSORY

To the angel of the Church of Smyrna write this:
Thus says the Lord, the first and the last,
the one who was dead and now lives:
I know your suffering and your poverty,
but you are rich indeed!

**Be true to your faith until death,
and I will give you the crown of life.**

Have no fear of the sufferings you will have to endure.

The devil will send some of you to prison to be tested.
Be true to your faith until death,
and I will give you the crown of life.
Revelation 2:8-9, 10

PRAYER

God of all creation,
you gave your bishop Polycarp
the privilege of being counted among the saints
who gave their lives in faithful witness to the gospel.
May his prayers give us the courage
to share with him the cup of suffering
and to rise to eternal glory.

We ask this through our Lord Jesus Christ, your Son,
who lives and reigns with you and the Holy Spirit,
one God, for ever and ever.

Our Father . . .

March 4

CASIMIR

Saint Casimir, son of the king of Poland, was born in 1458. He practiced the Christian virtues with special regard to chastity and kindness to the poor and was zealous in the faith, particularly in his devotion to the holy eucharist and the Virgin Mary. Casimir died of consumption in 1484.

READING

A reading from the Life of Saint Casimir written by one who lived during his times

By the power of the Holy Spirit, Casimir burned with a sincere

59

and unpretentious love for almighty God. So rich was his love and so abundantly did it fill his heart, that it flowed out from his inner spirit toward his fellow men. As a result nothing was more pleasant, nothing more desirable for him, than to share his belongings, and even to dedicate and give his entire self to Christ's poor, to strangers, to the sick, to those in captivity and to all who suffer. To widows, orphans and the afflicted, he was not only a guardian and patron but a father, son and brother.

He actively took up the cause of the needy and unfortunate and embraced it as his own; for this reason the people called him the patron of the poor. Though the son of a king and descendant of a noble line, he was never haughty in his conversation or dealings with anyone, no matter how humble or obscure.

He always preferred to be counted among the meek and poor of spirit, among those who are promised the kingdom of heaven, rather than among the famous and powerful men of this world.

RESPONSORY

Invest your wealth according to the command of the Most High.

It will yield a profit far greater than gold.

Strive for justice, reverence, faith and love;
always be patient and gentle.

It will yield a profit far greater than gold.
Sirach 29:11; 1 Timothy 6:11

PRAYER

All-powerful God,
to serve you is to reign:
by the prayers of Saint Casimir,
help us to serve you in holiness and justice.

Grant this through our Lord Jesus Christ, your Son,

who lives and reigns with you and the Holy Spirit,
one God, for ever and ever.

Our Father . . .

March 7

PERPETUA AND FELICITY, MARTYRS
Memorial

Saints Perpetua and Felicity suffered martyrdom in the persecution by the Roman Emperor at Carthage in 203. A most accurate
account of their death still exists, derived partly from their own
testimonies and partly from a writer of the period.

READING

A reading from the story of the death of the holy martyrs of
Carthage

The day of the martyrs' victory dawned. They marched from
their cells into the amphitheater, as if into heaven, with cheerful
looks and graceful bearing. If they trembled it was for joy and
not for fear.

Perpetua was the first to be thrown down, and she fell prostrate.
She got up and, seeing that Felicity was prostrate, went over
and reached out her hand to her and lifted her up. Both stood up
together. Rousing herself as if from sleep (so deeply had she
been in spiritual ecstasy), she began to look around. To
everyone's amazement she said: "When are we going to be led
to the beasts?" When she heard that it had already happened
she did not at first believe it until she saw the marks of violence
on her body and her clothing.

The people, however, had demanded that the martyrs be led to
the middle of the amphitheater. They wanted to see the sword

thrust into the bodies of the victims, so that their eyes might share in the slaughter. Without being asked they went where the people wanted them to go; but first they kissed one another, to complete their witness with the customary kiss of peace.

Bravest and happiest martyrs! You were called and chosen for the glory of our Lord Jesus Christ.

RESPONSORY

Christ Jesus is seated at God's right hand,
and there he pleads on our behalf.

What can separate us from the love of Christ?
Not suffering, hardship, persecution,
not hunger, destitution, peril or sword.

In all of these trials the victory is ours,
because of Christ who loves us.

What can separate us from the love of Christ?
Not suffering, hardship, persecution,
not hunger, destitution, peril or sword.

PRAYER

Father,
your love gave the Saints Perpetua and Felicity
courage to suffer a cruel martyrdom.
By their prayers, help us to grow in love of you.

We ask this through our Lord Jesus Christ, your Son,
who lives and reigns with you and the Holy Spirit,
one God, for ever and ever.

Our Father . . .

March 8

JOHN OF GOD, RELIGIOUS

Saint John of God was born in Portugal in 1495. After a hazardous period in the military service, he chose the better way of life and devoted himself entirely to the care of the sick. Founding a hospital in Granada, Spain, he selected assistants who later formed the Order of Hospitallers of Saint John of God. He was most distinguished for his charity to the needy and the sick. Saint John died in Granada in 1550.

READING

A reading from a letter by Saint John of God, religious

If we look forward to receiving God's mercy, we can never fail to do good so long as we have the strength. For if we share with the poor, out of love for God, whatever he has given to us, we shall receive according to his promise a hundredfold in eternal happiness. What a fine profit, what a blessed reward! With outstretched arms he begs us to turn toward him, to weep for our sins, and to become the servants of love, first for ourselves then for our neighbors. Just as water extinguishes a fire, so love wipes away sin.

So many poor people come here that I very often wonder how we can care for them all, but Jesus Christ provides all things and nourishes everyone. Many of them come to the house of God, because the city of Granada is large and very cold, especially now in winter. More than a hundred and ten are now living here, sick and healthy, servants and pilgrims. Since this house is open to everyone, it receives the sick of every type and condition: the crippled, the disabled, lepers, mutes, the insane, paralytics, those suffering from scurvy and those bearing the afflictions of old age, many children, and above all countless pilgrims and travelers, who come here, and for whom we furnish the fire, water, and salt, as well as the utensils to cook their food. And for all of this no payment is requested, yet Christ provides.

I work here on borrowed money, a prisoner for the sake of Jesus Christ. And often my debts are so pressing that I dare not go out of the house for fear of being seized by my creditors. Whenever I see so many poor brothers and neighbors of mine suffering beyond their strength and overwhelmed with so many physical or mental ills which I cannot alleviate, then I become exceedingly sorrowful; but I trust in Christ, who knows my heart. And so I say: "Woe to the man who trusts in men rather than in Christ."

RESPONSORY

Share your bread with the hungry and destitute,
and take the poor and homeless into your own house.

**Then your light will break forth like the dawn;
you holiness will go before you.**

When you see a man who is naked, clothe him,
and do not scorn your brother.

**Then your light will break forth like the dawn;
your holiness will go before you.**
Isaiah 58:7-8

PRAYER

Father,
you gave John of God
love and compassion for others.
Grant that by doing good for others
we may be counted among the saints in your kingdom.

We ask this through our Lord Jesus Christ, your Son,
who lives and reigns with you and the Holy Spirit,
one God, for ever and ever.

Our Father . . .

March 9

FRANCES OF ROME, RELIGIOUS

Saint Frances was born at Rome in 1384. While still young she married and had three sons. Though living during a time of plague and poverty, she gave her goods to the poor and looked after the needs of the sick. She was remarkable in this active work for the destitute and also in cultivating the virtues of humility and patience. In 1425 she founded the Congregation of Oblates under the rule of Saint Benedict. Saint Frances died in 1440.

READING

A reading from the Life of Saint Frances of Rome by one of her followers

God not only tested the patience of Frances with respect to her material wealth, but he also tested her especially through long and serious illnesses which she had to undergo. And yet no one ever observed in her a tendency toward impatience. She never exhibited any displeasure when she complied with an order, no matter how foolish.

With peace of soul she always reconciled herself to the will of God and gave him thanks for all that happened.

God had not chosen her to be holy merely for her own advantage. Rather the gifts he conferred upon her were to be for the spiritual and physical advantage of her neighbor. For this reason he made her so lovable that anyone with whom she spoke would immediately feel captivated by love for her and ready to help her in everything she wanted. She seemed able to subdue the passions of every type of person with a single word and lead them to do whatever she asked.

For this reason people flocked to Frances from all directions, as to a safe refuge. No one left her without being consoled, although she openly rebuked them for their sins and fearlessly reproved them for what was evil and displeasing to God.

Many different diseases were rampant in Rome. Fatal diseases and plagues were everywhere, but the saint ignored the risk of contagion and displayed the deepest kindness toward the poor and the needy. Her empathy would first bring them to atone for their sins. Then she would help them by her eager care, and urge them lovingly to accept their trials, however difficult, from the hand of God. She would encourage them to endure their sufferings for love of Christ, since he had previously endured so much for them.

For thirty years Frances continued this service to the sick and the stranger. During epidemics like this it was not only difficult to find doctors to care for the body but even priests to provide remedies for the soul. She herself would seek them out and bring them to those who were disposed to receive the sacraments of penance and the Eucharist.

RESPONSORY

May you be blessed by the Lord our God,
for all the people know you are a woman of virtue.

The Lord has so glorified your name,
that your praise will never pass from the memory of man.
For all the people know you are a woman of virtue.
Ruth 3:10, 11; Judith 13:25

PRAYER

Merciful Father,
in Frances of Rome

you have given us a unique example of love in marriage
as well as in religious life.
Keep us faithful in your service,
and help us to see and follow you
in all the aspects of life.

We ask this through our Lord Jesus Christ, your Son,
who lives and reigns with you and the Holy Spirit,
one God, for ever and ever.

Our Father . . .

March 17

PATRICK, BISHOP
Commemoration

Saint Patrick was born in Great Britain about the year 385. As a
young man he was captured and sold as a slave in Ireland where
he had to tend sheep. Having escaped from slavery, he chose to
enter the priesthood, and later, as a bishop, he tirelessly
preached the gospel to the people of Ireland where he converted many to the faith and established the Church. He died at
Down in 461.

READING

A reading from the Confession of Saint Patrick, bishop

I came to the Irish peoples to preach the Gospel and endure the
taunts of unbelievers, putting up with reproaches about my
earthly pilgrimage, suffering many persecutions, even bondage,
and losing my birthright of freedom for the benefit of others.

If I am worthy, I am ready also to give up my life, without
hesitation and most willingly, for Christ's name. I want to
spend myself for that country, even in death, if the Lord should
grant me this favor.

67

It is among that people that I want to wait for the promise made by him, who assuredly never tells a lie. He makes this promise in the Gospel: "They shall come from the east and west and sit down with Abraham, Isaac and Jacob." This is our faith: believers are to come from the whole world.

RESPONSORY

God has given me the grace
to be a minister of Christ Jesus among the Gentiles,
and to assume the priestly duty of preaching the Gospel,

**so that the Gentiles might be received as an acceptable
    offering,
consecrated by the Holy Spirit.**

In my spirit I serve the Father
by preaching the Gospel of his Son.

**So that the Gentiles might be received as an acceptable
    offering,
consecrated by the Holy Spirit.**
Romans 15:15-16, 1:9

PRAYER

God our Father,
you sent Saint Patrick
to preach your glory to the people of Ireland.
By the help of his prayers,
may all Christians proclaim your love to all men.

Grant this through our Lord Jesus Christ, your Son,
who lives and reigns with you and the Holy Spirit,
one God, for ever and ever

Our Father . . .

March 18

CYRIL OF JERUSALEM, BISHOP AND DOCTOR
Commemoration

Saint Cyril was born of Christian parents in 315. He succeeded
Maximus as bishop of Jerusalem in 348. He was involved in the
dispute over Arianism and was more than once punished with
exile. His most famous book explained to the people the true
teachings of the faith and of Scripture and also the traditions of
the Church. He died in 386.

The following reading gives some of Saint Cyril's advice to those
who were preparing for baptism and confirmation.

READING

A reading from a catechetical instruction by Saint Cyril of
Jerusalem, bishop

Children of justice, follow John's exhortation: "Make straight
the way of the Lord." Remove all obstacles and stumbling blocks
so that you will be able to go straight along the road to eternal
life. Through a sincere faith prepare yourselves so that you may
be free to receive the Holy Spirit.

My brothers, this is a truly great occasion. Approach it with
caution. You are standing in front of God and in the presence of
the hosts of angels. The Holy Spirit is about to impress his seal
on each of your souls. You are about to be pressed into the
service of a great king.

And so prepare yourselves to receive the sacrament. The gleam-
ing white garments you are about to put on are not the prepara-
tion I am speaking of, but rather the devotion of a clean conscience.

True teaching was in his mouth;
no evil was ever found on his lips.

He walked with me in goodness and in peace.

My hand will be a steady help to him,
my arm will give him strength.

He walked with me in goodness and in peace.
Malachi 2:6; Psalm 89:22

PRAYER

Father,
through Cyril of Jerusalem
you led your Church to a deeper understanding
of the mysteries of salvation.
Let his prayers help us to know your Son better
and to have eternal life in all its fullness.

We ask this through our Lord Jesus Christ, your Son,
who lives and reigns with you and the Holy Spirit,
one God, for ever and ever.

Our Father . . .

March 19

JOSEPH, HUSBAND OF MARY
Solemnity

Today the Church honors Saint Joseph who was the guardian
and protector of Jesus and Mary. He was a man of faith who
trusted firmly in God. We look to him today as our guardian and
protector against the dangers that threaten us.

A reading from a sermon by Saint Bernardine of Siena, priest

There is a general rule concerning all special graces granted to any human being. Whenever the divine favor chooses someone to receive a special grace, or to accept a lofty vocation, God adorns the person chosen with all the gifts of the Spirit needed to fulfill the task at hand.

This general rule is especially verified in the case of Saint Joseph, the foster-father of our Lord and the husband of the Queen of our world, enthroned above the angels. He was chosen by the eternal Father as the trustworthy guardian and protector of his greatest treasures, namely, his divine Son and Mary, Joseph's wife. He carried out this vocation with complete fidelity until at last God called him, saying: "Good and faithful servant, enter into the joy of your Lord."

Remember us, Saint Joseph, and plead for us to your foster-child. Ask your most holy bride, the Virgin Mary, to look kindly upon us, since she is the mother of him who with the Father and the Holy Spirit lives and reigns eternally. Amen.

God has made me a father to the king
and master of all his household.

He has raised me up,
that he might save many people (alleluia).

The Lord is my helper and protector;
he is my savior.

He has raised me up,
that he might save many people (alleluia).
See Genesis 45:8; 50:20; Sirach 51:2

Father,
you entrusted our savior to the care of Saint Joseph.
By the help of his prayers
may your Church continue to serve its Lord, Jesus Christ,
who lives and reigns with you and the Holy Spirit,
one God, for ever and ever.

Our Father . . .

March 23

TURIBIUS DE MONGROVEJO, BISHOP
Commemoration

Saint Turibius was born in Spain around the year 1538. He taught law at the University of Salamanca, and in 1580 he was chosen as bishop of Lima and journeyed to America. Burning with apostolic zeal, he called together many councils and synods which successfully promoted the reform of religion throughout the whole region. He vigorously defended the laws of the Church and earnestly looked after the people committed to his care by visiting them frequently. He devoted much of his time and attention to the care of the native Indian population. He died in 1606.

The following reading tells us some of the things a good bishop does for his people. As we read it, we can see how it applies to Saint Turibius.

READING

A reading from the decree on the pastoral office of bishops in the Church of the Second Vatican Council

In exercising their duty of teaching, bishops are to proclaim the Gospel of Christ before men, a task that stands out among their

principal duties. In the strength of the Spirit they are to call men
to faith, or confirm them in a living faith. They are to set before
them the mystery of Christ in its entirety, that is, those truths
which are necessary in order to know Christ, as well as the
divinely revealed way of glorifying God and so attaining to eternal happiness.

Moreover, they are to make it clear that earthly realities and
human institutions are themselves directed, in the plan of God
the creator, toward man's salvation, and are thus able to make
no small contribution to the building up of the body of Christ.

In discharging their duty as father and shepherd, bishops
should be among their people as those who serve, good
shepherds who know their sheep and whose sheep know them.
They should be outstanding in their spirit of love and concern
for all, true fathers whose God-given authority all obey with
joyful heart. They should unite and mold the entire family of
their flock so that all are made aware of their responsibilities and
are able to live and work in loving communion with each other.

RESPONSORY

Be shepherds of God's flock;
give them good example,

and when the chief shepherd appears,
he will give you a crown of unfading glory.

You must have at heart every member of the flock,
for the Holy Spirit has made you their shepherds.
You must rule over the Church of God.

And when the chief shepherd appears,
he will give you a crown of unfading glory.
1 Peter 5:2, 3-4; Acts 20:28

Lord,
through the apostolic work of Saint Turibius
and his unwavering love of truth,
you helped your Church to grow.
May your chosen people continue to grow
in faith and holiness.

Grant this through our Lord Jesus Christ, your Son,
who lives and reigns with you and the Holy Spirit,
one God, for ever and ever.

Our Father, . . .

March 25

ANNUNCIATION
Solemnity

Saint Luke tells us that the Angel Gabriel was sent by God to the Virgin Mary to announce to her that she was to be the mother of Jesus. The angel said to her: "You have found favor with God. You shall conceive and bear a son and give him the name of Jesus" (Luke 1:30-31). Mary accepted the angel's message, and said: "I am the servant of the Lord. Let it be done to me as you say." At that moment Jesus was conceived as man, although he would not be born until nine months later. So what we celebrate today is not only the angel's message to Mary, but the fact that Jesus became man.

READING

A reading from a letter by Saint Leo the Great, pope

Lowliness is assured by majesty, weakness by power, mortality by eternity. To pay the debt of our sinful state, a nature that is incapable of suffering was joined to one that could suffer. Thus, in keeping with the healing that we needed, one and the same mediator between God and men, the man Jesus Christ, was able to die in one nature, and unable to die in the other.

He who is true God was therefore born in the complete and perfect nature of a true man, whole in his own nature, whole in ours.

He took the nature of a servant without stain of sin, enlarging our humanity without diminishing his divinity.

Thus the Son of God enters this lowly world. He comes down from the throne of heaven, yet does not separate himself from the Father's glory. He is born in a new condition, by a new birth.

He was born in a new condition, for invisible in his own nature he became visible in ours. Beyond our grasp, he chose to come within our grasp. Existing before time began, he began to exist at a moment in time. Incapable of suffering as God, he did not refuse to be a man, capable of suffering. Immortal, he chose to be subject to the laws of death.

He who is true God is also true man.

One and the same person—this must be said over and over again—is truly the Son of God and truly the son of man.

RESPONSORY

Receive, O Virgin Mary, the word
which the Lord has made known to you by the message of the
    angel:
You will conceive and give birth to a son, both God and man,
and you will be called blessed among women (alleluia).

A virgin, you will indeed bear a son;
ever chaste and holy, you will be the mother of our savior.
And you will be called blessed among women (alleluia).
See Luke 1:31, 42

75

God our Father,
your Word became man and was born of the Virgin Mary.
May we become more like Jesus Christ,
whom we acknowledge as our redeemer, God and man.

We ask this through our Lord Jesus Christ, your Son,
who lives and reigns with you and the Holy Spirit,
one God, for ever and ever.

Our Father . . .

EASTER

Easter celebrates the resurrection of Christ from the dead. It is the holiest and greatest celebration of the year for as Saint Paul says: " . . . if Christ has not been raised, our preaching is void of content and your faith is empty too" (1 Corinthians 15:14).

READING

A reading from a letter of Melito of Sardis, bishop

The Lord, though he was God, became man. He suffered for the sake of those who suffer, he was bound for those in bonds, condemned for the guilty, buried for those who lie in the grave; but he rose from the dead, and cried aloud: "Who will contend with me? Let him confront me." I have freed the condemned, brought the dead back to life, raised men from their graves. Who has anything to say against me? I, he said, am the Christ; I have destroyed death, triumphed over the enemy, trampled hell underfoot, bound the strong one, and taken men up to the heights of heaven: I am the Christ.

Come, then, all you nations of men, receive forgiveness for the sins that defile you. I am your forgiveness. I am the Passover that brings salvation. I am the lamb who was immolated for you. I am your ransom, your life, your resurrection, your light, I am your salvation and your king. I will bring you to the heights of heaven. With my own right hand I will raise you up, and I will show you the eternal Father.

RESPONSORY

Praised be the God and Father of our Lord Jesus Christ;
in his great mercy he has given us new life in hope

by raising Jesus Christ from the dead, alleluia.

Free your minds from all that holds them down;
learn self-control and put your full trust in God
who offers you his grace.

By raising Jesus Christ from the dead, alleluia.
1 Peter 1:3-13

PRAYER

God of unchanging power and light,
look with mercy and favor on your entire Church.
Bring lasting salvation to mankind,
so that the world may see the fallen lifted up,
the old made new,
and all things brought to perfection,
through him who is their origin,
our Lord Jesus Christ,
who lives and reigns for ever and ever.

Our Father . . .

April 2

FRANCIS OF PAOLA, HERMIT

Saint Francis was born at Paola in Italy in 1416. He founded a congregation of hermits, which was later entitled the Order of Minims, and approved by the Apostolic See in 1506. He died at Tours in France in 1507.

READING

A reading from a letter by Saint Francis of Paola

Fix your minds on the passion of our Lord Jesus Christ. Inflamed with love for us, he came down from heaven to redeem us. For our sake he endured every torment of body and soul and shrank from no bodily pain. He himself gave us an example of perfect patience and love. We, then, are to be patient in adversity.

Take pains to refrain from sharp words. Pardon one another so that later on you will not remember the injury. The recollection of an injury is itself wrong. It adds to our anger, nurtures our sin and hates what is good. It is a rusty arrow and poison for the soul. It puts all virtue to flight.

Be peace-loving. Peace is a precious treasure to be sought with great zeal. You are well aware that our sins arouse God's anger. You must change your life, therefore, so that God in his mercy will pardon you. What we conceal from men is known to God. Be converted, then, with a sincere heart. Live your life that you may receive the blessing of the Lord. Then the peace of God our Father will be with you always.

RESPONSORY

Though we are always alive,
we are continually being handed over to death
for the sake of Jesus,

so that the life of Jesus may be revealed in our mortal bodies (alleluia).

Even though our outward body is failing,
the inner man is being renewed with each passing day.

So that the life of Jesus may be revealed in our mortal bodies (alleluia).

PRAYER

Father of the lowly,
you raised Saint Francis of Paola
to the glory of your saints.
By his example and prayers,
may we come to the rewards
you have promised the humble.

We ask this through our Lord Jesus Christ, your Son,
who lives and reigns with you and the Holy Spirit,
one God, for ever and ever.

Our Father . . .

April 4

ISIDORE, BISHOP AND DOCTOR

Saint Isidore was born around the year 560 at Seville in Spain.
After his father's death he was raised by his brother Leander. He
was appointed bishop of Seville, and wrote many learned
works. As bishop, he called together several councils in Spain
and presided over them with wisdom. He died in 636.

READING

A reading from the Book of Maxims by Saint Isidore, bishop

Prayer purifies us, reading instructs us. Both are good when both are possible. Otherwise, prayer is better than reading.

If a man wants to be always in God's company, he must pray regularly and read regularly. When we pray, we talk to God; when we read, God talks to us.

All spiritual growth comes from reading and reflection. By reading we learn what we did not know; by reflection we retain what we have learned.

Reading the holy Scriptures confers two benefits. It trains the mind to understand them; it turns man's attention from the follies of the world and leads him to the love of God.

The conscientious reader will be more concerned to carry out what he has read than merely to acquire knowledge of it. In reading we aim at knowing, but we must put into practice what we have learned in our course of study.

The more you devote yourself to a study of the sacred utterances, the richer will be your understanding of them, just as the more the soil is tilled, the richer the harvest.

The man who is slow to grasp things but who really tries hard is rewarded, equally he who does not cultivate his God-given intellectual ability is condemned for despising his gifts and sinning by sloth.

Learning unsupported by grace may get into our ears; it never reaches the heart. But when God's grace touches our innermost minds to bring understanding, his word which has been received by the ear sinks deep into the heart.

RESPONSORY

When a teacher of the law becomes a disciple of the kingdom of
    heaven,

**he is like the head of a household
who is able to take from his storeroom treasures new and old
(alleluia).**

Wisdom makes its home in a discerning heart,
and it can even teach those who are foolish.

**He is like the head of a household
who is able to take from his storeroom treasures new and old
(alleluia).**
Matthew 13:52; Proverbs 14:33

PRAYER

Lord,
hear the prayers we offer in commemoration of Saint Isidore.
May your Church learn from his teaching
and benefit from his intercession.

Grant this through our Lord Jesus Christ, your Son,
who lives and reigns with you and the Holy Spirit,
one God, for ever and ever.

Our Father . . .

April 5

VINCENT FERRER, PRIEST

Saint Vincent Ferrer was born at Valencia in Spain in 1350. He
joined the Dominican Order and taught theology. As a
preacher, he traveled through many regions and instructed
many people to observe the true teachings of their faith and to
reform their lives. He died at Vannes in France in 1419.

A reading from a book On the Spiritual Life by Saint Vincent Ferrer, priest

If you truly want to help the soul of your neighbor, you should approach God first with all your heart. Ask him simply to fill you with charity, the greatest of all virtues; with it you can accomplish what you desire.

RESPONSORY

Proclaim the message, in season and out of season;

refute falsehood, correct error, call to obedience (alleluia).

I preached repentance to the people,
that they might turn to God.

Refute falsehood, correct error, call to obedience (alleluia).
2 Timothy 4:2; Acts 26:20

PRAYER

Father,
you called Saint Vincent Ferrer
to preach the gospel of the last judgment.
Through his prayers may we come with joy
to meet your Son in the kingdom of heaven,
where he lives and reigns with you and the Holy Spirit,
one God, for ever and ever.

Our Father . . .

April 7

JOHN BAPTIST DE LA SALLE, PRIEST
Memorial

Saint John Baptist de la Salle was born in France in 1651. After ordination to the priesthood, he devoted himself to the education of boys and the founding of schools for the poor. He brought his companions together as a religious congregation, for the sake of which he endured many sufferings. He died in 1719.

READING

A reading from a meditation by Saint John Baptist de la Salle, priest

Be driven by the love of God because Jesus Christ died for all, that those who live may live not for themselves but for him who died and rose for them.

Above all, let your charity and zeal show how you love the Church. Your work is for the Church, which is the body of Christ.

RESPONSORY

The people brought little children to Jesus that he might touch them,
but the disciples tried to discourage them.
Jesus saw this and said:
Let the little children come to me, and do not prevent them, for the kingdom of God belongs to such as these (alleluia).

Embracing them and placing his hands upon them,
he blessed them.

Let the little children come to me, and do not prevent them, for the kingdom of God belongs to such as these (alleluia).
Mark 10:13-14, 16

Father,
you chose Saint John Baptist de la Salle
to give young people a Christian education.
Give your Church teachers who will devote themselves
to helping your children grow
as Christian men and women.

We ask this through our Lord Jesus Christ, your Son,
who lives and reigns with you and the Holy Spirit,
one God, for ever and ever.

Our Father . . .

April 11

STANISLAUS, BISHOP AND MARTYR

Saint Stanislaus was born in Poland around the year 1030. He studied in Paris and was ordained to the priesthood. In 1071 he succeeded Bishop Lambert at Cracow. In this post he ruled as a good shepherd by helping the poor and visiting his clerics every year. When Stanislaus dared to reprove the king for his wicked life, that ruler had him put to death.

We can learn to imitate the bravery of Saint Stanislaus by following the advice we shall find in today's reading.

READING

A reading from a letter by Saint Cyprian, bishop and martyr

Dear brethren, let us arm ourselves with all our might, let us prepare ourselves for the struggle by innocence of heart, integrity of faith, dedication to virtue.

Let us take this armor and defend ourselves with these spiritual defenses from heaven, so that we may be able to resist the threats of the devil, and fight back on the evil day.

Let us put on the breastplate of righteousness so that our hearts may be safeguarded, proof against the arrows of the enemy.

Let us with fortitude bear the shield of faith to protect us by extinguishing all the burning arrows that the enemy may launch against us.

Dear brethren, have all this firmly fixed in your hearts. If the day of persecution finds us thinking on these things, and meditating upon them, the soldier of Christ, trained by Christ's commands and instructions, does not begin to panic at the thought of battle, but is ready for the crown of victory.

RESPONSORY

For the law of God this holy man engaged in combat even unto
    death.
He feared no wicked threats;
his faith was founded on solid rock (alleluia).

He renounced earthly joys,
and so gained the kingdom of heaven.
His faith was founded on solid rock (alleluia).

PRAYER

Father,
to honor you, Saint Stanislaus faced martyrdom with courage.
Keep us strong and loyal in our faith until death.

Grant this through our Lord Jesus Christ, your Son,

who lives and reigns with you and the Holy Spirit,
one God, for ever and ever.

Our Father . . .

April 13

MARTIN I, POPE AND MARTYR

Saint Martin was born at Todi in Italy. He became a member of
the clergy of Rome and was elected pope in 649. He convened
the council which condemned the heresy of the Monothelites,
who denied that Christ had both a human and a divine will. In
653 he was taken prisoner by the Emperor Constans and detained in Constantinople where he was forced to suffer many
indignities. Finally, he died in exile in 659.

Today's reading is from one of Saint Martin's letters which he
wrote while he was in exile. We can see how lonely he was, and
yet how he trusted in God.

READING

A reading from a letter by Saint Martin, pope

Indeed, I have been amazed and continue to be amazed at the
lack of perception and callousness of those who were once con-
nected with me, both my friends and my relatives. They have all
completely forgotten about my unhappy state, and do not care
to know where I am, whether I am alive or dead.

But "God wishes all men to be saved and to come to a knowledge of the truth" through the prayers of Peter. Hence I pray
that God will strengthen their hearts in the orthodox faith, help

them to stand firm against every heretic and enemy of the
Church, and guard them unshaken. In this way, together with
me in my humiliation, they will receive the crown of justice in
the true faith from the hand of our Lord and Savior Jesus Christ.
For the Lord himself will take care of this lowly body of mine as
befits his providence, whether this means unending suffering or
some small consolation. Why am I anxious? "The Lord is near."
But my hope is in his compassion that he will not delay in
putting an end to this course which he has assigned to me.

RESPONSORY

I have fought the good fight,
I have run the race to the finish,
I have kept the faith;

now a crown of holiness awaits me (alleluia).

Nothing has seemed worthwhile to me except to know Christ,
to be one with him in his sufferings,
to bear his death in my body.

Now a crown of holiness awaits me (alleluia).
2 Timothy 4:7-8; Philippians 3:8-10

PRAYER

Merciful God, our Father,
neither hardship, pain, nor the threat of death
could weaken the faith of Saint Martin.
Through our faith, give us courage
to endure whatever sufferings the world may inflict upon us.

We ask this through our Lord Jesus Christ, your Son,
who lives and reigns with you and the Holy Spirit,
one God, for ever and ever.

Our Father . . .

April 21

ANSELM, BISHOP AND DOCTOR

Saint Anselm was born in northern Italy. He entered the Benedictine Order at the monastery of Bec in France. While he quickly progressed in the spiritual life, he taught theology to his fellow students. He went to England where he was appointed archbishop of Canterbury. He fought vigorously for the freedom of the Church, and for this he was twice exiled. He has achieved fame for his writings, especially those on mystical theology. He died in 1109.

READING

A reading from one of the works of Saint Anselm, bishop

O God, let me know you and love you so that I may find joy in you; and if I cannot do so fully in this life, let me at least make some progress every day, until at last that knowledge, love and joy come to me in all their plenitude. While I am here on earth let me know you fully; let my love for you grow deeper here, so that there I may love you fully. On earth then I shall have great joy in hope, and in heaven complete joy in the fulfillment of my hope.

O Lord, through your Son you command us, no, you counsel us to ask, and you promise that you will hear us so that our joy may be complete. Give me then what you promise to give through your Truth. You, O God, are faithful; grant that I may receive my request, so that my joy may be complete.

RESPONSORY

We honor Anselm, an outstanding doctor and a disciple of Lanfranc.

While an abbot he was greatly loved by his fellow monks, but he was called to serve as a bishop.

He fought strenuously for the freedom of holy Church, alleluia.

He steadfastly asserted that the Church, the bride of Christ, was not a slave but free.

He fought strenuously for the freedom of holy Church, alleluia.

PRAYER

Father,
you called Saint Anselm
to study and teach the sublime truths you have revealed.
Let your gift of faith come to the aid of our understanding
and open our hearts to your truth.

Grant this through our Lord Jesus Christ, your Son,
who lives and reigns with you and the Holy Spirit,
one God, for ever and ever.

Our Father . . .

April 23

GEORGE, MARTYR

The veneration of Saint George began as early as the fourth century at Lydda in Palestine, where a church was built in his honor. From antiquity this veneration has spread throughout both the East and the West.

READING

A reading from a sermon by Saint Peter Damian, bishop

Saint George was a man who abandoned one army for another: he gave up the rank of tribune to enlist as a soldier for Christ. Eager to encounter the enemy, he first stripped away his worldly wealth by giving all he had to the poor. Then, free and unencumbered, bearing the shield of faith, he plunged into the thick of the battle, an ardent soldier for Christ.

Clearly what he did serves to teach us a valuable lesson: if we are afraid to strip ourselves of our worldly possessions, then we are unfit to make a strong defense of the faith.

Dear brothers, let us not only admire the courage of this fighter in heaven's army but follow his example. Let us be inspired to strive for the reward of heavenly glory.

We must now cleanse ourselves, as Saint Paul tells us, from all defilement of body and spirit, so that one day we too may deserve to enter that temple of blessedness to which we now aspire.

RESPONSORY

For the law of God this holy man engaged in combat even unto
    death.
He feared no wicked threats;

his faith was founded on solid rock, alleluia.

He renounced earthly joys,
and so gained the kingdom of heaven.

His faith was founded on solid rock, alleluia.

PRAYER

Lord,
hear the prayers of those who praise your mighty power.
As Saint George was ready to follow Christ in suffering and
    death,
so may he be ready to help us in our weakness.

We ask this through our Lord Jesus Christ, your Son,
who lives and reigns with you and the Holy Spirit,
one God, for ever and ever.

Our Father . . .

April 24

FIDELIS OF SIGMARINGEN, PRIEST AND MARTYR

Saint Fidelis was born in the town of Sigmaringen in Germany
in 1578. He entered the Order of Friars Minor Capuchins and led
an austere life of penance, vigils and prayer. Continuously engaged in preaching the word of God, he was commissioned by
the Sacred Congregation for the Propagation of the Faith to
preach in a part of Switzerland where the Catholic faith was
persecuted. In 1622 he was attacked by a band of heretics and
suffered martyrdom.

READING

A reading from a eulogy for Saint Fidelis of Sigmaringen, priest
and martyr

Pope Benedict XIV praised Fidelis as a confessor of the Catholic
faith in these words: "He practiced the fullness of charity in
bringing consolation and relief to his neighbors as well as strangers. With a father's love he embraced all those who were in
trouble. He supported great numbers of poor people with the
alms he had collected from every quarter.

"With wealth collected from the powerful and from princes, he
comforted widows and orphans in their loneliness. He was always helping prisoners in their spiritual and bodily needs. He
showed constant zeal in visiting and comforting the sick whom
he would win back to God and prepare for their last struggle."

In addition to this charity, he was faithful in truth as well as in name. His zeal for defending the Catholic faith was unsurpassed and he preached it tirelessly. A few days before he shed his blood to bear witness to his preaching, he gave his last sermon. These are the words he left as a testament: "O Catholic faith, how solid, how strong you are. How deeply rooted, 'how firmly founded on a solid rock.' Heaven and earth will pass away, but you can never pass away. From the beginning the whole world opposed you, but you mightily triumphed over everything. 'This is the victory that overcomes the world, our faith.' It has subjected powerful kings to the rule of Christ; it has bound nations to his service.

"What made the holy apostles and martyrs endure fierce agony and bitter torments, except faith, and especially faith in the resurrection?

"It is living faith 'that expresses itself through love.' It is this that makes us put aside the goods of the present in the hope of future goods. It is because of faith that we exchange the present for the future."

RESPONSORY

I have fought the good fight,
I have run the race to the finish,
I have kept the faith;

now a crown of holiness awaits me, alleluia.

Nothing has seemed worthwhile to me except to know Christ,
to be one with him in his sufferings,
to bear his death in my body.

Now a crown of holiness awaits me, alleluia.
2 Timothy 4:7-8; Philippians 3:8-10

Father,
you filled Saint Fidelis with the fire of your love
and gave him the privilege of dying
that the faith might live.
Let his prayers keep us firmly grounded in your love,
and help us to come to know the power of Christ's resurrection.

We ask this through our Lord Jesus Christ, your Son,
who lives and reigns with you and the Holy Spirit,
one God, for ever and ever.

Our Father . . .

April 25

MARK, EVANGELIST
Feast

Saint Mark, a cousin of Barnabas, accompanied Saint Paul on his
first missionary journey and later went with him to Rome. He
was a disciple of Saint Peter whose teaching was the basis for
Mark's gospel. Mark is said to be the founder of the church of
Alexandria.

READING

A reading from the book Against Heresies by Saint Irenaeus,
bishop

The Church, which has spread everywhere, even to the ends of
the earth, received the faith from the apostles and their disciples. By faith, we believe in one God, the almighty Father "who
made heaven and earth and the sea and all that is in them." We
believe in one Lord Jesus Christ, the Son of God, who became
man for our salvation. And we believe in the Holy Spirit who
through the prophets foretold God's plan: the coming of our

beloved Lord Jesus Christ, his birth from the Virgin, his passion, his resurrection from the dead, his ascension into heaven, and his final coming from heaven in the glory of his Father, to "recapitulate all things" and to raise all men from the dead, so that, by the decree of his invisible Father, he may make a just judgment in all things and so that "every knee should bow in heaven and on earth and under the earth" to Jesus Christ our Lord and our God, our Savior and our King, and "every tongue confess him."

The Church, spread throughout the whole world, received this preaching and this faith and now preserves it carefully, dwelling as it were in one house. Having one soul and one heart, the Church holds this faith, preaches and teaches it consistently as though by a single voice. For though there are different languages, there is but one tradition.

Just as God's creature, the sun, is one and the same the world over, so also does the Church's preaching shine everywhere to enlighten all men who want to come to a knowledge of truth.

RESPONSORY

Tell all the nations how glorious God is, alleluia, alleluia.

Tell all the nations how glorious God is, alleluia, alleluia.

Make known his wonders to every people,
alleluia, alleluia.

Glory to the Father . . .

Tell all the nations how glorious God is, alleluia, alleluia.

PRAYER

Father,
you gave Saint Mark
the privilege of proclaiming your gospel.

May we profit by his wisdom
and follow Christ more faithfully.

Grant this through our Lord Jesus Christ, your Son,
who lives and reigns with you and the Holy Spirit,
one God, for ever and ever.

Our Father . . .

April 28

PETER CHANEL, PRIEST AND MARTYR

Saint Peter Chanel was born in France in 1803. After ordination
to the priesthood, he was engaged in pastoral work for a few
years. He then joined the Marists and journeyed to Oceania to
preach the gospel. Despite many hardships he converted some
of the natives to the faith. Out of hatred for the faith, a band of
native warriors killed him in 1841 on the island of Futuna.

READING

A reading from a sermon honoring Saint Peter, priest and martyr.

As soon as Peter embraced religious life in the Society of Mary,
he was sent at his own request to the missions of Oceania, and
landed on the island of Futuna in the Pacific Ocean, where the
name of Christ had never before been preached. A lay brother
who was constantly at his side gave the following account of his
life in the missions.

"Because of his labors he was often burned by the heat of the
sun, and famished with hunger, and he would return home wet
with perspiration and completely exhausted. Yet he always remained in good spirits, courageous and energetic, as if he were
returning from a pleasure jaunt, and this would happen almost
every day.

95

"He could never refuse anything to the Futunians, even to those who persecuted him; he always made excuses for them and never rejected them, even though they were often rude and troublesome. He displayed an unparalleled mildness toward everyone on all occasions without exception. It is no wonder then that the natives used to call him the 'good-hearted-man.' He once told a fellow religious: 'In such a difficult mission one has to be holy.' "

Quietly he preached Christ and the Gospel, but there was little response. Still with invincible perseverance he pursued his missionary task on both the human and religious level, relying on the example and words of Christ: "There is one who sows and another who reaps." And he constantly prayed for help from the Mother of God, to whom he was especially devoted.

By his preaching of Christianity he destroyed the cult of the evil spirits, which the chieftains of the Futunians encouraged in order to keep the tribe under their rule. This was the reason they subjected Peter to a most cruel death, hoping that by killing him the seeds of the Christian religion which he had sowed would be annihilated.

On the day before his martyrdom he had said: "It does not matter if I die. Christ's religion is so deeply rooted on this island that it cannot be destroyed by my death."

The blood of this martyr benefited, in the first place, the natives of Futuna, for a few years later they were all converted to the faith of Christ. But it benefited as well the other islands of Oceania, where Christian churches, which claim Peter as their first martyr, are now flourishing.

RESPONSORY

So great a harvest, and so few to gather it in;

pray to the Lord of the harvest,
beg him to send out laborers for his harvest, alleluia.

You will receive power when the Holy Spirit comes upon you, and you will be my witnesses to the ends of the earth.
Pray to the Lord of the harvest,
beg him to send out laborers for his harvest, alleluia.
Luke 10:2; Acts 1:8

PRAYER

Father,
you called Saint Peter Chanel to work for your Church
and gave him the crown of martyrdom.
May our celebration of Christ's death and resurrection
make us faithful witnesses to the new life he brings,
for he lives and reigns with you and the Holy Spirit,
one God, for ever and ever.

Our Father . . .

April 29

CATHERINE OF SIENA, VIRGIN AND DOCTOR
Memorial

Saint Catherine was born at Siena in 1347. While still a young girl, she sought the way of perfection and entered the Third Order of Saint Dominic. On fire with love of God and neighbor, she established peace and concord between cities, vigorously fought for the rights and freedom of the Pope and promoted the renewal of religious life. She also composed works of doctrine and spiritual inspiration. She died in 1380.

READING

A reading from the dialogue On Divine Providence by Saint Catherine of Siena, virgin and doctor

Eternal Trinity, Godhead, mystery deep as the sea, you could give me no greater gift than the gift of yourself. For you are a fire ever burning and never consumed, which itself consumes all the selfish love that fills my being. Yes, you are a fire that takes away the coldness, illuminates the mind with its light and causes me to know your truth. And I know that you are beauty and wisdom itself. The food of angels, you gave yourself to man in the fire of your love.

RESPONSORY

My sister and my beloved, open yourself to me,
you are a coheir of my Kingdom
and you have understood the hidden mysteries of my truth.

You are enriched with the gift of my Spirit,
cleansed of all sin by the shedding of my blood, alleluia.

Go forth from the quiet of contemplation
and courageously bear witness to my truth.

You are enriched with the gift of my Spirit,
cleansed of all sin by the shedding of my blood, alleluia.

PRAYER

Father,
in meditating on the sufferings of your Son
and in serving your Church,
Saint Catherine was filled with the fervor of your love.
By her prayers,
may we share in the mystery of Christ's death
and rejoice in the revelation of his glory,
for he lives and reigns with you and the Holy Spirit,
one God, for ever and ever.

Our Father . . .

April 30

PIUS V, POPE

Saint Pius V was born in Italy in 1504. He entered the Dominican Order and taught theology. After being ordained a bishop
and named a cardinal, he became pope in 1566. He worked hard
to reform the Church as begun at the Council of Trent. He promoted the spread of the faith and made changes to improve the
liturgy. He died on May 1, 1572.

In today's reading, Saint Augustine points out the importance of
the pope in the Church. Saint Pius V was a holy pope who lived
up to these ideals.

READING

A reading from a treatise on John by Saint Augustine, bishop

Now the apostle Peter, because of the primacy of his apostleship, stood as a symbol of the entire Church.

In himself he was by nature one man, by grace one Christian, by
a more abundant grace an apostle and the chief of the apostles.
But Christ said to him: "To you I shall give the keys of the
kingdom of heaven and whatever you will bind upon the earth
will be bound also in heaven and whatever you will forgive
upon the earth will be forgiven also in heaven." Now these
words applied to the entire Church. In this life it is shaken by
various trials, as if by rains, floods and tempests, but it does not
fall because it is founded upon the rock from which Peter received his name.

The Lord said: "Upon this rock I shall build my Church" because Peter has first said: "You are Christ, the Son of the living
God." The Lord was really saying: "I shall build my Church
upon the rock which you have acknowledged." For the "rock
was Christ," and upon this foundation even Peter himself was
raised up.

The Church, which is founded upon Christ, received from him the keys of the kingdom of heaven, that is, the power of binding and forgiving sins, in the person of Peter. Therefore this Church, by loving and following Christ, is set free from evil.

RESPONSORY

If you warn the virtuous man to avoid sin,
and he does not sin,
he shall surely live
and you shall save your own life, alleluia.

Be careful of what you do and teach,
and you will save yourself
and all who listen to you.
And you shall save your own life, alleluia.
Ezekiel 3:21, 1 Timothy 4:16

PRAYER

Father,
you chose Saint Pius V as pope of your Church
to protect the faith and give you more fitting worship.
By his prayers,
help us to celebrate your holy mysteries
with a living faith and an effective love.

We ask this through our Lord Jesus Christ, your Son,
who lives and reigns with you and the Holy Spirit,
one God, for ever and ever.

Our Father . . .

May 1

JOSEPH THE WORKER

Saint Joseph was not only the protector of Mary, his wife, and Jesus, his foster son. He was also a man who had to work to keep the Holy Family fed and clothed and housed. We honor him today because he is the kind of father any married man ought to be.

Joseph shows us that work is not something to be avoided. It is God's way of helping us to help others.

Our reading today gives us the reason why we, like Saint Joseph, should work for the Lord and for all people.

READING

A reading from the epistle to the Colossians

"Whatever you do, work at it with your whole being. Do it for the Lord rather than for men, since you know full well you will receive an inheritance from him as your reward."

RESPONSORY

The Lord God put man in the garden of Eden
to cultivate the garden and care for it, alleluia.

From the beginning of time this has been man's lot.
To cultivate the garden and care for it, alleluia.
See Genesis 2:15

PRAYER

God our Father,
creator and ruler of the universe,

101

in every age you call man
to develop and use his gifts for the good of others.
With Saint Joseph as our example and guide,
help us to do the work you have asked
and come to the rewards you have promised.

We ask this through our Lord Jesus Christ, your Son,
who lives and reigns with you and the Holy Spirit,
one God, for ever and ever.

Our Father...

May 2

ATHANASIUS, BISHOP AND DOCTOR
Memorial

Saint Athanasius was born at Alexandria in Egypt in 295. He
accompanied Bishop Alexander to the Council of Nicaea, and
succeeded him as bishop of Alexandria. He fought courageously
against the Arian heresy. For this he suffered many hardships
and was exiled several times. His writings are outstanding in
their explanation and defense of the true teachings of the faith.
He died in 373.

READING

A reading from a talk by Saint Athanasius, bishop

The Word of God, incorporeal, incorruptible and immaterial,
entered our world.

Out of his loving-kindness for us he came to us, and we see this
in the way he revealed himself openly to us. Taking pity on
mankind's weakness, and moved by our corruption, he could
not stand aside and see death have the mastery over us. He did
not want creation to perish and his Father's work in fashioning

man to be in vain. He therefore took to himself a body, no different from our own, for he did not wish simply to be in a body or only to be seen.

By dying for others, he immediately banished death for all mankind. The corruption of death no longer holds any power over mankind, thanks to the Word, who has come to dwell among us through his one body.

You will be my spokesman.
I will make you a solid wall of brass to these people.

They will fight against you,
but they shall not prevail,
for I am with you, alleluia.

False teachers will arise.
They will secretly bring in destructive heresies
and deny the Master who saved them.

They will fight against you,
but they shall not prevail,
for I am with you, alleluia.
Jeremiah 15:19, 20; 2 Peter 2:1

Father,
you raised up Saint Athanasius
to be an outstanding defender
of the truth of Christ's divinity.
By his teaching and protection
may we grow in your knowledge and love.

Grant this through our Lord Jesus Christ, your Son,
who lives and reigns with you and the Holy Spirit,
one God, for ever and ever.

Our Father . . .

May 3

PHILIP AND JAMES, APOSTLES
Feast

Philip was born at Bethsaida. At first a disciple of John the
Baptist, he became a follower of Christ. James, a cousin of the
Lord and the son of Alphaeus, ruled over the Church at
Jerusalem, wrote an epistle and converted many of the Jewish
people to the faith. He led an austere life and suffered martyr-
dom in the year 62.

READING

From the treatise On the Treatment of Heretics by Tertullian,
priest

Our Lord Jesus Christ himself declared what he was, what he
had been, how he was carrying out his Father's will, what obligations he demanded of men. This he did during his earthly life,
either publicly to the crowds or privately to his disciples. Twelve
of these he picked out to be his special companions, appointed
to teach the nations.

They then went out into the whole world and proclaimed to the
nations the same doctrinal faith.

They set up churches in every city.

Every family has to be traced back to its origins. That is why we
can say that all these great churches constitute that one original
Church of the apostles; for it is from them that they all come.

The only way in which we can prove what the apostles
taught—that is to say, what Christ revealed to them—is through
those same churches. They were founded by the apostles themselves, who first preached to them by what is called the living
voice and later by means of letters.

The Lord had said clearly in former times: "I have many more things to tell you, but you cannot endure them now." But he went on to say: "When the Spirit of truth comes, he will lead you into the whole truth." Thus Christ shows us that the apostles had full knowledge of the truth, for he had promised that they would receive the "whole truth" through the Spirit of truth.

RESPONSORY

You have made them rulers over all the earth, alleluia, alleluia.

You have made them rulers over all the earth, alleluia, alleluia.

They will always remember your name, O Lord, alleluia, alleluia.

Glory to the Father . . .

You have made them rulers over all the earth, alleluia, alleluia.

PRAYER

God our Father,
every year you give us joy
on the festival of the apostles Philip and James.
By the help of their prayers
may we share in the suffering, death, and resurrection
of your only Son
and come to the eternal vision of your glory.

We ask this through our Lord Jesus Christ, your Son,
who lives and reigns with you and the Holy Spirit,
one God, for ever and ever.

Our Father . . .

May 12

NEREUS AND ACHILLEUS, MARTYRS

Saints Nereus and Achilleus were at first in military service, but both left the military once they had converted to the faith. For this faith they were condemned to death, probably during the reign of Diocletian. Their sepulcher is preserved in a cemetery near Rome, and a church has been constructed in their honor. Saints Nereus and Achilleus followed in the footsteps of Christ through their sufferings and death. In the following reading Saint Cyprian points out how we can follow Christ and what our reward will be.

READING

A reading from a letter of Saint Cyprian, bishop and martyr

Holy Scripture speaks of the sufferings which consecrate God's martyrs and sanctify them by the very testing of pain: "Though in the eyes of men they suffered torments, their hope is full of immortality."

The Lord himself is an example of all this in his own person. He teaches us that only those who have followed him along his way arrive at his kingdom: "He who loves his life in this world will lose it. And he who hates his life in this world will save it for eternal life." And again he says: "Do not fear those who kill the body, but cannot kill the soul; fear rather him who can kill both body and soul and send them to hell." Paul too admonishes us, that as we desire to gain the Lord's promises we must imitate the Lord in all things. "We are God's children," he tells us. "If children, we are also heirs of God, and coheirs with Christ, if only we suffer with him, that we may also be glorified with him."

The Lord shall wipe away every tear from the eyes of his saints,
and there shall no longer be mourning,
nor crying, nor pain,

for all that used to be has passed away.

They shall never again know hunger or thirst,
nor shall the sun and the dry winds beat down on them.

For all that used to be has passed away.
Revelation 21:4; 7:16

PRAYER

Father,
we honor Saints Nereus and Achilleus for their courage
in dying to profess their faith in Christ.
May we experience the help of their prayers
at the throne of your mercy.

Grant this through our Lord Jesus Christ, your Son,
who lives and reigns with you and the Holy Spirit,
one God, for ever and ever.

Our Father...

On the same day,

May 12

PANCRAS, MARTYR

Saint Pancras, martyr, died at Rome probably during the persecutions. His tomb over which Pope Symmachus built a church is preserved.

In the following reading, Saint Bernard teaches us how to apply to ourselves the lesson of courage we can learn from a martyr like Saint Pancras.

A reading from a sermon by Saint Bernard, abbot

God himself descended to be near those who are saddened in spirit, to be with us in our tribulation. One day "we shall be caught up together in the clouds to meet the Lord in the air; and so we shall always be with the Lord"—provided, however, that we are concerned here below to have him with us, as our companion on the journey, who will restore us to our true country or, better, as one who is now on our way and our true country hereafter.

"If God is with us who can be against us?" And if he then rescues us, who will steal us from his hand? Lastly, if he honors us, who can dishonor us? If he honors us, who can humiliate us?

RESPONSORY

For the law of God this holy man engaged in combat even unto
    death.
He feared no wicked threats;

his faith was founded on solid rock, alleluia.

He renounced earthly joys,
and so gained the kingdom of heaven.

His faith was founded on solid rock, alleluia.

PRAYER

God of mercy,
give your Church joy and confidence
through the prayers of Saint Pancras.
Keep us faithful to you
and steadfast in your service.

We ask this through our Lord Jesus Christ, your Son,

who lives and reigns with you and the Holy Spirit,
one God, for ever and ever.

Our Father . . .

May 14

MATTHIAS, APOSTLE
Feast

Because he had been a witness to the resurrected Lord, Saint
Matthias was chosen by the other apostles to take the place of
Judas. The Acts of the Apostles (1:15-26) tells of how he was
numbered among the Twelve.

In our reading today Saint John Chrysostom speaks of the part
the Spirit of the Lord Jesus played in the choice of Matthias.

READING

A reading from a homily on the Acts of the Apostles by Saint
John Chrysostom, bishop

"In those days, Peter stood up in the midst of the disciples and
said . . ." As the fiery spirit to whom the flock was entrusted by
Christ and as the leader in the band of the apostles, Peter always
took the initiative in speaking: "My brothers, we must choose
from among our number." He left the decision to the whole
body, at once augmenting the honor of those elected and avoid-
ing any suspicion of partiality.

Did not Peter then have the right to make the choice himself?
Certainly he had the right, but he did not want to give the
appearance of showing special favor to anyone. "And they
nominated two," we read, "Joseph, who was called Barsabbas
and surnamed Justus, and Matthias." He himself did not nomi-
nate them; all present did. But it was he who brought the issue

forward, pointing out that it was not his own idea but had been suggested to him by a scriptural prophecy.

And they all prayed together, saying: "You, Lord, know the hearts of men; make your choice known to us. You, not we." Appropriately they said that he knew the hearts of men, because the choice was to be made by him, not by others.

They spoke with such confidence, because someone had to be appointed. They did not say "choose" but "make known to us" the chosen one; "the one you choose," they said, fully aware that everything was being preordained by God.

RESPONSORY

Lord, you know the hearts of all.

**Show us the one whom you have chosen
to assume this ministry and apostleship, alleluia.**

They cast lots and the choice fell upon Matthias,
and he was added to the eleven apostles.

**Show us the one whom you have chosen
to assume this ministry and apostleship, alleluia.**
Acts 1:24-25

PRAYER

Father,
you called Saint Matthias to share in the mission of the apostles.
By the help of his prayers
may we receive with joy the love you share with us
and be counted among those you have chosen.

We ask this through our Lord Jesus Christ, your Son,
who lives and reigns with you and the Holy Spirit,
one God, for ever and ever.

Our Father . . .

May 15

ISIDORE

Isidore was born in Madrid, Spain, and spent his life working as a farm laborer, while at the same time devoting himself to prayer. Many miracles are attributed to his intercession.

In the following reading Saint Augustine tells us what it means to follow Christ. Saint Isidore followed Christ in this way.

READING

A reading from a sermon by Saint Augustine, bishop

"If anyone wishes to come after me, let him deny himself, take up his cross and follow me." The Lord's command seems difficult and painful: that anyone who wishes to follow him must deny himself. But his command is not really difficult or painful, since he himself helps us to do what he commands. True also are his own words: "My yoke is mild and my burden is light." For love makes easy whatever is difficult in his commands.

What does it mean, "let him take up his own cross?" It means he must endure many things that are painful; that is the way he must follow me.

But hold out, be steadfast, endure, bear the delay, and you have carried the cross.

RESPONSORY

This holy man worked wonders in the sight of God;
he praised the Lord with his whole heart.
May he intercede for sinful mankind.

He was a man without bitterness,
his life a living praise to God.

He avoided all evil deeds and kept himself sinless to the end.
May he intercede for sinful mankind.

PRAYER

Lord God,
all creation is yours, and you call us to serve you
by caring for the gifts that surround us.
May the example of Saint Isidore urge us
to share our food with the hungry
and to work for the salvation of mankind.

We ask this through our Lord Jesus Christ, your Son,
who lives and reigns with you and the Holy Spirit,
one God, for ever and ever.

Our Father . . .

May 18

JOHN I, POPE AND MARTYR

Saint John was born in Italy and elected bishop of the Church of Rome in 523. He went to Emperor Justin in Constantinople as an ambassador of King Theodoric, who was ruler of Italy. On his return he was captured by the king, who was displeased at the outcome of the embassy, and cast into prison at Ravenna where he died in 526.

Today's reading reminds us that people who suffer for what is right, as Saint John did, give us an example of how we ought to live.

READING

A reading from a letter by Saint John of Avila, priest

112

Dear brothers and sisters, I pray God may open your eyes and let you see what hidden treasures he bestows on us in the trials from which the world thinks only to flee. Shame turns into honor when we seek God's glory. Present affliction becomes the source of heavenly glory. To those who suffer wounds in fighting his battles God opens his arms in loving, tender friendship.

That is why he [Christ] tells us that if we want to join him, we shall travel the way he took. It is surely not right that the Son of God should go his way on the path of shame while the sons of men walk the way of worldly honor: "The disciple is not above his teacher, nor the servant greater than his master."

RESPONSORY

Though we are always alive,
we are continually being handed over to death
for the sake of Jesus,

so that the life of Jesus may be revealed in our mortal bodies, alleluia.

Even though our outward body is failing,
the inner man is being renewed with each passing day.

So that the life of Jesus may be revealed in our mortal bodies, alleluia.
2 Corinthians 4:11, 16

PRAYER

God our Father,
rewarder of all who believe,
hear our prayers
as we celebrate the martyrdom of Pope John.
Help us to follow him in loyalty to the faith.

Grant this through our Lord Jesus Christ, your Son,

who lives and reigns with you and the Holy Spirit,
one God, for ever and ever.

Our Father . . .

May 20

BERNARDINE OF SIENA, PRIEST

Saint Bernardine was born in Italy in 1380. He entered the Friars
Minor and, after being ordained to the priesthood, traveled
throughout Italy preaching with great success. He increased devotion to the holy name of Jesus and fostered learning and discipline in his Order. He also wrote works on theology. Saint
Bernardine died in 1444.

We can get some idea of Saint Bernardine's love for the holy
name of Jesus from today's reading.

READING

A reading from a sermon by Saint Bernardine of Siena, priest

When a fire is lit to clear a field, it burns off all the dry and
useless weeds and thorns. When the sun rises and darkness is
dispelled, robbers, night-prowlers and burglars hide away. So
when Paul's voice was raised to preach the Gospel to the nations, like a great clap of thunder in the sky, his preaching was a
blazing fire carrying all before it. It was the sun rising in full
glory. Infidelity was consumed by it, false beliefs fled away, and
the truth appeared like a great candle lighting the whole world
with its brilliant flame.

By word of mouth, by letters, by miracles and by the example of
his own life, Saint Paul bore the name of Jesus wherever he

went. He praised the name of Jesus "at all times," but never more than when "bearing witness to his faith."

Moreover, the Apostle did indeed carry this name "before the Gentiles and kings and the sons of Israel" as a light to enlighten all nations. And this was his cry wherever he journeyed: "The night is passing away, the day is at hand. Let us then cast off the works of darkness and put on the armor of light; let us conduct ourselves honorably as in the day." Paul himself showed forth the burning and shining-light set upon a candlestick, everywhere proclaiming "Jesus, and him crucified."

And so the Church, the bride of Christ strengthened by his testimony, rejoices with the psalmist, singing: "O God from my youth you have taught me, and I still proclaim your wondrous deeds." The psalmist exhorts her to do this, as he says: "Sing to the Lord, and bless his name, proclaim his salvation day after day." And this salvation is Jesus, her savior.

RESPONSORY

I will always praise your name,

and will sing a hymn of thanksgiving to you, alleluia.

In you I will rejoice and be glad;
I will sing to your name, Most High.

And will sing a hymn of thanksgiving to you, alleluia.
Sirach 51:15; Psalm 9:3

PRAYER

Father,
you gave Saint Bernardine a special love
for the holy name of Jesus.
By the help of his prayers,

115

may we always be alive with the spirit of your love.

We ask this through our Lord Jesus Christ, your Son,
who lives and reigns with you and the Holy Spirit,
one God, for ever and ever.

Our Father . . .

May 25

VENERABLE BEDE, PRIEST AND DOCTOR

Saint Bede was born near one of the famous monasteries in
England in 673. After his schooling he entered the monastery.
Ordained to the priesthood, he spent his ministry in teaching
and writing. Saint Bede wrote theological and historical works
and explained sacred Scripture. He died in 735.

READING

A reading from a letter on the death of the Venerable Bede, by
the monk Cuthbert

On Tuesday before the feast of the Ascension, Bede's breathing
became labored and a slight swelling appeared in his legs.
Nevertheless, he gave us instruction all day long and dictated
cheerfully the whole time. It seemed to us, however, that he
knew very well that his end was near, and so he spent the whole
night giving thanks to God.

At daybreak on Wednesday he told us to finish the writing we
had begun. We worked until nine o'clock, when we went in
procession with the relics as the custom of the day required. But
one of our community, a boy named Wilbert, stayed with him

and said to him: "Dear master, there is still one more chapter to finish in that book you were dictating. Do you think it would be too hard for you to answer any more questions?" Bede replied: "Not at all; it will be easy. Take up your pen and ink, and write quickly," and he did so.

At three o'clock, Bede said to me: "I have a few treasures in my private chest, some pepper, napkins, and a little incense. Run quickly and bring the priests of our monastery, and I will distribute among them these little presents that God has given me."

When the priests arrived he spoke to them and asked each one to offer Masses and prayers for him regularly. They gladly promised to do so. The priests were sad, however, and they all wept, especially because Bede had said that he thought they would not see his face much longer in this world. Yet they rejoiced when he said: 'If it so please my Maker, it is time for me to return to him who created me and formed me out of nothing when I did not exist. I have lived a long time, and the righteous Judge has taken good care of me during my whole life. The time has come for my departure, and I long to die and be with Christ. My soul yearns to see Christ, my King, in all his glory." He said many other things which profited us greatly, and so he passed the day joyfully till evening.

When evening came, young Wilbert said to Bede, "Dear master, there is still one sentence that we have not written down." Bede said: "Quick, write it down." In a little while, Wilbert said: "There; now it is written down." Bede said: "Good. You have spoken the truth; it is finished. Hold my head in your hands, for I really enjoy sitting opposite the holy place where I used to pray; I can call upon my Father as I sit there."

And so Bede, as he lay upon the floor of his cell, sang: "Glory be to the Father, and to the Son and to the Holy Spirit." And when he had named the Holy Spirit, he breathed his last breath.

During all of my years in the monastery
I spent long hours in meditating on the sacred Scriptures;
I was always faithful to the holy rule
and to the daily chanting of the hours.

I found delight in constant study, teaching and writing.

The man who obeys God's law and teaches others to do so
will be great in the kingdom of heaven.

I found delight in constant study, teaching and writing.

PRAYER

Lord,
you have enlightened your Church
with the learning of Saint Bede.
In your love
may your people learn from his wisdom
and benefit from his prayers.

Grant this through our Lord Jesus Christ, your Son,
who lives and reigns with you and the Holy Spirit,
one God, for ever and ever.

Our Father . . .

On the same day May 25

GREGORY VII, POPE

This pope, whose name was Hildebrand, was born in Italy about
the year 1028. He was educated at Rome and entered the monastic life. He helped the popes of his time through many missions
on behalf of Church reform, and in 1073 ascended to the chair of
Saint Peter under the name of Gregory VII. Driven from Rome
by a hostile king, he died a refugee at Salerno in 1085.

A reading from a letter by Saint Gregory VII, pope

Now, my dearest brothers, listen carefully to what I tell you. All those throughout the world who are numbered as Christian and who truly acknowledge the Christian faith know and believe that the blessed Peter, the prince of the apostles, is the father of all Christians and, after Christ, the first shepherd, and that the holy Roman Church is the mother and teacher of all the churches. Therefore, if you believe this and hold to it without hesitation, I ask you and enjoin upon you by Almighty God—I, your brother and unworthy teacher as I am—to support and assist your father and your mother if you wish to have, through them, the remission of all your sins, along with blessing and grace in this world and in the life to come.

May almighty God, from whom all good things come, continually enlighten your minds and fill them with love for him and for your neighbor, so that by your devotion you may deserve to make this father and mother of whom I have spoken your debtors and enter without shame into their company. Amen.

RESPONSORY

The Lord glorified him in the sight of kings,
and gave him commandments for his people.
God revealed to him his glory, alleluia.

The Lord chose him to be a servant,
a shepherd of his own Israel.
God revealed to him his glory, alleluia.
Sirach 45:3; Psalm 78:70, 71

PRAYER

Lord,
give your Church
the spirit of courage and love for justice

119

which distinguished Pope Gregory.
Make us courageous in condemning evil
and free us to pursue justice with love.

We ask this through our Lord Jesus Christ, your Son,
who lives and reigns with you and the Holy Spirit,
one God, for ever and ever.

Our Father . . .

On the same day May 25

MARY MAGDALENE DE PAZZI, VIRGIN

Saint Mary Magdalene was born at Florence, Italy in 1566 and
after a religious upbringing she entered the Carmelites. She led
a solitary life of prayer and self-denial, prayed fervently for
Church reform and directed her nuns on the road to perfection.
She was blessed by many gifts from God and died in 1607.

The following reading will help us to join Saint Mary Magdalene
in her love for the Holy Spirit.

READING

A reading from the writings by Saint Mary Magdalene de Pazzi,
virgin

Come, Holy Spirit. Spirit of truth, you are the reward of the
saints, the comforter of souls, light in the darkness, riches to the
poor, treasure to lovers, food for the hungry, comfort to those
who are wandering; to sum up, you are the one in whom all
treasures are contained.

Come! As you descended upon Mary that the Word might become flesh, work in us through grace as you worked in her
through nature and grace.

Come! Food of every chaste thought, fountain of all mercy, sum of all purity.

Come! Consume in us whatever prevents us from being consumed in you.

RESPONSORY

RESPONSORY

No eye has seen, no ear heard,
nor has the heart of man conceived,

the marvels God has prepared for those who love him.

These things God has revealed to us through his Spirit.

The marvels God has prepared for those who love him.
1 *Corinthians 2:9-10*

PRAYER

Father,
you love those who give themselves completely to your service,
and you filled Saint Mary Magdalene de Pazzi
with heavenly gifts and the fire of your love.
As we honor her today
may we follow her example of purity and charity.

Grant this through our Lord Jesus Christ, your Son,
who lives and reigns with you and the Holy Spirit,
one God, for ever and ever.

Our Father . . .

May 26

PHILIP NERI, PRIEST
Memorial

Saint Philip Neri was born at Florence in 1515. He went to Rome and began to work with young men among whom he fostered Christian life. He formed a society to take care of the poor and the sick. Ordained to the priesthood in 1551, he founded the Oratory where spiritual reading, singing and works of charity were practiced. He excelled in his love of neighbor and was always joyful in serving God. Saint Philip died in 1595.

In today's reading Saint Augustine speaks of what it means to serve the Lord joyfully the way Saint Philip did.

READING

A reading from a sermon by Saint Augustine, bishop

The Apostle tells us to rejoice, but in the Lord, not in the world. As a man cannot serve two masters, so one cannot rejoice both in the world and in the Lord.

This is said, not because we are not to rejoice while we are in this world, but in order that, even while we are still in this world, we may already rejoice in the Lord.

So, brethren, "rejoice in the Lord," not in the world. That is, rejoice in the truth, not in the wickedness; rejoice in the hope of eternity, not in the fading flower of vanity. That is the way to rejoice. Wherever you are on earth, however long you remain on earth, "the Lord is near, do not be anxious about anything."

RESPONSORY

Rejoice, brothers.

Strive for perfection;
encourage one another.
Live in harmony and peace,

and the God of peace and love will be with you.

May the God of hope fill you with all joy and peace
through your faith in him.

And the God of peace and love will be with you.
2 Corinthians 13:11; Romans 15:13

PRAYER

Father,
you continually raise up your faithful
to the glory of holiness.
In your love
kindle in us the fire of the Holy Spirit
who so filled the heart of Philip Neri.

We ask this through our Lord Jesus Christ, your Son,
who lives and reigns with you and the Holy Spirit,
one God, for ever and ever.

Our Father . . .

May 27

AUGUSTINE OF CANTERBURY, BISHOP

Saint Augustine was sent in 597 from Saint Andrew's monastery in Rome by Saint Gregory the Great to preach the gospel in England. He was aided there by King Ethelbert and chosen bishop of Canterbury. He converted many to the faith and established many dioceses. He died on May 26, about the year 605.

A reading from a letter by Saint Gregory the Great, pope

Who, dear brother, is capable of describing the great joy of believers when they have learned what the grace of Almighty God and your own cooperation achieved among the Angles? They abandoned the errors of darkness and were bathed with the light of holy faith. With full awareness, they trampled on the idols which they had previously adored with savage fear. They are now committed to Almighty God. They bow down to the ground in prayer lest their minds cling too closely to earthly things. Whose achievement is this? It is the achievement of him who said: "My Father is at work until now and I am at work as well."

RESPONSORY

Be imitators of me, my brothers,
and, as you have us as a model,
observe those who follow the example we set.

**Live according to what you have learned and accepted,
what you have heard me say or seen me do,
and the God of peace will be with you, alleluia.**

I plead with you, my brothers, in the name of our Lord Jesus
    Christ,
to agree among yourselves.

**Live according to what you have learned and accepted,
what you have heard me say or seen me do,
and the God of peace will be with you, alleluia.**
Philippians 3:17; 4:9; 1 Corinthians 1:10

PRAYER

Father,
by the preaching of Saint Augustine of Canterbury,
you led the people of England to the gospel.

May the fruits of his work continue in your Church.

Grant this through our Lord Jesus Christ, your Son,
who lives and reigns with you and the Holy Spirit,
one God, for ever and ever.

Our Father . . .

May 31

VISITATION
Feast

Today the Church remembers the visit the Virgin Mary paid to
her relative Elizabeth, who was going to have a baby.

This visit shows Mary's self-sacrifice in going to help Elizabeth,
for Mary herself was soon going to have a baby too. But more
important still, this visit marked the time when Mary was recognized as the mother of the savior.

When Mary entered the house, Elizabeth was filled with the
Holy Spirit and cried out: "Blest are you among women and
blest is the fruit of your womb. But who am I that the mother of
my Lord should come to me?"

It was then that Mary uttered her song in praise of the Lord:
"My soul proclaims the greatness of the Lord
and my spirit rejoices in God my savior.
For the Almighty has done great things for me,
and holy is his name."

READING

A reading from a homily by Saint Bede the Venerable, priest

"My soul proclaims the greatness of the Lord, and my spirit

rejoices in God my savior." With these words Mary first acknowledges the special gifts she has been given.

Above all other saints, she alone could truly rejoice in Jesus, her savior, for she knew that he who was the source of eternal salvation would be born in time in her body, in one person both her own son and her Lord.

"For the Almighty has done great things for me, and holy is his name." Mary attributes nothing to her own merits. She refers all her greatness to the gift of one whose essence is power and whose nature is greatness, for he fills with greatness and strength the small and the weak who belive in him.

She did well to add: "and holy is his name," to warn those who heard, and indeed all who would receive his words, that they must believe and call upon his name. For they too could share in everlasting holiness and true salvation according to the words of the prophet: "and it will come to pass, that everyone who calls on the name of the Lord will be saved." This is the name she spoke of earlier when she said "and my spirit rejoices in God my savior."

RESPONSORY

Hail Mary, full of grace, the Lord is with you, alleluia, alleluia.
Hail Mary, full of grace, the Lord is with you, alleluia, alleluia.

Blessed are you among women, and blessed is the fruit of your
    womb,
alleluia, alleluia.

Glory to the Father . . .
Hail Mary, full of grace, the Lord is with you, alleluia, alleluia.

Eternal Father,
you inspired the Virgin Mary, mother of your Son,
to visit Elizabeth and assist her in her need.
Keep us open to the working of your Spirit,
and with Mary may we praise you for ever.

We ask this through our Lord Jesus Christ, your Son,
who lives and reigns with you and the Holy Spirit,
one God, for ever and ever.

Our Father . . .

PENTECOST
Solemnity

Today we celebrate the feast of Pentecost. On this day the Holy Spirit appeared before the apostles in tongues of fire and gave them his spiritual gifts. He sent them out to preach to the whole world, and to proclaim that all who believe and are baptized shall be saved.

READING

A reading from an essay Against Heresies by Saint Irenaeus, bishop

Luke says that the Spirit came down on the disciples at Pentecost, after the Lord's ascension, with power to open the gates of life to all nations and to make known to them the new covenant. So it was that men of every language joined in singing one song of praise to God, and scattered tribes, restored to unity by the Spirit, were offered to the Father as first fruits of all nations.

This was why the Lord had promised to send the Advocate: he was to prepare us as an offering to God. Like dry flour, which cannot become one lump of dough, one loaf of bread, without moisture, we who are many could not become one in Jesus Christ without the water that comes down from heaven. And like parched ground, which yields no harvest unless it receives moisture, we who were once like a waterless tree could never have lived and borne fruit without this abundant rainfall from above. Through the baptism that liberates us from change and decay we have become one in soul.

RESPONSORY

On the day of Pentecost
they had all gathered together in one place.
Out of the heavens suddenly there came

the sound of great wind,
which filled the whole house, alleluia.

The disciples had gathered together in one room.
Suddenly there came a sound from heaven.
The sound of great wind,
which filled the whole house, alleluia.
Acts 2:1-2

PRAYER

God our Father,
let the Spirit you sent on your Church
to begin the teaching of the gospel
continue to work in the world
through the hearts of all who believe.

We ask this through our Lord Jesus Christ, your Son,
who lives and reigns with you and the Holy Spirit,
one God, for ever and ever.

Our Father . . .

128

Sunday after Pentecost

TRINITY SUNDAY
Solemnity

Today the Church pays honor to the Holy Trinity—one God in three divine persons. This is a great mystery. That is, we can only believe it is true because God has given us the gift of faith.

READING

A reading from the first letter to Serapion by Saint Athanasius, bishop

It will not be out of place to consider the ancient tradition, teaching and faith of the Catholic Church, which was revealed by the Lord, proclaimed by the apostles and guarded by the fathers. For upon this faith the Church is built, and if anyone were to lapse from it, he would no longer be a Christian.

We acknowledge the Trinity, holy and perfect, to consist of the Father, the Son and the Holy Spirit. Accordingly, in the Church, one God is preached, one God who is "above all things and through all things and in all things." God is "above all things" as Father, for he is principle and source; he is "through all things" through the Word; and he is "in all things" in the Holy Spirit.

This is Paul's teaching in his second letter to the Corinthians: "The grace of our Lord Jesus Christ and the love of God and the fellowship of the Holy Spirit be with you all." For grace and the gift of the Trinity are given by the Father through the Son in the Holy Spirit. Just as grace is given from the Father through the Son, so there could be no giving of the gift to us except in the Holy Spirit. But when we share in the Spirit, we possess the love of the Father, the grace of the son and the fellowship of the Spirit himself.

Let us adore the Father, and the Son and the Holy Spirit;

let us praise and exalt God above all for ever.

Blessed be God in the firmament of heaven;
all praise, all glory to him for ever.

Let us praise and exalt God above all for ever.

PRAYER

Father,
you sent your Word to bring us truth
and your Spirit to make us holy.
Through them we come to know the mystery of your life.
Help us to worship you, one God in three Persons,
by proclaiming and living our faith in you.

Grant this through our Lord Jesus Christ, your Son,
who lives and reigns with you and the Holy Spirit,
one God, for ever and ever.

Our Father . . .

Sunday after Trinity Sunday

CORPUS CHRISTI
Solemnity

All Masses celebrate the presence of Christ under the form of
bread and wine. Today, however, the Church asks us to fix our
attention most specially on this sacred mystery so that we may
learn to love Christ in the eucharist more and more each day.

A reading from a work by Saint Thomas Aquinas, priest

Since it was the will of God's only-begotten Son that men and women should share in his divinity, he assumed our nature in order that by becoming man he might make men gods. He offered his body to God the Father on the altar of the cross as a sacrifice for our reconciliation. He shed his blood so that we might be redeemed from our wretched state of bondage and cleansed from all sin. But to ensure that the memory of so great a gift would abide with us for ever, he left his body as food and his blood as drink for the faithful to consume in the form of bread and wine.

What could be more wonderful than this? No other sacrament has greater healing power; through it sins are purged away, vitues are increased, and the soul is enriched with an abundance of every spiritual gift.

RESPONSORY

He gave them bread from heaven, alleluia, alleluia.

He gave them bread from heaven, alleluia, alleluia.

Man has eaten the bread of angels,
alleluia, alleluia.

Glory to the Father . . .

He gave them bread from heaven, alleluia, alleluia.

PRAYER

Lord Jesus Christ,
you gave us the eucharist
as the memorial of your suffering and death.
May our worship of this sacrament of your body and blood
help us to experience the salvation you won for us

and the peace of the kingdom
where you live with the Father and the Holy Spirit,
one God, for ever and ever.

Our Father . . .

Friday After the Second Sunday After Pentecost

SACRED HEART
Solemnity

Today the Church reminds us of Christ's love for us in giving up
the last drop of blood from his Sacred Heart for our salvation.

READING

A reading from a work by Saint Bonaventure, bishop

It was a divine decree that permitted one of the soldiers to open
his [Christ's] sacred side with a lance. This was done so that the
Church might be formed from the side of Christ as he slept the
sleep of death on the cross, and so that the Scripture might be
fulfilled: "They shall look on him whom they pierced." The
blood and water which poured out at that moment were the
price of our salvation. Flowing from the secret abyss of our
Lord's heart as from a fountain, this stream gave the sacraments
of the Church the power to confer the life of grace, while for
those already living in Christ it became a spring of living water
welling up to life everlasting.

Arise, then, beloved of Christ! Run with eager desire to this
source of life and light, all you who are vowed to God's service.

RESPONSORY

Take my yoke upon you and learn from me.

Take my yoke upon you and learn from me.

For I am gentle and humble of heart.

Learn from me.

Glory to the Father . . .

Take my yoke upon you and learn from me.

PRAYER

Father,
we rejoice in the gifts of love
we have received from the heart of Jesus your Son.
Open our hearts to share his life
and continue to bless us with his love.

We ask this through our Lord Jesus Christ, your Son,
who lives and reigns with you and the Holy Spirit,
one God, for ever and ever.

Our Father . . .

Saturday following the Second Sunday after Pentecost

IMMACULATE HEART OF MARY

We sometimes speak of loving someone or believing something
"with our whole heart." We mean that we have or believe truly
and sincerely with every fiber of our being.

No merely human person has ever loved God with the deep and
pure love of our Lady. It is this spotless and loving heart of Mary
which the Church celebrates today.

133

A reading from a sermon by Saint Lawrence Justinian, bishop

How entirely blessed was the mind of the Virgin which, through the indwelling and guidance of the Spirit, was always and in every way open to the power of the Word of God.

Imitate her, O faithful soul. Enter into the deep recesses of your heart so that you may be purified spiritually and cleansed from your sins. God places more value on good will in all we do than on the works themselves. Therefore, whether we give ourselves to God in the work of contemplation or whether we serve the needs of our neighbor by good works, we accomplish these things because the love of Christ urges us on. The acceptable offering of the spiritual purification is accomplished not in a man-made temple but in the recesses of the heart where the Lord Jesus freely enters.

RESPONSORY

O pure and holy virgin,
how can I find words to praise your beauty?

The highest heavens cannot contain God whom you carried in your womb.

Blessed are you among women,
and blessed is the fruit of your womb.

The highest heavens cannot contain God whom you carried in your womb.

PRAYER

Father,
you prepared the heart of the Virgin Mary
to be a fitting home for your Holy Spirit.
By her prayers
may we become a more worthy temple of your glory.

Grant this through our Lord Jesus Christ, your Son,
who lives and reigns with you and the Holy Spirit,
one God, for ever and ever.

Our Father . . .

June 1

JUSTIN, MARTYR
Memorial

Saint Justin, philosopher and martyr, was born of pagan parents
in Syria at the beginning of the second century. Following his
conversion to the faith he wrote many works in defense of religion. He also opened a school at Rome in which public debates
were held. Justin was martyred along with several companions
during the reign of Marcus Aurelius around the year 165.

READING

A reading from the Acts of the martyrdom of Saint Justin and his
companion saints

The saints were seized and brought before the prefect of Rome,
whose name was Rusticus. As they stood before the judgment
seat, Rusticus the prefect said to Justin: "Above all, have faith in
the gods and obey the emperors." Justin said: "We cannot be
accused or condemned for obeying the commands of our Savior,
Jesus Christ."

Rusticus said: "What system of teaching do you profess?" Justin
said: "I have tried to learn about every system, but I have accepted the true doctrines of the Christians, though these are not
approved by those who are held fast by error."

The prefect Rusticus said: "Are those doctrines approved by
you, wretch that you are?" Justin said: "Yes, for I follow them
with their correct teaching."

The prefect Rusticus said: "What sort of teaching is that?" Justin said: "Worship the God of the Christians. We hold him to be from the beginning the one creator and maker of the whole creation, of things seen and things unseen. We worship also the Lord Jesus Christ, the Son of God."

Rusticus said: "You are a Christian, then?" Justin said: "Yes, I am a Christian."

The prefect said to Justin: "You are called a learned man and think you know what is true teaching. Listen: if you were scourged and beheaded, are you convinced that you would go up to heaven?" Justin said: "I hope that I shall enter God's house if I suffer in that way. For I know that God's favor is stored up until the end of the whole world for all who have lived good lives."

The prefect Rusticus said: "Do you have an idea that you will go up to heaven to receive some suitable rewards?" Justin said: "It is not an idea that I have; it is something I know well and hold to be most certain."

The prefect Rusticus said: "Now let us come to the point at issue, which is necessary and urgent. Gather round then and with one accord offer sacrifice to the gods." Justin said: "No one who is right-thinking stoops from true worship to false worship."

The prefect Rusticus said: "If you do not do as you are commanded you will be tortured without mercy." Justin said: "We hope to suffer torment for the sake of our Lord Jesus Christ, and so be saved."

In the same way the other martyrs also said: "Do what you will. We are Christians; we do not offer sacrifice to idols."

The prefect Rusticus pronounced sentence, saying: "Let those who have refused to sacrifice to the gods and to obey the command of the emperor be scourged and led away to suffer capital punishment according to the ruling of the laws." Glorifying God, the holy martyrs were beheaded, and so fulfilled their witness of martyrdom in confessing their faith in their Savior.

RESPONSORY

I have preached faith in our Lord Jesus Christ
and now I fear no danger.

I do not count my life more precious than my work,
which is to finish my course,
the task of preaching and proclaiming the good news of God's
grace.

I am not ashamed of the Gospel,
for it is God's power at work,
bringing salvation to all who believe in it,
Jew first and then Greek.

I do not count my life more precious than my work,
which is to finish my course,
the task of preaching and proclaiming the good news of God's
grace.
Acts 20:21, 24; Romans 1:16

PRAYER

Father,
through the folly of the cross
you taught Saint Justin the sublime wisdom of Jesus Christ.
May we too reject falsehood
and remain loyal to the faith.

We ask this through our Lord Jesus Christ, your Son,
who lives and reigns with you and the Holy Spirit,
one God, for ever and ever.

Our Father . . .

June 2

MARCELLINUS AND PETER, MARTYRS

Pope Damasus is our authority for the martyrdom of Saints Marcellinus and Peter. He received this information from the executioner himself. They were beheaded in a grove, but their bodies were moved and buried in a cemetery on a Roman road. Once peace had been restored, the Church built a basilica over their tombs.

READING

A reading from the exhortation to Martyrdom by Origen, priest

"The more we share in the sufferings of Christ, the more we share, through him, in his consolation." We should be extremely eager to share in Christ's sufferings and to let them be multiplied in us if we desire the superabundant consolation that will be given to those who mourn.

In Christ and with Christ the martyrs disarm principalities and the powers of evil and share in his triumph over them, for their share in Christ's sufferings makes them sharers also in the mighty deeds those sufferings accomplished. But I entreat you "not to give offense to anyone. Be very patient and show in every way that you are servants of God."

RESPONSORY

Our struggle is not against human enemies
but against the principalities and powers, against the evil spirits.
Stand firm and let the truth be the belt around your waist.

Put on the armor of God;
then you will be able to stand firm when the worst happens;
you will fulfill all your duties and hold your ground.
Stand firm and let the truth be the belt around your waist.
Ephesians 6:12, 14, 13

Father,
may we benefit from the example
of your martyrs Marcellinus and Peter,
and be supported by their prayers.

Grant this through our Lord Jesus Christ, your Son,
who lives and reigns with you and the Holy Spirit,
one God, for ever and ever.

Our Father . . .

June 3

CHARLES LWANGA AND COMPANIONS, MARTYRS
Memorial

Owing to religious hatred, many faithful Christians were killed
in Uganda by King Mwanga during the years 1885-1887. Some
of them had enjoyed the good graces of the king at his court,
and some were even related to him. Among them, Charles
Lwanga and his twenty-one companions, adhering steadfastly
to the Catholic faith, were put to death, some by sword, others
by burning, because they would not accede to the king's unreasonable demands.

READING

A reading from the homily at the canonization of the martyrs of
Uganda by Pope Paul VI

The African martyrs add another page to the Church's roll of
honor—an occasion both of mourning and of joy.

These African martyrs herald the dawn of a new age. If only the
mind of man might be directed not toward persecutions and

religious conflicts but toward a rebirth of Christianity and civilization!

Africa has been washed by the blood of these latest martyrs, and first of this new age (and, God willing, let them be the last, although such a holocaust is precious indeed). Africa is reborn free and independent.

RESPONSORY

We are warriors now, fighting on the battlefield of faith,
and God sees all we do;
the angels watch and so does Christ.

What honor and glory and joy, to do battle
    in the presence of God,
and to have Christ approve our victory.

Let us arm ourselves in full strength
and prepare ourselves for the ultimate struggle
with blameless hearts, true faith and unyielding courage.

What honor and glory and joy, to do battle
    in the presence of God,
and to have Christ approve our victory.

PRAYER

Father,
you have made the blood of the martyrs
the seed of Christians.
May the witness of Saint Charles and his companions
and their loyalty to Christ in the face of torture
inspire countless men and women
to live the Christian faith.

We ask this through our Lord Jesus Christ, your Son,
who lives and reigns with you and the Holy Spirit,
one God, for ever and ever.

Our Father . . .

June 5

BONIFACE, BISHOP AND MARTYR
Memorial

Saint Boniface was born in England about the year 673. He entered the monastic life at Exeter but in 719 went to Germany to preach the gospel. He made many converts there and was consecrated bishop. He attracted many companions by whose help he founded or restored dioceses in Bavaria, Thuringia and Franconia. He also convened councils and promulgated laws. While preaching the gospel to the Frisians, Saint Boniface was killed by pagans in 754. His body is buried in the monastery of Fulda.

READING

A reading from a letter by Saint Boniface, bishop and martyr

In her voyage across the ocean of this world, the Church is like a great ship being pounded by the waves of life's different stresses. Our duty is not to abandon ship but to keep her on her course.

Let us stand fast in what is right and prepare our souls for trial. Let us wait upon God's strengthening aid and say to him: "O Lord, you have been our refuge in all generations."

Let us trust in him who has placed this burden upon us. What we ourselves cannot bear let us bear with the help of Christ. For he is all-powerful and he tells us: "My yoke is easy and my burden is light."

Let us continue the fight on the day of the Lord. "The days of anguish and of tribulation have overtaken us; if God so wills, "let us die for the holy laws of our fathers," so that we may deserve to obtain an eternal inheritance with them.

I have longed to give you the Gospel,
and more than that, to give you my very life;

you have become very dear to me.

My little children, I am like a mother giving birth to you,
until Christ is formed in you.

You have become very dear to me.

1 Thessalonians 2:8; Galatians 4:19

PRAYER

Lord,
your martyr Boniface
spread the faith by his teaching
and witnessed to it with his blood.
By the help of his prayers
keep us loyal to our faith
and give us the courage to profess it in our lives.

Grant this through our Lord Jesus Christ, your Son,
who lives and reigns with you and the Holy Spirit,
one God, for ever and ever.

Our Father . . .

June 6

NORBERT, BISHOP

Saint Norbert was born in Germany around the year 1080. He
was converted from a worldly life and, embracing the religious
state, was ordained to the priesthood in 1115. He was famous for
his preaching, particularly throughout France and Germany.
Gathering together some companions, he laid the foundations
of the Premonstratensian Order, for which he also founded

monasteries. Elected Archbishop of Magdeburg in 1126, he spread the faith to nearby pagan nations. Saint Norbert died in 1134.

A reading from the life of Saint Norbert, bishop

Norbert established a clergy dedicated to the ideals of the Gospel and the apostolic Church. They were chaste and poor. They wore the clothing and the symbols of the new man; that is to say, they wore "the religious habit and exhibited the dignity proper to the priesthood." Norbert asked them "to live according to the norms of the Scriptures with Christ as their model.

The priests lived in community, where they continued the work of the apostles.

When Norbert was appointed as archbishop, he urged his brothers to carry the faith to the lands of the Wends.

"Faith was the outstanding virtue of Norbert's life, as charity had been the hallmark of Bernard of Clairvaux's." Affable and charming, amiable to one and all, "he was at ease in the company of the humble and the great alike." Finally, he was a most eloquent preacher; after long meditation "he would preach the word of God" and with his fiery eloquence purged vices, refined virtues and filled souls of good will with the warmth of wisdom.

Proclaim the message, in season and out of season; refute falsehood, correct error, call to obedience;

endure all hardships and spread the Gospel.

Keep watch over the whole flock which the Holy Spirit has given you to rule and guide, as a shepherd of the Church of God.

Endure all hardships and spread the Gospel.
2 Timothy 4:2, 5; Acts 20:28

PRAYER

Father,
you made the bishop Norbert
an outstanding minister of your Church,
renowned for his preaching and pastoral zeal.
Always grant to your Church faithful shepherds
to lead your people to eternal salvation.

We ask this through our Lord Jesus Christ, your Son,
who lives and reigns with you and the Holy Spirit,
one God, for ever and ever.

Our Father...

June 9

EPHREM, DEACON AND DOCTOR

Saint Ephrem was born of a Christian family in northern Asia around the year 306. He became a deacon and founded a theological school. He lived a life of prayer and sacrifice. But he also found time to write books and preach against false teachings. He died in 373.

READING

A reading from a sermon by Saint Ephrem, deacon

Lord, shed upon our darkened souls the brilliant light of your wisdom so that we may be enlightened and serve you with renewed purity. Sunrise marks the hour for men to begin their toil, but in our souls, Lord, prepare a dwelling for the day that will never end. Through our unremitting zeal for you, Lord, set upon us the sign of your day that is not measured by the sun.

In your sacrament we daily embrace you and receive you into our bodies; make us worthy to experience the resurrection for which we hope. Teach us to find our joy in your favor!

Savior, your crucifixion marked the end of your mortal life; teach us to crucify ourselves and make way for our life in the Spirit.

RESPONSORY

He loved the Lord with his whole heart
and daily sang praises to his Maker.

**He chose musicians to stand before the altar
to provide sweet music for the psalms.**

He did this so that men might praise the holy name of the Lord
and the sanctuary might resound with music from the rising to
    the setting of the sun.

**He chose musicians to stand before the altar
to provide sweet music for the psalms.**

PRAYER

Lord,
in your love fill our hearts with the Holy Spirit,
who inspired the deacon Ephrem to sing the praise of your
    mysteries
and gave him strength to serve you alone.

Grant this through our Lord Jesus Christ, your Son,
who lives and reigns with you and the Holy Spirit,
one God, for ever and ever.

Our Father . . .

June 11

BARNABAS, APOSTLE

Memorial

Born in Cyprus, Barnabas is numbered among the first of the faithful at Jerusalem. He preached the gospel at Antioch and, as a companion of Saint Paul, accompanied him on his first journey. He was also present at the Council of Jerusalem. Upon returning to his own country, he continued to spread the gospel and eventually died there.

READING

A reading from an essay on the Gospel of Saint Matthew by Saint Chromatius, bishop

"You are the light of the world." The Lord called his disciples the salt of the earth because they seasoned with heavenly wisdom the hearts of men, rendered insipid by the devil. Now he calls them the light of the world because they have been enlightened by him, the true and everlasting light, and have themselves become a light in the darkness.

Since he is the Sun of Justice, he fittingly calls his disciples the light of the world. The reason for this is that through them, as through shining rays, he has poured out the light of the knowledge of himself upon the entire world. For by manifesting the light of truth, they have dispelled the darkness of error from the hearts of men.

Moreover, we too have been enlightened by them. We have been made light out of darkness as the Apostle says: "For once you were darkness, but now you are light in the Lord; walk as children of light." He says another time: "For you are not sons of the night and darkness, but you are all sons of light and of day."

Therefore, because we rejoice in having been freed from the

146

darkness of error, we should always walk in the light as children
of light.

RESPONSORY

When Barnabas arrived in Antioch
and saw God's grace at work there,
he rejoiced,

for he was a good man,
filled with the Holy Spirit and with faith.

He encouraged all to stand firm in their commitment to
the Lord.

For he was a good man,
filled with the Holy Spirit and with faith.
Acts 11:23-24

PRAYER

God our Father,
you filled Saint Barnabas with faith and the Holy Spirit
and sent him to convert the nations.
Help us to proclaim the gospel by word and deed.

We ask this through our Lord Jesus Christ, your Son,
who lives and reigns with you and the Holy Spirit,
one God, for ever and ever.

Our Father . . .

June 13

ANTHONY OF PADUA, PRIEST AND DOCTOR
Memorial

Saint Anthony was born in Lisbon, Portugal, near the end of the twelfth century. He joined the Canons Regular of Saint Augustine, but, shortly after ordination to the priesthood, transferred to the Friars Minor to devote himself to spreading the faith among African peoples. He had his greatest success, however, preaching in France and Italy and converting heretics. He was the first member of this Order to teach theology to his brethren. His sermons are notable for their learning and gentleness. Saint Anthony died at Padua in 1231.

READING

A reading from a sermon by Saint Anthony of Padua, priest

Actions speak louder than words; let your words teach and your actions speak. We are full of words but empty of actions, and therefore are cursed by the Lord, since he himself cursed the fig tree when he found no fruit but only leaves. It is useless for a man to flaunt his knowledge of the law if he undermines its teaching by his actions.

But the apostles "spoke as the Spirit gave them the gift of speech." Happy the man whose words issue from the Holy Spirit and not from himself!

We should speak, then, as the Holy Spirit gives us the gift of speech. Our humble and sincere request to the Spirit for ourselves should be that we may bring the day of Pentecost to fulfillment, insofar as he infuses us with his grace, by using our bodily senses in a perfect manner by keeping the commandments. Likewise we shall request that we may be filled with a keen sense of sorrow and with fiery tongues for confessing the faith so our deserved reward may be to stand in the blazing splendor of the saints and to look upon the triune God.

148

The just man shall blossom like the lily;

he shall flourish for ever in the courts of our God.

He will be praised by all of God's chosen ones.

He shall flourish for ever in the courts of our God.
See Hosea 14:6; Psalm 92:13; Ecclesiasticus 24:4

PRAYER

Almighty God,
you have given Saint Anthony to your people
as an outstanding preacher
and a ready helper in time of need.
With his assistance may we follow the gospel of Christ
and know the help of your grace in every difficulty.

Grant this through our Lord Jesus Christ, your Son,
who lives and reigns with you and the Holy Spirit,
one God, for ever and ever.

Our Father . . .

June 19

ROMUALD, ABBOT

Saint Romuald was born in Ravenna in the middle of the tenth century. He embraced the hermit's life and for many years traveled through various lands seeking solitude and establishing small monasteries while directing himself to a life of perfection by the practice of virtues. He died around the year 1027.

A reading from the life of Saint Romuald by Saint Peter Damian

Romuald lived in the vicinity of the city of Parenzo for three years. In the first year he built a monastery and appointed an abbot with monks. For the next two years he remained there in seclusion.

Wherever the holy man might arrange to live, he would follow the same pattern. First he would build an oratory with an altar in a cell; then he would shut himself in and forbid access.

Finally, after he had lived in many places, perceiving that his end was near, he returned to the monastery he had built in the valley of Castro. While he awaited with certainty his approaching death, he ordered a cell to be constructed there with an oratory in which he might isolate himself and preserve silence until death.

Accordingly the hermitage was built, since he had made up his mind that he would die there. His body began to grow more and more oppressed by afflictions and was already failing. One day he began to feel the loss of his physical strength under all the harassment of increasingly violent afflictions. As the sun was beginning to set, he instructed two monks who were standing by to go out and close the door of the cell behind them; they were to come back to him at daybreak to celebrate matins. They were so concerned about his end that they went out reluctantly and did not rest immediately. On the contrary, since they were worried that their master might die, they lay hidden near the cell and watched this precious treasure. For some time they continued to listen attentively until they heard neither movement nor sound. Rightly guessing what had happened, they pushed open the door, rushed in quickly, lit a candle and found the holy man lying on his back, his blessed soul snatched up into heaven.

The Lord has blessed you in all that you have done;
he has watched over your progress as you journeyed through
the vast desert.

The Lord your God has been with you;
no need of yours has been forgotten.

As a father teaches his son,
so the Lord your God was disciplining you.

The Lord your God has been with you;
no need of yours has been forgotten.

PRAYER

Father,
through Saint Romuald
you renewed the life of solitude and prayer in your Church.
By our self-denial as we follow Christ
bring us the joy of heaven.

We ask this through our Lord Jesus Christ, your Son,
who lives and reigns with you and the Holy Spirit,
one God, for ever and ever.

Our Father . . .

June 21

ALOYSIUS GONZAGA, RELIGIOUS
Memorial

Saint Aloysius was born of a princely family in 1568 near
Mantua in Lombardy. Instructed in piety by his mother, he manifested an inclination to religious life. He legally delivered his
share of the ancestral goods to his brother and entered the Society of Jesus. While serving the sick during a plague, he himself
contracted the disease and died in 1591.

151

A reading from a letter to his mother by Saint Aloysius

May the comfort and grace of the Holy Spirit by yours for ever, most honored lady. Your letter found me lingering still in this region of the dead, but now I must rouse myself to make my way on to heaven at last and to praise God for ever in the land of the living; indeed I had hoped that before this time my journey there would have been over. If charity, as Saint Paul says, means "to weep with those who weep and rejoice with those who are glad," then, dearest mother, you shall rejoice exceedingly that God in his grace and his love for you is showing me the path to true happiness, and assuring me that I shall never lose him.

Take care above all things, most honored lady, not to insult God's boundless loving kindness; you would certainly do this if you mourned as dead one living face to face with God, one whose prayers can bring you in your troubles more powerful aid than they ever could on earth. And our parting will not be for long; we shall see each other again in heaven; we shall be united with our Savior; there we shall praise him with heart and soul, sing of his mercies for ever, and enjoy eternal happiness.

RESPONSORY

You upheld me because of my innocence;

you let me stand in your sight for ever.

I would rather lie at the threshold of the house of my God than live in the tents of the wicked.

You let me stand in your sight for ever.
Psalm 41:13; 84:11

PRAYER

Father of love,

giver of all good things,
in Saint Aloysius you combined remarkable innocence
with the spirit of penance.
By the help of his prayers
may we who have not followed his innocence
follow his example of penance.

Grant this through our Lord Jesus Christ, your Son,
who lives and reigns with you and the Holy Spirit,
one God, for ever and ever.

Our Father . . .

June 22

PAULINUS OF NOLA, BISHOP

Saint Paulinus was born at Bordeaux in France in 355. He held
public office, married and had a son. Desirous of an austere life,
he received baptism and, having disposed of all worldly goods,
began to live the monastic life in 393, in Italy. He later was made
bishop and assisted pilgrims. He worked to help the poor and
suffering. He also composed poems remarkable for their fine
language. Saint Paulinus died in 431.

READING

A reading from a letter by Saint Paulinus of Nola, bishop

I give thanks and boast in the Lord, who, one and the same
throughout the world, produces his love in his people through
the Holy Spirit whom he pours out upon all flesh.

But you should know everything about me and you should be
aware that I am a sinner of long standing. It is not so long ago
that "I was led out of darkness and the shadow of death"; only
recently have I begun to breathe in the air of life; only recently
have I put my hand to the plough and taken up the cross of
Christ.

Blessed is the man who is found without fault,
who does not make gold his life's object,
who does not put his trust in wealth.

His future will be secure in the Lord.

He was able to sin, but did not;
he was able to do wrong, but would not.

His future will be secure in the Lord.
Sirach 31:8, 11, 10

PRAYER

Lord,
you made Saint Paulinus
renowned for his love of poverty
and concern for his people.
May we who celebrate his witness to the gospel
imitate his example of love for others.

We ask this through our Lord Jesus Christ, your Son,
who lives and reigns with you and the Holy Spirit,
one God, for ever and ever.

Our Father . . .

On the same day, June 22

JOHN FISHER, BISHOP AND MARTYR, AND
THOMAS MORE, MARTYR

Saint John Fisher was born in 1469. After completing his
theological studies at Cambridge in England, he was ordained to
the priesthood. Appointed bishop of Rochester, he led a most
austere life and fulfilled his pastoral role by frequently visiting
the faithful. He also composed works against the errors of the
time.

Saint Thomas More was born in 1477 and was educated at Oxford. He married and had one son and three daughters. While Chancellor in the King's Court, he wrote works on the governance of the realm and in defense of the Faith.

Both were beheaded in 1535 by order of King Henry VIII, whom they had resisted in the matter of his divorce: John Fisher on June 22 and Thomas More on July 6. While detained in prison, Bishop Fisher was named to the College of Cardinals of the Holy Roman Church by Pope Paul III.

READING

A reading from a letter written in prison to his daughter, Margaret, by Saint Thomas More

Although I know well, Margaret, that because of my past wickedness I deserve to be abandoned by God, I cannot but trust in his merciful goodness. His grace has strengthened me until now and made me content to lose goods, land, and life as well, rather than to swear against my conscience. God's grace has given the king a gracious frame of mind toward me, so that as yet he has taken from me nothing but my liberty. In doing this His Majesty has done me such great good with respect to spiritual profit that I trust that among all the great benefits he has heaped so abundantly upon me I count my imprisonment the very greatest. I cannot, therefore, mistrust the grace of God.

By the merits of his bitter passion joined to mine and far surpassing in merit for me all that I can suffer myself, his bounteous goodness shall release me from the pains of purgatory and shall increase my reward in heaven besides.

I will not mistrust him, Meg, though I shall feel myself weakening and on the verge of being overcome with fear. I shall remember how Saint Peter at a blast of wind began to sink because of his lack of faith, and I shall do as he did: call upon Christ and pray to him for help. And then I trust he shall place his holy hand on me and in the stormy seas hold me up from drowning.

And finally, Margaret, I know this well: that without my fault he will not let me be lost. I shall, therefore, with good hope commit myself wholly to him. And if he permits me to perish for my faults, then I shall serve as praise for his justice. But in good faith, Meg, I trust that his tender pity shall keep my poor soul safe and make me commend his mercy.

And, therefore, my own good daughter, do not let your mind be troubled over anything that shall happen to me in this world. Nothing can come but what God wills. And I am very sure that whatever that be, however bad it may seem, it shall indeed be the best.

RESPONSORY

When the martyrs of Christ were suffering,
they turned their minds to heavenly things and cried out:

Help us, O Lord, to complete your work without wavering.

Look down upon your servants
and upon the works of your hands.

Help us, O Lord, to complete your work without wavering.

PRAYER

Father,
you confirm the true faith
with the crown of martyrdom.
May the prayers of Saints John Fisher and Thomas More
give us the courage to proclaim our faith
by the witness of our lives.

Grant this through our Lord Jesus Christ, your Son,
who lives and reigns with you and the Holy Spirit,
one God, for ever and ever.

Our Father . . .

June 24

BIRTH OF JOHN THE BAPTIST
Solemnity

Saint John was the one who prepared the people to receive Jesus as the Chosen One of God. In the following reading, Saint Augustine tells us why Saint John is so great and why the Church pays him such special honor.

READING

A reading from a sermon by Saint Augustine, bishop

The Church observes the birth of John as a hallowed event. We have no such commemoration for any other fathers; but it is significant that we celebrate the birthdays of John and of Jesus. This day cannot be passed by. And even if my explanation does not match the dignity of the feast, you may still meditate on it with great depth and profit.

John appears as the boundary between the two testaments, the old and the new. That he is a sort of boundary the Lord himself bears witness, when he speaks of "the law and the prophets up until John the Baptist." Thus he represents times past and is the herald of the new era to come. As a representative of the past, he is born of aged parents; as a herald of the new era, he is declared to be a prophet while still in his mother's womb. For when yet unborn he leapt in his mother's womb at the arrival of blessed Mary. In that womb he had already been designated a prophet, even before he was born; it was revealed that he was to be Christ's precursor, before they ever saw one another. These are divine happenings, going beyond the limits of our human frailty.

When John was preaching the Lord's coming he was asked·

"Who are you?" And he replied: "I am the voice of one crying in the wilderness." The voice is John, but the Lord "in the beginning was the Word." John was a voice that lasted only for a time; Christ, the Word in the beginning, is eternal.

RESPONSORY

You, my child, shall be called the prophet of the Most High,

for you will go before the Lord to prepare his way.

To give his people knowledge of salvation
by the forgiveness of their sins.

For you will go before the Lord to prepare his way.
Luke 1:76-77

PRAYER

God our Father,
you raised up John the Baptist
to prepare a perfect people for Christ the Lord.
Give your Church joy in spirit
and guide those who believe in you
into the way of salvation and peace.

We ask this through our Lord Jesus Christ, your Son,
who lives and reigns with you and the Holy Spirit,
one God, for ever and ever.

Our Father . . .

June 27

CYRIL OF ALEXANDRIA, BISHOP AND DOCTOR

Saint Cyril was born in 370 and lived a monastic life. He was ordained a priest and succeeded his uncle as bishop of

Alexandria in 412. He had a preeminent role at the Council of Ephesus; he fought bravely against the doctrines of Nestorius, who taught that there were two persons in Christ. Saint Cyril also wrote many learned works explaining and defending the Catholic faith. He died in 444.

READING

A reading from a letter by Saint Cyril of Alexandria, bishop

That anyone could doubt the right of the holy Virgin to be called the Mother of God fills me with astonishment. Surely she must be the Mother of God if our Lord Jesus Christ is God, and she gave birth to him! Our Lord's disciples may not have used those exact words, but they delivered to us the belief those words enshrine, and this has also been taught us by the holy fathers.

The divinely inspired Scriptures affirm that the Word of God was made flesh, that is to say, he was united to a human body endowed with a rational soul. He undertook to help the descendants of Abraham, fashioning a body for himself from a woman and sharing our flesh and blood, to enable us to see in him not only God, but also, by reason of this union, a man like ourselves.

It is held, therefore, that there is in Emmanuel two entities, divinity and humanity. Yet our Lord Jesus Christ is nonetheless one, the one true Son, both God and man; not a defied man on the same footing as those who share the divine nature by grace, but true God who for our sake appeared in human form. We are assured of this by Saint Paul's declaration: "When the fullness of time came, God sent his Son, born of a woman, born under the law, to redeem those who were under the law and to enable us to be adopted as sons."

RESPONSORY

This holy man worked wonders in the sight of God;
he praised the Lord with his whole heart.

May he intercede for sinful mankind.

This priest of the Lord meditated on his commandments day
and night.

May he intercede for sinful mankind.

PRAYER

Father,
the bishop Cyril courageously taught
that Mary was the Mother of God.

May we who cherish this belief
receive salvation through the incarnation of Christ your Son,
who lives and reigns with you and the Holy Spirit,
one God, for ever and ever.

Our Father . . .

June 28

IRENAEUS, BISHOP AND MARTYR
Memorial

Saint Irenaeus was born around the year 130. Educated at
Smyrna, in what is now Turkey, he became the disciple of Saint
Polycarp, bishop of that city. In the year 177 he was ordained a
priest at Lyons in France and shortly thereafter was made
bishop of that city. He composed works defending the Catholic
faith against heretics, and it is said that he received the martyr's
crown around the year 200.

READING

A reading from an essay Against the Heresies by Saint Irenaeus,
bishop

The glory of God gives life; those who see God receive life. Men will therefore see God if they are to live; through the vision of God they become immortal and attain to God himself.

God is the source of all activity throughout creation. He cannot be seen or described in his own nature and in all his greatness by any of his creatures. Yet he is certainly not unknown. Through his Word the whole creation learns that there is one God the Father, who holds all things together and gives them their being. As it is written in the Gospel: "No man has ever seen God, except the only-begotten Son, who is in the bosom of the Father; he has revealed him."

From the beginning the Son is the one who teaches us about the Father; he is with the Father from the beginning.

The Word revealed God to men and presented men to God. Life in man is the glory of God; the life of man is the vision of God. If the revelation of God through creation gives life to all who live upon the earth, much more does the manifestation of the Father through the Word give life to those who see God.

RESPONSORY

True teaching was in his mouth;
no evil was ever found on his lips.

He walked with me in goodness and in peace.

My hand will be a steady help to him;
my arm will give him strength.

He walked with me in goodness and in peace.
Malachi 2:6; Psalm 89:22

PRAYER

Father,
you called Saint Irenaeus to uphold your truth
and bring peace to your Church.

161

By his prayers renew us in faith and love
that we may always be intent
on fostering unity and peace.

Grant this through our Lord Jesus Christ, your Son,
who lives and reigns with you and the Holy Spirit,
one God, for ever and ever.

Our Father . . .

June 29

PETER AND PAUL, APOSTLES
Solemnity

Saint Peter is the "rock" on whom Christ founded his Church.
Saint Paul is the apostle chosen by Christ especially to preach to
the Gentiles the Good News of the Kingdom. The Church today
celebrates the memory of these two great pillars of the faith in
one glorious solemnity.

READING

A reading from a sermon by Saint Augustine, bishop

This day has been made holy by the passion of the blessed
apostles Peter and Paul. We are, therefore, not talking about
some obscure martyrs. "For their voice has gone forth to all the
world, and to the ends of the earth their message." These martyrs realized what they taught; they pursued justice, they confessed the truth, they died for it.

Saint Peter, the first of the apostles and a fervent lover of Christ,
merited to hear these words: "I say to you that you are Peter,"
for he had said: "You are the Christ, the Son of the living God."
Then Christ said: "And I say to you that you are Peter, and on
this rock I will build my Church." On this rock I will build the
faith that you now confess, and on your words: "You are the

162

Christ, the Son of the living God," I will build my Church.

As you are aware, Jesus chose his disciples before his passion and called them apostles; and among these almost everywhere Peter alone deserved to represent the entire Church. And because of that role which he alone had, he merited to hear the words: "To you I shall give the keys of the kingdom of heaven." For it was not one man who received the keys, but the entire Church considered as one.

Both apostles share the same feast day, for these two were one; and even though they suffered on different days, they were as one. Peter went first, and Paul followed. And so we celebrate this day made holy for us by the apostles' blood. Let us embrace what they believed, their life, their labors, their sufferings, their preaching and their confession of faith.

RESPONSORY

The apostles proclaimed the word of God and preached it faithfully.

The apostles proclaimed the word of God and preached it faithfully.

They bore witness to the resurrection of Jesus Christ.

And preached it faithfully.

Glory to the Father . . .

The apostles proclaimed the word of God and preached it faithfully.

PRAYER

God our Father,
today you give us the joy
of celebrating the feast of the apostles Peter and Paul.
Through them your Church first received the faith.

Keep us true to their teaching.

Grant this through our Lord Jesus Christ, your Son,
who lives and reigns with you and the Holy Spirit,
one God, for ever and ever.

Our Father . . .

June 30

FIRST MARTYRS OF THE CHURCH OF ROME

In the first persecution against the Church, begun by the Emperor Nero after the burning of Rome in 64, many of the faithful were tortured and slain. The pagan writer Tacitus testifies to these events in his history, as does Clement, bishop of Rome, in his letter to the Corinthians.

READING

A reading from a letter to the Corinthians by Clement I, pope

It was through jealousy and envy that the greatest and most upright pillars of the Church were persecuted and struggled unto death. Let us set before our eyes the good apostles. First of all, Peter, who because of unreasonable jealousy, suffered not merely once or twice but many times, and, having thus given his witness, went to the place of glory that he deserved. It was through jealousy and conflict that Paul showed the way to the prize for perseverance. He was put in chains seven times, sent into exile, and stoned; a herald both in the east and the west, he achieved a noble fame by his faith. He taught justice to all the world and, when he had reached the limits of the western world, he gave his witness before those in authority; then he left this world and was taken up into the holy place, a superb example of endurance.

164

Around these men with their holy lives there gathered a great throng of the elect, who, though victims of jealousy, gave us the finest example of endurance in the midst of many indignities and tortures.

We are writing this, beloved, not only for your admonition but also as a reminder to ourselves; for we are placed in the same arena, and the same contest lies before us. Hence we ought to put aside vain and useless concerns and should consider what is good, pleasing and acceptable in the sight of him who made us. Let us fix our gaze on the blood of Christ, realizing how precious it is to his Father, since it was shed for our salvation and brought the grace of repentance to all the world.

RESPONSORY

They handed their bodies over to be tortured for their faith in
   God,
and so they earned an everlasting reward.

They have undergone great persecution
and have washed their robes in the blood of the Lamb.
And so they earned an everlasting reward.
Revelation 7:14

PRAYER

Father,
you sanctified the Church of Rome
with the blood of its first martyrs.
May we find strength from their courage
and rejoice in their triumph.

We ask this through our Lord Jesus Christ, your Son,
who lives and reigns with you and the Holy Spirit,
one God, for ever and ever.

Our Father . . .

July 3

THOMAS, APOSTLE
Feast

Saint Thomas is remembered for his disbelief in Christ's resurrection from the dead. When confronted by the risen Lord, his disbelief gave way to belief and he proclaimed the Easter faith of the Church: "My Lord and my God!" Nothing certain is known of his life except for this evidence in the gospels. He is said to have subsequently preached the gospel to the people of India. Since the fourth century the celebration of the transference of his body to Edessa in Mesopotamia has been commemorated on July 3.

READING

A reading from a homily on the gospels by Saint Gregory the Great, pope

"Thomas, one of the twelve, called the Twin, was not with them when Jesus came." He was the only disciple absent; on his return he heard what had happened but refused to believe it. The Lord came a second time; he offered his side for the disbelieving disciple to touch, held out his hands, and showing the scars of his wounds, healed the wound of his disbelief.

Dearly beloved, what do you see in these events? Do you really believe that it was by chance that this chosen disciple was absent, then came and heard, heard and doubted, doubted and touched, touched and believed? It was not by chance but in God's providence. In a marvelous way God's mercy arranged that the disbelieving disciple, in touching the wounds of his master's body, should heal our wounds of disbelief. The disbelief of Thomas has done more for our faith than the faith of the other disciples. As he touches Christ and is won over to belief, every doubt is cast aside and our faith is strengthened. So the disciple who doubted, then felt Christ's wounds, becomes a witness to the reality of the resurrection.

Touching Christ, he cried out: "'My Lord and my God.' Jesus said to him: 'Because you have seen me, Thomas, you have believed.'" Paul said: "Faith is the guarantee of things hoped for, the evidence of things unseen." It is clear, then, that faith is the proof of what cannot be seen. What is seen gives knowledge, not faith. When Thomas saw and touched, why was he told: "You have believed because you have seen me?" Because what he saw and what he believed were different things. God cannot be seen by mortal man. Thomas saw a human being, whom he acknowledged to be God, and said: "My Lord and my God." Seeing, he believed; looking at one who was true man, he cried out that this was God, the God he could not see.

What follows is reason for great joy: "Blessed are those who have not seen and have believed." There is here a particular reference to ourselves. We are included in these words, but only if we follow up our faith with good works. The true believer practices what he believes. But of those who pay only lip service to faith, Paul has this to say: "They profess to know God, but they deny him in their works." Therefore James says: "Faith without works is dead."

RESPONSORY

This life was made visible;
we have seen it and we proclaim to you

**the eternal life which was with the Father
and has appeared to us.**

We have seen it with our own eyes
and with our own hands we have touched the Word of life;
what we have seen and heard we declare to you.

**The eternal life which was with the Father
and has appeared to us.**
1 John 1:2, 1

Almighty Father,
as we honor Thomas the apostle,
let us always experience the help of his prayers.
May we have eternal life by believing in Jesus,
whom Thomas acknowledged as Lord,
for he lives and reigns with you and the Holy Spirit,
one God, for ever and ever.

Our Father . . .

July 4

ELIZABETH OF PORTUGAL

Saint Elizabeth was born of a Spanish royal family in 1271. As a young maiden she was given in marriage to the king of Portugal and bore him two children. She bravely endured afflictions and troubles through prayer and works of charity. When her husband died she distributed her property to the poor and received the habit of the Third Order of Saint Francis. After ending a serious dispute between her son and son-in-law, she died in 1331. Saint Elizabeth was a true peacemaker.

READING

A reading from a sermon attributed to Peter Chrysologus, bishop

"Blessed are the peacemakers," the evangelist said, dearest brethren, "for they shall be called sons of God."

Peace lends strength to our prayers; it is the way our petitions can reach God easily and can be credited; it is the plenitude which fills our desires. Peace is the mother of love, the bond of concord and the manifest sign of a pure soul, one which seeks to please God, which seeks to be fulfilled and has its desire rewarded. Peace must be preserved according to the Lord's precepts, as Christ said: "I leave you peace, my peace I give you," that is, as I left you in peace, in peace shall I find you. As Christ left the world, he wished to leave the gift he wanted to find when he returned.

Now you see, dearest brethren, why we should love peace and cultivate harmony: because they beget and nurture love. But you know also from the apostle John that, "Love comes from God," and that whoever is not with God does not possess love.

Love peace, and all the world will be tranquil and quiet.

RESPONSORY

Share your bread with the hungry,
and take the poor and homeless into your own house.

Then your light will break forth like the dawn
and your holiness will go before you.

When you see a man who is naked, clothe him,
and do not scorn your brother.

Then your light will break forth like the dawn
and your holiness will go before you.
Isaiah 58:7-8

PRAYER

Father of peace and love,
you gave Saint Elizabeth the gift of reconciling enemies.
By the help of her prayers
give us the courage to work for peace among men,
that we may be called the sons of God.

We ask this through our Lord Jesus Christ, your Son,
who lives and reigns with you and the Holy Spirit,

one God, for ever and ever.

Our Father . . .

July 5
ANTHONY ZACCARIA, PRIEST

Saint Anthony was born at Cremona in Italy in 1502. He studied medicine at Padua. After his ordination to the priesthood, he founded the Society of Clerics of Saint Paul, also known as the Barnabites. The Society did much to reform the morals of the faithful. He died in 1539.

READING

A reading from a sermon to fellow members of his society by Saint Anthony Zaccaria, priest

"We are fools for Christ's sake": our holy guide and most revered patron was speaking about himself and the rest of the apostles, and about the other people who profess the Christian and apostolic way of life. We should love and feel compassion for those who oppose us, rather than abhor and despise them, since they harm themselves and do us good, and adorn us with crowns of everlasting glory while they incite God's anger against themselves. And even more than this, we should pray for them and not be overcome by evil, but overcome evil by goodness. We should heap good works "like red-hot coals" of burning love "upon their heads," as our Apostle urges us to do, so that when they become aware of our tolerance and gentleness they may undergo a change of heart and be prompted to turn in love to God.

In his mercy God has chosen us, unworthy as we are, out of this world, to serve him and thus to advance in goodness and to bear the greatest possible fruit of love in patience.

170

I have preached faith in our Lord Jesus Christ,
and now I fear no danger.

**I do not count my life more precious than my work,
which is to finish my course,
the task of proclaiming and preaching
the good news of God's grace.**

I am not ashamed of the Gospel.

**I do not count my life more precious than my work,
which is to finish my course,
the task of proclaiming and preaching
the good news of God's grace.**

Acts 20:21, 24; Romans 1:16

PRAYER

Lord,
enable us to grasp in the spirit of Saint Paul,
the sublime wisdom of Jesus Christ,
the wisdom which inspired Saint Anthony Zaccaria
to preach the message of salvation in your Church.

Grant this through our Lord Jesus Christ, your Son,
who lives and reigns with you and the Holy Spirit,
one God, for ever and ever.

Our Father . . .

July 6

MARIA GORETTI, VIRGIN AND MARTYR

Saint Maria was born of a poor family in Italy in 1890. Near
Nettuno she spent a difficult childhood assisting her mother in
domestic duties. She was of a pious nature and often at prayer.
In 1902 she was stabbed to death, preferring to die rather than
be raped.

171

A reading from a homily at the canonization of Saint Maria
Goretti by Pope Pius XII

It is well known how this young girl had to face a bitter struggle
with no way to defend herself. Without warning a vicious
stranger burst upon her, bent on raping her and destroying her
childlike purity. In that moment of crisis she could have spoken
to her Redeemer in the words of that classic, *The Imitation of
Christ*: "Though tested and plagued by a host of misfortunes, I
have no fear so long as your grace is with me. It is my strength,
stronger than any adversary; it helps me and gives me guidance." With splendid courage she surrendered herself to God
and his grace and so gave her life to protect her virginity.

The life of a simple girl—I shall concern myself only with
highlights—we can see as worthy of heaven. Even today people
can look upon it with admiration and respect. Parents can learn
from her story how to raise their God-given children in virtue,
courage and holiness; they can learn to train them in the
Catholic faith so that, when put to the test, God's grace will
support them and they will come through undefeated, un-
scathed and untarnished.

From Maria's story carefree children and young people with
their zest for life can learn not to be led astray by attractive
pleasures which are not only ephemeral and empty but also
sinful. Instead they can fix their sights on achieving Christian
moral perfection, however difficult that course may prove. With
determination and God's help all of us can attain that goal by
persistent effort and prayer.

Not all of us are expected to die a martyr's death, but we are all
called to the pursuit of Christian virtue.

So let us all, with God's grace, strive to reach the goal that the
example of the virgin martyr, Saint Maria Goretti, sets before us.
Through her prayers to the Redeemer may all of us, each in his
own way, joyfully try to follow the inspiring example of Maria

Goretti who now enjoys eternal happiness in heaven.

How beautiful you are, virgin of Christ;
the Lord has given you the gift of perpetual virginity.

Nothing can rob you of your reward
or separate you from the love of the Son of God.
The Lord has given you the gift of perpetual virginity.

PRAYER

Father,
source of innocence and lover of chastity,
you gave Saint Maria Goretti the privilege
of offering her life in witness to Christ.
As you gave her the crown of martyrdom,
let her prayers keep us faithful to your teaching.

We ask this through our Lord Jesus Christ, your Son,
who lives and reigns with you and the Holy Spirit,
one God, for ever and ever.

Our Father . . .

July 11
BENEDICT, ABBOT
Memorial

Saint Benedict was born at Nursia in Italy about the year 480.
Educated at Rome, he began to live a hermit's life at Subiaco
where he gathered disciples, and then departed for Monte Cassino. There he established the famous monastery and composed
the Benedictine Rule. Because this rule was adopted throughout

Europe, he received the title of patriarch of Western monasticism. He died on March 21, 547, but since the end of the eighth century, his memory has been observed on this day.

READING

A reading from the Rule of Benedict, abbot

Girded with a faith and the performance of good works, let us follow in his [Christ's] paths by the guidance of the Gospel; then we shall deserve to see him "who has called us into his kingdom." If we wish to attain a dwelling place in his kingdom we shall not reach it unless we hasten there by our good deeds.

Just as there exists an evil fervor, a bitter spirit, which divides us from God and leads us to hell, so there is a good fervor which sets us apart from evil inclinations and leads us toward God and eternal life. No one should follow what he considers to be good for himself, but rather what seems good for another. Let them put Christ before all else; and may he lead us all to everlasting life.

RESPONSORY

Wishing to please God alone,
Benedict left his home and patrimony
to enter the religious life.
He lived as a hermit in the presence of the all-seeing God.

He withdrew from the world of men,
knowingly unacquainted with its ways
and wisely unlearned in its wisdom.
He lived as a hermit in the presence of the all-seeing God.

PRAYER

God our Father,

you made Saint Benedict an outstanding guide
to teach men how to live in your service.
Grant that by preferring your love to everything else,
we may walk in the way of your commandments.

We ask this through our Lord Jesus Christ, your Son,
who lives and reigns with you and the Holy Spirit,
one God, for ever and ever.

Our Father . . .

July 13

HENRY

Saint Henry was born in Bavaria in 973. He succeeded his father
and was later elected Emperor. He was most remarkable for his
work in Church reform and for fostering missionary activity. He
died in 1024 and was enrolled among the saints by Pope Eugene
III in 1146.

READING

A reading from the ancient Life of Saint Henry

After the most blessed servant of God had been anointed king,
he was not satisfied with the anxieties of his realm; so, in order
to attain the crown of immortality he determined to campaign
for the King of all, for to serve him is to rule. [He wrote:] "By the
most salutary instructions of sacred eloquence we are taught
and advised to abandon temporal riches, to lay aside earthly
goods, and to strive to reach the eternal and everlasting dwelling places in heaven. For present glory is fleeting and meaning-
less, while it is possessed, unless in it we can glimpse something
of heaven's eternity. But God's mercy toward the human race
provided a useful remedy when he made the reward for earthly
existence a share in our heavenly country."

The Lord made him rich;
he protected him from his enemies,
and he saved him from ambush.

He gave him unending glory.

He guided the just man on the straight path
and showed him God's kingdom.

He gave him unending glory.
Wisdom 10:11-12, 14, 10

PRAYER

Lord,
you filled Saint Henry with your love
and raised him from the cares of an earthly kingdom
to eternal happiness in heaven.
In the midst of the changes of this world,
may his prayers keep us free from sin
and help us on our way toward you.

Grant this through our Lord Jesus Christ, your Son,
who lives and reigns with you and the Holy Spirit,
one God, for ever and ever.

Our Father . . .

July 14

CAMILLUS DE LELLIS, PRIEST

Saint Camillus was born in Italy in 1550. He first entered the
military profession, but upon his conversion he devoted himself
to the care of the sick. His studies completed, he was ordained
to the priesthood and founded a society which established hospitals and cared for the sick. He died in Rome in 1614.

A reading from the life of Saint Camillus, by his companion

Let me begin with holy charity. It is the root of all the virtues and Camillus' most characteristic trait. I can attest that he was on fire with this holy virtue—not only toward God, but also toward his fellow men, and especially toward the sick. The mere sight of the sick was enough to soften and melt his heart and make him utterly forget all the pleasures, enticements and interests of this world. When he was taking care of his patients, he seemed to spend and exhaust himself completely, so great was his devotion and compassion. He would have loved to take upon himself all their illness, their every affliction, could he but ease their pain and relieve their weakness.

In the sick he saw the person of Christ. His reverence in their presence was as great as if he were really and truly in the presence of his Lord.

To enkindle the enthusiasm of his religious brothers for this all-important virtue, he used to impress upon them the consoling words of Jesus Christ: "I was sick and you visited me." He seemed to have these words truly graven on his heart, so often did he say them over and over again.

Great and all-embracing was Camillus' charity. Not only the sick and dying, but every other needy or suffering human being found shelter in his deep and kind concern.

RESPONSORY

Support the weak;
always strive to do good for all,

for this is God's will for you in Christ Jesus.

Welcome one another as Christ has welcomed you,
for the glory of God.

For this is God's will for you in Christ Jesus.

1 Thessalonians 5:14, 15, 18; Romans 15:7

Father,
you gave Saint Camillus a special love for the sick.
Through his prayers inspire us with your grace,
so that by serving you in our brothers and sisters
we may come safely to you at the end of our lives.

We ask this through our Lord Jesus Christ, your Son,
who lives and reigns with you and the Holy Spirit,
one God, for ever and ever.

Our Father . . .

July 15

BONAVENTURE, BISHOP AND DOCTOR
Memorial

Saint Bonaventure was born about the year 1218. He studied
philosophy and theology at Paris and, having earned the title
Master, he taught his fellow members of the Order of Friars
Minor with great success. He was elected Minister General of
the Order, a position he filled with prudence and wisdom. After
being made Cardinal-Bishop of Albano, he died at the Council
of Lyons in 1274. His writings did much to illuminate the study
of both theology and philosophy.

READING

A reading from the Journey of the Mind to God by Saint
Bonaventure

Christ is both the way and the door. Christ is the staircase and
the vehicle, like the "throne of mercy over the Ark of the Covenant," and "the mystery hidden from the ages." A man should
turn his full attention to this throne of mercy, and should gaze at
him hanging on the cross, full of faith, hope and charity, de-

voted, full of wonder and joy, marked by gratitude, and open to praise and jubilation. Then such a man will make with Christ a "pasch," that is, a passing-over. Through the branches of the cross he will pass over the Red Sea, leaving Egypt and entering the desert. There he will taste the hidden manna, and rest with Christ in the sepulcher, as if he were dead to things outside. He will experience, as much as is possible for one who is still living, what was promised to the thief who hung beside Christ: "Today you will be with me in paradise."

RESPONSORY

All who keep God's commandments live in God
and God lives in them.

We know that he dwells in us,
by the Spirit he has given us.

In his Holy Spirit God created wisdom,
which he has poured forth upon all creation
and has offered to those who love him.

We know that he dwells in us,
by the Spirit he has given us.
1 John 3:24; Sirach 1:8, 9

PRAYER

All-powerful Father,
may we who celebrate the feast of Saint Bonaventure
always benefit from his wisdom
and follow the example of his love.

Grant this through our Lord Jesus Christ, your Son,
who lives and reigns with you and the Holy Spirit,
one God, for ever and ever.

Our Father . . .

July 16

OUR LADY OF MOUNT CARMEL

Sacred Scripture celebrated the beauty of Carmel where the prophet Elijah defended the purity of Israel's faith in the living God. In the twelfth century, hermits withdrew to that mountain and later founded the Order devoted to the contemplative life under the patronage of Mary, the holy Mother of God.

READING

A reading from a sermon by Saint Leo the Great, pope

A royal virgin of the house of David is chosen. She is to bear a holy child, one who is both God and man. She is to conceive him in her soul before she conceives him in her body. In the face of so unheard of an event she is to know no fear through ignorance of the divine plan; the angel tells her what is to be accomplished in her by the Holy Spirit. She believes, and her faith is confirmed by the witness of a previous wonder; against all expectation Elizabeth is made fruitful. God has enabled a barren woman to be with child; he must be believed when he makes the same promise to a virgin.

The Son of God who was "in the beginning with God, through whom all things were made, without whom nothing was made," became man to free him from eternal death. He stooped down to take up our lowliness without loss to his own glory. He remained what he was; he took up what he was not. He wanted to join the very nature of a servant to that nature in which he is equal to God the Father.

Dearly beloved, this kind of birth was fitting for Christ, the power and wisdom of God: a birth in which he was one with us in our human nature but far above us in his divinity. If he were not true God, he would not be able to bring us healing; if he were not true man, he would not be able to give us an example.

Let us recall the memory of the glorious Virgin Mary,
whose humility God favored.

**Having received the angel's message,
she conceived the Savior of the world.**

Let us praise Christ,
as we celebrate this feast of the admirable Mother of God.

**Having received the angel's message,
she conceived the Savior of the world.**

PRAYER

Father,
may the prayers of the Virgin Mary protect us
and help us to reach Christ her Son
who lives and reigns with you and the Holy Spirit,
one God, for ever and ever.

Our Father . . .

July 21

LAWRENCE OF BRINDISI, PRIEST AND DOCTOR

Saint Lawrence of Brindisi was born in 1559. He entered the
Capuchin Friars, taught theology to his fellow religious, and
was chosen to fill positions of leadership in his order. He became famous throughout Europe as an effective and forceful
preacher. He wrote many works explaining the faith and died at
Lisbon in 1619.

READING

A reading from a sermon by Saint Lawrence of Brindisi, priest

There is a spiritual life that we share with the angels of heaven and with the divine spirits, for like them we have been formed in the image and likeness of God. The bread that is necessary for living this life is the grace of the Holy Spirit and the love of God. But grace and love are nothing without faith, since without faith it is impossible to please God. "Faith comes through hearing, and what is heard is the word of Christ." The preaching of the word of God, then, is necessary for the spiritual life, just as the planting of seed is necessary for bodily life.

The word of God is a light to the mind and a fire to the will. It enables man to know God and to love him. Against the hardness of a heart that persists in wrongdoing, it acts as a hammer. Against the world, the flesh and the devil it serves as a sword that destroys all sin.

RESPONSORY

You who preach the good news to Zion,
climb up to the top of a high mountain

and proclaim to the cities of Judah:
Here is your God.

Follow me; go and preach the kingdom of God.

And proclaim to the cities of Judah:
Here is your God.
Isaiah 40:9; Luke 9:59, 60

PRAYER

Lord,
for the glory of your name and the salvation of souls
you gave Lawrence of Brindisi
courage and right judgment.
By his prayers,
help us to know what we should do
and give us the courage to do it.

We ask this through our Lord Jesus Christ, your Son,
who lives and reigns with you and the Holy Spirit,
one God, for ever and ever.

Our Father . . .

July 22

MARY MAGDALENE
Memorial

Mary Magdalene was one of Christ's disciples and was present
when he died. Early on the morning of the resurrection, she
was, according to Saint Mark's account (16:9), the first to see the
risen Lord. By the twelfth century particularly, devotion to Saint
Mary Magdalene was widespread in the western Church.

READING

A reading from a homily on the Gospels by Gregory the Great,
pope

When Mary Magdalene came to the tomb and did not find the
Lord's body, she thought it had been taken away and so informed the disciples. After they came and saw the tomb, they
too believed what Mary had told them. The text then says: "The
disciples went back home," and it adds: "but Mary wept and
remained standing outside the tomb."

We should reflect on Mary's attitude and the great love she felt
for Christ; for though the disciples had left the tomb, she remained. She was still seeking the one she had not found, and
while she sought she wept; burning with the fire of love, she
longed for him who she thought had been taken away. And so it
happened that the woman who stayed behind to seek Christ
was the only one to see him. For perseverance is essential to any
good deed, as the voice of truth tell us: "Whoever perseveres to
the end will be saved."

Mary, do not weep; the Lord is risen from the dead.

Mary, do not weep; the Lord is risen from the dead.

Go to my brothers and say to them:

The Lord is risen from the dead.

Glory to the Father . . .

Mary, do not weep; the Lord is risen from the dead.

PRAYER

Father,
your Son first entrusted to Mary Magdalene
the joyful news of his resurrection.
By her prayers and example
may we proclaim Christ as our living Lord
and one day see him in glory,
for he lives and reigns with you and the Holy Spirit,
one God, for ever and ever.

Our Father . . .

July 23

BRIDGET, RELIGIOUS

Saint Bridget was born in Sweden in 1303. She married and gave birth to eight children for whom she was a devoted mother. After her husband's death she continued to live in the world but devoted herself to the ascetic life as a member of the Third Order of Saint Francis. She then founded a religous order and, journeying to Rome for the sake of penance, became a model of great virtue to all. She also wrote many works in which she related her mystical experiences. Saint Bridget died at Rome in 1373.

A reading from the prayers attributed to Saint Bridget

Eternal praise be to you, my Lord Jesus Christ, for the time you endured on the cross the greatest torments and sufferings for us sinners. The sharp pain of your wounds fiercely penetrated even to your blessed soul and cruelly pierced your most sacred heart till finally you sent forth your spirit in peace, bowed your head, and humbly commended yourself into the hands of God your Father, and your whole body remained cold in death.

Blessed may you be, my Lord Jesus Christ. For our salvation you allowed your side and heart to be pierced with a lance; and from that side water and your precious blood flowed out abundantly for our redemption.

Unending honor be to you, my Lord Jesus Christ. On the third day you rose from the dead and appeared to those you had chosen. And after forty days you ascended into heaven before the eyes of many witnesses, and there in heaven you gathered together in glory those you love, whom you had freed from hell.

Rejoicing and eternal praise be to you, my Lord Jesus Christ, who sent the Holy Spirit into the hearts of your disciples and increased the boundless love of God in their spirits.

Blessed are you and praiseworthy and glorious for ever, my Lord Jesus.

RESPONSORY

Christ loved us, and poured out his blood
to free us from our sins.

He has made of us a kingdom of priests.

Live then in love, even as Christ loved us
and gave himself up for us.

He has made of us a kingdom of priests.

PRAYER

Lord our God,
you revealed the secrets of heaven to Saint Bridget
as she meditated on the suffering and death of your Son.
May your people rejoice in the revelation of your glory.

Grant this through our Lord Jesus Christ, your Son,
who lives and reigns with you and the Holy Spirit,
one God, for ever and ever.

Our Father . . .

July 25

JAMES, APOSTLE
Feast

Saint James, son of Zebedee and brother of Saint John the apostle, was born at Bethsaida. He was present at most of the miracles performed by Christ and was put to death by Herod around the year 42. He is especially honored at Compostella in Spain where a famous church is dedicated to his name.

READING

A reading from a homily on Matthew by Saint John
Chrysostom, bishop

The sons of Zebedee press Christ: "Promise that one may sit at your right side and the other at your left." What does he do? He wants to show them that it is not a spiritual gift for which they are asking, and that if they knew what their request involved,

186

they would never dare make it. So he says: "You do not know what you are asking," that is, what a great and splendid thing it is and how much beyond the reach even of the heavenly powers. Then he continues: "Can you drink the cup which I must drink and be baptized with the baptism which I must undergo?" He is saying: "You talk of sharing honors and rewards with me, but I must talk of struggle and toil. Now is not the time for rewards or the time for my glory to be revealed. Earthly life is the time for bloodshed, war and danger."

He also calls his suffering a baptism, to show that it will effect a great cleansing of the entire world.

The disciples really do not know what they are saying. How does Christ reply: "You will indeed drink my cup and be baptized with my baptism. But seats at my right and left side are not mine to give; they belong to those for whom the Father has prepared them." Thus, after lifting their minds to higher goals and preparing them to meet and overcome all that will make them desolate, he sets them straight on their request.

RESPONSORY

These men while on earth founded the Church of Christ with their own blood.
They drank the cup of the Lord
and became the friends of God.

Their voice has gone out to the limits of the earth, their words to the ends of the world.
They drank the cup of the Lord
and became the friends of God.

PRAYER

Almighty Father,
by the martyrdom of Saint James

you blessed the work of the early Church.
May his profession of faith give us courage
and his prayers bring us strength.

We ask this through our Lord Jesus Christ, your Son,
who lives and reigns with you and the Holy Spirit,
one God, for ever and ever.

Our Father . . .

July 26

JOACHIM AND ANN, PARENTS OF MARY
Memorial

From an ancient tradition, going back even to the second century, the parents of the Virgin Mary are known by the names of Joachim and Ann. Devotion to Saint Ann is found in the sixth century in the East, and by the tenth century it was widespread in the West. Saint Joachim was likewise honored, but at a more recent date.

READING

A reading from a sermon by Saint John Damascene, bishop

Joachim and Ann, how blessed a couple! All creation is indebted to you. For at your hands the Creator was offered a gift excelling all other gifts: a chaste mother, who alone was worthy of him.

Joachim and Ann, how blessed and spotless a couple! You will be known by the fruit you have borne, as the Lord says: "By their fruits you will know them." The conduct of your life pleased God and was worthy of your daughter. For by the chaste and holy life you led together, you have fashioned a jewel of virginity: she who remained a virgin before, during and after giving birth. She alone for all time would maintain her virginity in mind and soul as well as in body.

188

Joachim and Ann, how chaste a couple! While leading a devout and holy life in your human nature, you gave birth to a daughter nobler than the angels, whose queen she now is.

In the tender compassion of our God, the Lord has come to us.

In the tender compassion of our God, the Lord has come to us.

He has raised up Jesus, our savior.

The Lord has come to us.

Glory to the Father . . .

In the tender compassion of our God, the Lord has come to us.

God of our fathers,
you gave Saints Joachim and Ann
the privilege of being the parents of Mary,
the mother of your incarnate Son.
May their prayers help us to attain
the salvation you have promised to your people.

Grant this through our Lord Jesus Christ, your Son,
who lives and reigns with you and the Holy Spirit,
one God, for ever and ever.

Our Father . . .

July 29

MARTHA

Memorial

Saint Martha was a sister of Mary and Lazarus. When she received the Lord as a guest at Bethany, she looked after him with devoted attention. She begged the Lord to raise her brother, Lazarus, from the dead.

READING

A reading from a sermon by Saint Augustine, bishop

Our Lord's words teach us that though we labor among the many distractions of this world, we should have but one goal. For we are but travelers on a journey without as yet a fixed abode; we are on our way, not yet in our native land; we are in a state of longing, not yet of enjoyment. But let us continue on our way, and continue without sloth or respite, so that we may ultimately arrive at our destination.

Martha and Mary were sisters, related not only by blood but also by religious aspirations. They stayed close to our Lord and both served him harmoniously when he was among them. Martha welcomed him as travelers are welcomed. But in her case, the maidservant received her Lord, the creature her Creator, to serve him bodily food while she was to be fed by the Spirit.

No one of you should say: "Blessed are they who have deserved to receive Christ into their homes!" Do not grieve or complain that you were born in a time when you can no longer see God in the flesh. He did not in fact take this privilege from you. As he says: "Whatever you have done to the least of my brothers, you did to me."

RESPONSORY

After Jesus had raised Lazarus from the dead,

they gave a dinner for him at Bethany,

and Martha served at table.

Mary took a pound of costly perfume
and anointed the feet of Jesus.

And Martha served at table.

PRAYER

Father,
your Son honored Saint Martha
by coming to her home as a guest.
By her prayers
may we serve Christ in our brothers and sisters
and be welcomed by you into heaven, our true home.

We ask this through our Lord Jesus Christ, your Son,
who lives and reigns with you and the Holy Spirit,
one God, for ever and ever.

Our Father . . .

July 30

PETER CHRYSOLOGUS, BISHOP AND DOCTOR

Saint Peter Chrysologus was born about the year 380 in Italy
and there entered the priesthood. He was elected bishop of
Ravenna in 424 and instructed his flock by his learned sermons
and writings. He died around the year 450.

READING

A reading from a sermon by Saint Peter Chrysologus, bishop

Christ is born that by his birth he might restore our nature. He became a child, was fed, and grew that he might inaugurate the one perfect age to remain for ever as he created it. He supports man that man might no longer fall. And the creature he had formed of earth he now makes heavenly, and what he endowed with a human soul he now vivifies to become a heavenly spirit. In this way he fully raised man to God, and left in him neither sin, nor death, nor pain, nor anything earthly, with the grace of our Lord Christ Jesus, who lives and reigns with the Father in the unity of the Holy Spirit now and for ever, for all the ages of eternity. Amen.

RESPONSORY

Come near to Christ, the living stone;

you too must be living stones, built up in him.

Jesus is the stone which has become the cornerstone.

You too must be living stones, built up in him.
1 Peter 2:4, 5; Psalm 118:22

PRAYER

Father,
you made Peter Chrysologus
an outstanding preacher of your incarnate Word.
May the prayers of Saint Peter help us to cherish
the mystery of our salvation
and make its meaning clear in our love for others.

Grant this through our Lord Jesus Christ, your Son,
who lives and reigns with you and the Holy Spirit,
one God, for ever and ever.

Our Father . . .

July 31

IGNATIUS OF LOYOLA, PRIEST
Memorial

Saint Ignatius was born in 1491 at Loyola in Spain. He spent his early years at court and as a soldier. Later he was converted to God and undertook theological studies at Paris where he attracted his first followers. Afterward at Rome he joined them together as the first members of the Society of Jesus. He exercised a most fruitful apostolate both by his written works and in the training of his disciples who won great praise for their renewal of the Church. He died at Rome in 1556.

READING

A reading from the life of Saint Ignatius from his own words by Luis Gonzalez

Ignatius was passionately fond of reading worldly books of fiction and tales of knight-errantry. When he felt he was getting better [from a wound he had received in battle,] he asked for some of these books to pass the time. But no book of that sort could be found in the house; instead they gave him a life of Christ and a collection of the lives of saints written in Spanish.

By constantly reading these books he began to be attracted to what he found narrated there. Sometimes in the midst of his reading he would reflect on what he had read. Yet at other times he would dwell on many of the things which he had been accustomed to dwell on previsouly. But at this point our Lord came to his assistance, insuring that these thoughts were followed by others which arose from his current reading.

While reading the life of Christ our Lord or the lives of the saints, he would reflect and reason with himself: "What if I should do what Saint Francis or Saint Dominic did?" In this way he let his mind dwell on many thoughts; they lasted a while until other things took their place. Then those vain and worldly images would come into his mind and remain a long time.

But there was a difference. When Igantius reflected on worldly thoughts, he felt intense pleasure; but when he gave them up out of weariness, he felt dry and depressed. Yet when he thought of living the rigorous sort of life he knew the saints had lived, he not only experienced pleasure when he actually thought about it, but even after he dismissed these thoughts, he still experienced great joy. Yet he did not pay attention to this, nor did he appreciate it, until one day, in a moment of insight he began to marvel at the difference. Then he understood his experience. Thoughts of one kind left him sad, the others full of joy.

RESPONSORY

Whoever speaks should proclaim God's message;
whoever ministers should serve by the power that God gives,

so that in all of you God may be glorified through Jesus Christ.

Before all else be constant in your love for one another.
So that in all of you God may be glorified through Jesus Christ.
1 Peter 4:11, 8

PRAYER

Father,
you gave Saint Ignatius of Loyola to your Church
to bring greater glory to your name.
May we follow his example on earth
and share the crown of life in heaven.

We ask this through our Lord Jesus Christ, your Son,
who lives and reigns with you and the Holy Spirit,
one God, for ever and ever.

Our Father . . .

August 1

ALPHONSUS LIGUORI, BISHOP AND DOCTOR

Memorial

Saint Alphonsus was born at Naples in 1696. He was a lawyer, but he left the legal profession and entered the priesthood. Later he founded the Congregation of the Most Holy Redeemer. To help make people better Christians, he spent much time preaching and writing books on moral theology, of which he is considered a master. He was chosen bishop of Saint' Agata dei Goti, but soon resigned his office to work as a simple priest. Saint Alphonsus died in 1787.

READING

A reading from a sermon by Saint Alphonsus Liguori, bishop

All holiness and perfection of soul lies in our love for Jesus Christ our God, who is our redeemer and our supreme good.

Has not God in fact won for himself a claim on all our love? From all eternity he has loved us. And it is in this vein that he speaks to us: "O man, consider carefully that I first loved you. You had not yet appeared in the light of day, nor did the world yet exist, but already I loved you. From all eternity I have loved you."

Since God knew that man is enticed by favors, he wished to bind him to his love by means of his gifts: I want to catch men with the snares, those chains of love in which they allow themselves to be entrapped, so that they will love me. And all the gifts which he bestowed on man were given to this end. He gave him a soul, made in his likeness. He endowed him with memory, intellect and will; he gave him a body equipped with the senses. It was for him that he created heaven and earth and such an abundance of things. He made all these things out of love for man, so that all creation might serve man, and man in turn might love God out of gratitude for so many gifts.

But he did not wish to give us only beautiful creatures; the truth is that to win for himself our love, he went so far as to bestow upon us the fullness of himself. The eternal Father went so far as to give us his only Son. When he saw that we were all dead through sin and deprived of his grace, what did he do? He sent his beloved Son to make reparation for us and to call us back to a sinless life.

RESPONSORY

The Lord fulfills the desires of those who fear him;
he hears their cry and saves them.
The Lord watches over all who love him.

Everyone who is a child of God does not sin,
for God's grace remains in him.
The Lord watches over all who love him.
Psalm 145:19-20; 1 John 3:9

PRAYER

Father,
you constantly build up your Church
by the lives of your saints.
Give us grace to follow Saint Alphonsus
in his loving concern for the salvation of men,
and so come to share his reward in heaven.

Grant this through our Lord Jesus Christ, your Son,
who lives and reigns with you and the Holy Spirit,
one God, for ever and ever.

Our Father . . .

August 2

EUSEBIUS OF VERCELLI, BISHOP

Saint Eusebius was born at the beginning of the fourth century
in Sardinia. He became a member of the Roman clergy and in
345 was elected first bishop of Vercelli. He spread religion by his
preaching and established the monastic life in his diocese. Because of his faith he was driven into exile by Emperor
Constantius and endured much suffering. Returning to his
country, he worked tirelessly to strengthen the faith. He died at
Vercelli in 371.

READING

A reading from a letter by Saint Eusebius of Vercelli, bishop

Dearly beloved, I rejoice in your faith, in the salvation that
comes from faith, in your good works, which are not confined to
your own surroundings but spread far and wide. Like a farmer
tending a sound tree, untouched by ax or fire because of its fruit,
I want not only to serve you in the body, good people that you
are, but also to give my life for your well-being.

So I beg you to keep the faith with all vigilance, to preserve
harmony, to be earnest in prayer, to remember me always, so
that the Lord may grant freedom to his Church which is suffering throughout the world, and that I may be set free from the
sufferings that weigh upon me, and so be able to rejoice with
you.

RESPONSORY

This is a man who loved his brethren and ever prayed for them.

This is a man who loved his brethren and ever prayed for them.

He spent himself in their service

and ever prayed for them.

Glory to the Father . . .

This is a man who loved his brethren and ever prayed for them.

PRAYER

Lord God,
Saint Eusebius affirmed the divinity of your Son.
By keeping the faith he taught,
may we come to share the eternal life of Christ,
who lives and reigns with you and the Holy Spirit,
one God, for ever and ever.

Our Father . . .

August 4

JOHN VIANNEY, PRIEST
Memorial

Saint John Vianney was born in France in 1786. After overcoming many difficulties, he was ordained a priest. He was entrusted with a parish in the town of Ars. He cared for this parish in a marvelous way by his preaching, his mortification, prayer and good works. Since he was renowned for great skill in helping penitents, people came to him from many regions and devoutly accepted his counsels. He died in 1859.

READING

A reading from the cathechetical instructions by Saint John Mary Vianney, priest

My little children, reflect on these words: the Christian's treasure is not on earth but in heaven. Our thoughts, then, ought to be directed to where our treasure is. This is the glorious duty of man: to pray and to love. If you pray and love, that is where a man's happiness lies.

Prayer is nothing else but union with God. In this intimate union, God and the soul are fused together like two bits of wax that no one can ever pull apart. This union of God with a tiny creature is a lovely thing. It is a happiness beyond understanding.

My little children, your hearts are small, but prayer stretches them and makes them capable of loving God. Through prayer we receive a foretaste of heaven and something of paradise comes down upon us. Prayer never leaves us without sweetness. It is honey that flows into the soul and makes all things sweet. When we pray properly, sorrows disappear like snow before the sun.

Some men immerse themselves as deeply in prayer as fish in water, because they give themselves totally to God. O, how I love these noble souls!

How unlike them we are! How often we come to church with no idea of what to do or what to ask for. And yet, whenever we go to any human being, we know well enough why we go. And still worse, there are some who seem to speak to the good God like this: "I will only say a couple of things to you, and then I will be rid of you." I often think that when we come to adore the Lord, we would receive everything we ask for, if we would ask with living faith and with a pure heart.

RESPONSORY

Our troubles pass quickly,
and their burden seems light
when we compare them to the weight of eternal glory

which far exceeds the burden of our suffering.

No eye has seen, no ear heard,
nor has the heart of man conceived,
the marvels God has prepared for those who love him.

Which far exceeds the burden of our suffering.
2 Corinthians 4:17; 1 Corinthians 2:9

Father of mercy,
you made Saint John Vianney outstanding
in his priestly zeal and concern for your people.
By his example and prayers,
enable us to win our brothers and sisters
to the love of Christ
and come with them to eternal glory.

We ask this through our Lord Jesus Christ, your Son,
who lives and reigns with you and the Holy Spirit,
one God, for ever and ever.

Our Father . . .

August 5

DEDICATION OF SAINT MARY MAJOR

After the Council of Ephesus (431) in which the mother of Jesus
was acclaimed as Mother of God, Pope Sixtus III erected at
Rome on the Esquiline Hill a basilica dedicated to the honor of
the holy Mother of God. It was afterward called Saint Mary
Major and it is the oldest church in the West dedicated to the
honor of the Blessed Virgin Mary.

READING

A reading from a homily delivered at the Council of Ephesus by
Saint Cyril of Alexandria, bishop

Mary, Mother of God, we salute you. Precious vessel, worthy of
the whole world's reverence, you are an ever-shining light, the
crown of virginity, the symbol of orthodoxy, an indestructible
temple, the place that held him whom no place can contain,
mother and virgin. Because of you the holy gospels could say:
"Blessed is he who comes in the name of the Lord."

Who can put Mary's high honor into words? She is both mother and virgin.

Behold then the joy of the whole universe. Let the union of God and man in the Son of the Virgin Mary fill us with awe and adoration. Let us fear and worship the undivided Trinity as we sing the praise of the ever-virgin Mary, the holy temple of God, and of God himself, her Son. To him be glory for ever and ever. Amen.

RESPONSORY

Rejoice with me, all you who love the Lord,
for in my lowliness I have pleased the Most High.
From my womb I have given birth to a Son
who is both God and man.

From this day all generations will call me blessed,
for the Lord has looked with favor on his lowly servant.

From my womb I have given birth to a Son
who is both God and man.

PRAYER

Lord,
pardon the sins of your people.
May the prayers of Mary, the mother of your Son,
help to save us,
for by ourselves we cannot please you.

Grant this through our Lord Jesus Christ, your Son,
who lives and reigns with you and the Holy Spirit,
one God, for ever and ever.

Our Father . . .

August 6

TRANSFIGURATION

Feast

Today the Church celebrates the transfiguration of Christ, to honor him as the One who possesses in himself the glory of God. The scene on the mountain, where Jesus' face and garments shone like the brightest of lights, was a sign to the disciples that, after his death, he was going to rise in glory. It is also a sign to us that one day we too will rise in glory to be with him forever.

READING

A reading from a sermon on the transfiguration of the Lord by Anastasius of Sinai, bishop

Upon Mount Tabor, Jesus revealed to his disciples a heavenly mystery. While living among them he had spoken of the kingdom and of his second coming in glory, but to banish from their hearts any possible doubt concerning the kingdom and to confirm their faith in what lay in the future, he gave them on Mount Tabor a wonderful vision of his glory, a foreshadowing of the kingdom of heaven. It was as if he said to them: "As time goes by you may be in danger of losing your faith. To save you from this I tell you now that 'some standing here' listening to me 'will not taste death until they have seen the Son of Man coming' in the glory of his Father." Moreover, in order to assure us that Christ could command such power when he wished, the evangelist continues: "Six days later, Jesus took with him Peter, James and John, and led them up a high mountain where they were alone. There, before their eyes, he was transfigured. His face shone like the sun, and his clothes became as white as light. Then the disciples saw Moses and Elijah appear, and they were talking to Jesus."

These are the divine wonders we celebrate today; this is the saving revelation given us upon the mountain; this is the festival of Christ that has drawn us here.

Let us retire from the world, stand aloof from the earth, rise above the body, detach ourselves from creatures and turn to the Creator, to whom Peter exclaimed: "Lord, it is good for us to be here."

It is indeed good to be here, as you have said, Peter. It is good to be with Jesus and to remain here for ever. What greater happiness or higher honor could we have than to be with God, to be made like him and to live in his light?

RESPONSORY

His face shone like the sun;

when the disciples saw his glory,
they were filled with wonder and fear.

Suddenly Moses and Elijah appeared before them speaking with Jesus.

When the disciples saw his glory,
they were filled with wonder and fear.
Matthew 17:2, 3; see Luke 9:32, 34

PRAYER

God our Father,
in the transfigured glory of Christ your Son,
you strengthen our faith
by confirming the witness of your prophets,
and show us the splendor of your beloved sons and daughters.
As we listen to the voice of your Son,
help us to become heirs to eternal life with him
who lives and reigns with you and the Holy Spirit,
one God, for ever and ever.

Our Father . . .

August 7

SIXTUS II, POPE AND MARTYR, AND COMPANIONS, MARTYRS

Saint Sixtus was ordained bishop of the Church of Rome in 257. The following year, while celebrating the sacred liturgy in the cemetery of Saint Callistus, he was arrested by soldiers carrying out the edict of the Emperor Valerian. On the same day, August 6, he was put to death along with four deacons.

READING

A reading from a letter by Saint Cyprian, bishop and martyr

All the clergy [of Rome] are exposed to the imminent danger of being put to the test and prepared in a spirit of dedication for the divine glory of heaven.

The true state of affairs is this. Valerian has issued an edict to the Senate to the effect that bishops, presbyters and deacons shall suffer the death penalty without delay. Senators, distinguished men and members of the equestrian class are to be deprived of their rank and property, and if, after forfeiting their wealth and privileges, they still persist in professing Christianity, they too are to be sentenced to death. Ladies of the upper classes are to be deprived of their property and exiled. In the case of members of the imperial staff, any who have either previously confessed or will now confess to being Christians shall have their property confiscated and will be assigned as prisoners to the imperial estates.

To this decree the Emperor Valerian attached a copy of a letter he had sent to the provincial governors concerning us. Every day we are hoping that this letter will arrive, for we are standing firm in faith and ready to endure suffering, in expectation of winning the crown of eternal life through the help and mercy of the Lord. I must also inform you that Sixtus was put to death in a catacomb on the sixth of August, and four deacons with him. Moreover, the prefects in Rome are pressing this persecution zealously and without intermission to such a point that anyone brought before them is punished and his property is claimed by the treasury.

I ask you to make these facts known to the rest of our fellow bishops, in order that by the exhoration of their pastors the brethren everywhere may be strengthened and prepared for the spiritual combat. Let all our people fix their minds not on death but rather on immortality; let them commit themselves to the Lord in complete faith and unflinching courage and make their confession with joy rather than in fear, knowing that in this contest the soldiers of God and Christ are not slain but rather win their crowns.

RESPONSORY

We are being handed over to death for Jesus's sake

so that the life of Jesus may be revealed in our mortal bodies.

For your sake, O Lord, we are being put to death all day long, and we are treated like sheep for the slaughter.

So that the life of Jesus may be revealed in our mortal bodies.
2 Corinthians 4:11; Psalm 44:23

PRAYER

Father,
by the power of the Holy Spirit
you enabled Saint Sixtus and his companions to lay down their
    lives
for your word in witness to Jesus.
Give us the grace to believe in you
and the courage to profess our faith.

We ask this through our Lord Jesus Christ, your Son,
who lives and reigns with you and the Holy Spirit,
one God, for ever and ever.

Our Father . . .

On the same day, August 7

CAJETAN, PRIEST

Saint Cajetan was born at Vicenza in 1480. He studied law in
Padua and after being ordained a priest, he founded the Congregation of Clerks Regular at Rome to foster the Church's mission. He extended this congregation into the district of Venice
and into the kingdom of Naples. He was most earnest in prayer
and in love of neighbor. He died at Naples in 1547.

READING

A reading from a letter by Saint Cajetan, priest

I am a sinner and do not think much of myself; I have recourse
to the greatest servants of the Lord, that they may pray for you
to the blessed Christ and his Mother. But do not forget that all
the saints cannot endear you to Christ as much as you can yourself. It is entirely up to you. If you want Christ to love you and
help you, you must love him and always make an effort to
please him. Do not waver in your purpose, because even if all
the saints and every single creature should abandon you, he will
always be near you, whatever your needs.

You know, of course, that we are pilgrims in this world, on a
journey to our true home in heaven. The man who becomes
proud loses his way and rushes to death. While living here we
should strive to gain eternal life. Yet of ourselves we cannot
achieve this since we have lost it through sin; but Jesus Christ
has recovered it for us. For this reason we must always be grateful to him and love him. We must always obey him, and as far as
possible remain united with him.

He has offered himself to be our food. How wretched is the
man who knows nothing of such a gift! To us has been given
the opportunity to receive Christ, son of the Virgin Mary, and
we refuse him. Woe to the man who does not care enough to
receive him. My daughter, I want what is good for myself; I beg

206

the same for you. Now there is no other way to bring this about than to ask the Virgin Mary constantly to come to you with her glorious Son. Be bold! Ask her to give you her Son, who in the blessed sacrament of the altar is truly the food of your soul. Readily will she give him to you, still more readily will he come to you, giving you the strength to make your way fearlessly through this dark wood. In it large numbers of our enemies lie in wait, but they cannot reach us if they see us relying on such powerful help.

Nor, my child, must you merely receive Jesus Christ simply as a means to further your own plans. I want you to surrender to him, that he may welcome you and, as your divine Savior, do to you and in you whatever he wills.

RESPONSORY

Let us praise the fame of this holy man
and his boundless love.

Turning aside worldly pleasures,
he gained eternal life.

For to him life was Christ, and death was gain.

Turning aside worldly pleasures,
he gained eternal life.

PRAYER

Lord,
you helped Saint Cajetan
to imitate the apostolic way of life.
By his example and prayers
may we trust in you always
and be faithful in seeking your kingdom.

Grant this through our Lord Jesus Christ, your Son,
who lives and reigns with you and the Holy Spirit,

one God, for ever and ever.

Our Father . . .

August 8

DOMINIC, PRIEST
Memorial

Saint Dominic was born in Calaruega in Spain around the year 1170. He studied theology at Palencia and was made canon of the church of Osma. He worked effectively against heresy through preaching and good example. To carry on this work he gathered together companions and founded the Order of Preachers. He died at Bologna on August 6, 1221.

READING

A reading from various writings on the history of the Order of Preachers

Dominic possessed such great integrity and was so strongly motivated by divine love, that without a doubt he proved to be a bearer of honor and grace. And since a joyful heart animates the face, he displayed the peaceful composure of a spiritual man in the kindness he manifested outwardly and by the cheerfulness of his countenance.

Wherever he went he showed himself in word and deed to be a man of the Gospel. During the day no one was more community-minded or pleasant toward his brothers and associ- ates. During the night hours no one was more persistent in every kind of vigil and supplication. He seldom spoke unless it was with God, that is, in prayer, or about God; and in this matter he instructed his brothers.

Frequently he made a special personal petition that God would deign to grant him genuine charity in caring for and obtaining the salvation of men. For he believed that only then would he be truly a member of Christ, when he had given himself totally for the salvation of men, just as the Lord Jesus, the Savior of all, had offered himself completely for our salvation. So, for this work, after a lengthy period of careful and provident planning, he founded the Order of Friars Preachers.

In his conversations and letters he often urged the brothers of the Order to study constantly the Old and New Testaments. He always carried with him the gospel according to Matthew and the epistles of Paul, and so well did he study them that he almost knew them from memory.

Two or three times he was chosen bishop, but he always refused, preferring to live with his brothers in poverty. Of him Pope Gregory IX declared: "I knew him as a steadfast follower of the apostolic way of life. There is no doubt that he is in heaven, sharing in the glory of the apostles themselves."

RESPONSORY

This preacher of the new salvation leaped up like a flame.

His words burned like a torch.

True teaching was in his mouth;
no evil was ever found on his lips.

His words burned like a torch.
See Sirach 48:1; Malachi 2:6

PRAYER

Lord,
let the holiness and teaching of Saint Dominic
come to the aid of your Church.
May he help us now with his prayers
as he once inspired people by his preaching.

We ask this through our Lord Jesus Christ, your Son,
who lives and reigns with you and the Holy Spirit,
one God, for ever and ever.

Our Father . . .

August 10

LAWRENCE, DEACON AND MARTYR
Feast

Saint Lawrence was a deacon of the church of Rome. He became
a martyr during the persecution of Valerian four days after the
martyrdom of Pope Sixtus II and his four companions.
Lawrence's tomb is located in the field of Verano near the Via
Tiburtina where Constantine the Great built a basilica. Devotion
to Lawrence was widespread by the fourth century.

READING

A reading from a sermon by Saint Augustine, bishop

The Roman Church commends to us today the anniversary of
the triumph of Saint Lawrence. For on this day he trod the
furious pagan world underfoot and flung aside its allurements,
and so gained victory over Satan's attack on his faith.

As you have often heard, Lawrence was a deacon of the Church
at Rome. There he ministered the sacred blood of Christ; there
for the sake of Christ's name he poured out his own blood. Saint
John the apostle was evidently teaching us about the mystery of
the Lord's supper when he wrote: "Just as Christ laid down his
life for us, so we ought to lay down our lives for the brethren."
My brethren, Lawrence understood this and, understanding, he
acted on it. In his life he loved Christ; in his death he followed in
his footsteps.

Brethren, we too must imitate Christ if we truly love him. We shall not be able to render better return on that love than by modeling our lives on his. "Christ suffered for us, leaving us an example, that we should follow in his steps." The holy martyrs followed Christ even to shedding their life's blood, even to reproducing the very likeness of his passion. They followed him, but not they alone. It is not true that the bridge was broken after the martyrs crossed; nor is it true that after they had drunk from it, the fountain of eternal life dried up.

On no account may any class of people despair, thinking that God has not called them. Christ suffered for all. What the Scriptures say of him is true: "He desires all men to be saved and to come to knowledge of the truth."

I tell you again and again, my brethren, that on no account may any class of people despair, thinking that God has not called them. Christ suffered for all. What the Scriptures say of him is true: "He desires all men to be saved and to come to knowledge of the truth."

Let us understand, then, how a Christian must follow Christ even though he does not shed his blood for him, and his faith is not called upon to undergo the great test of the martyr's sufferings. The apostle Paul says of Christ our Lord: "Though he was in the form of God he did not consider equality with God a prize to be clung to." How unrivaled his majesty! "But he emptied himself, taking on the form of a slave, made in the likeness of men, and presenting himself in human form." How deep his humility!

Christ humbled himself. Christian, that is what you must make your own. "Christ became obedient." How is it that you are proud? When this humbling experience was completed and death itself lay conquered, Christ ascended into heaven. Let us follow him there, for we hear Paul saying: "If you have been raised with Christ, you must lift your thought on high, where Christ now sits at the right hand of God."

Blessed Lawrence cried out:
I worship my God
and serve only him.

So I do not fear your torture.

God is my rock; I take refuge in him.

So I do not fear your torture.

PRAYER

Father,
you called Saint Lawrence to serve you by love
and crowned his life with glorious martyrdom.
Help us to be like him
in loving you and doing your work.

Grant this through our Lord Jesus Christ, your Son,
who lives and reigns with you and the Holy Spirit,
one God, for ever and ever.

Our Father . . .

August 11

CLARE, VIRGIN
Memorial

Saint Clare was born at Assisi in 1193. She followed her fellow
citizen, Saint Francis, in a life of poverty and became mother
and foundress of an order of nuns. She led a life that was
austere, yet rich in works of charity and piety. She died in 1253.

A reading from a letter to Blessed Agnes of Prague by Saint Clare, virgin

He [Christ] is the splendor of eternal glory, "the brightness of eternal light, and the mirror without cloud."

Behold, I say, the birth of this mirror. Behold [Christ's] poverty even as he was laid in the manger and wrapped in swaddling clothes. What wondrous humility, what marvelous poverty! The King of angels, the Lord of heaven and earth resting in a manger! Look more deeply into the mirror and meditate on his humility, or simply on his poverty. Behold the many labors and sufferings he endured to redeem the human race. Then, in the depths of this very mirror, ponder his unspeakable love which caused him to suffer on the wood of the cross and to endure the most shameful kind of death. The mirror himself, from his position on the cross, warned passers-by to weigh carefully this act, as he said: "All of you who pass by this way, behold and see if there is any sorrow like mine." Let us answer his cries and lamentations with one voice and one spirit: "I will be mindful and remember, and my soul will be consumed within me."

RESPONSORY

Though my flesh and my heart may fail,

**God is my strength
and my portion for ever.**

I count all that this world offers as worthless,
that I may gain Christ
and be found in him.

**God is my strength
and my portion for ever.**
Psalm 73:26; Philippians 3:8, 9

God of mercy,
you inspired Saint Clare with the love of poverty.
By the help of her prayers
may we follow Christ in poverty of spirit
and come to the joyful vision of your glory
in the kingdom of heaven.

We ask this through our Lord Jesus Christ, your Son,
who lives and reigns with you and the Holy Spirit,
one God, for ever and ever.

Our Father . . .

August 13

PONTIAN, POPE AND MARTYR, AND HIPPOLYTUS, PRIEST AND MARTYR

Saint Pontian was ordained bishop of Rome in 231. In 235 he was banished to Sardinia by the Emperor Maximinus, along with the priest Hippolytus. There he resigned from his office and later died. His body was buried in the cemetery of Saint Callistus, while the body of Hippolytus was buried in a cemetery along the Via Tiburtina. The Roman Church sanctioned devotion to both martyrs at the beginning of the fourth century.

READING

A reading from a letter by Saint Cyprian, bishop and martyr

With what praises can I extol you, most valiant brothers? What words can I find to proclaim and celebrate your brave hearts and your persevering faith? Examined under the fiercest torture, you held out until your ordeal was consummated in glory. It was not you who yielded to the torments but rather the torments that yielded to you. No respite from pain was allowed by the instruments of your torture, but your very crowning signaled the end of pain. The cruel butchery was permitted to last the longer, not so that it might overthrow the faith that stood so firm, but rather that it might dispatch you men of God, more speedily to the Lord.

The crowd in wonder watched God's heavenly contest, this spiritual battle that was Christ's. They saw his servants standing firm, free in speech, undefiled in heart, endowed with supernatural courage, naked and bereft of the weapons of this world, but as believers equipped with the arms of faith. Tortured men stood there stronger than their torturers; battered and lacerated limbs triumphed over clubs and claws that tore them.

In the psalms, where the Holy Spirit speaks to us and counsels us, it is written: "Precious in the sight of God is the death of his holy ones." Rightly is that death called "precious," for at the price of blood it purchased immortality and won God's crown through the ultimate act of courage.

How blessed is this Church of ours, so honored and illuminated by God and ennobled in these our days by the glorious blood of martyrs! In earlier times it shone white with the good deeds of our brethren, and now it is adorned with the red blood of martyrs. Let each of us, then, strive for the highest degree of glory, whichever be the honor for which he is destined. May all Christians be found worthy of either the pure white crown of a holy life or the royal red crown of martyrdom.

RESPONSORY

We are warriors now, fighting on the battlefield of faith,
and God sees all we do;
the angels watch and so does Christ.

What honor and glory and joy, to do battle
in the presence of God,
and to have Christ approve our victory.

Let us arm ourselves
and prepare ourselves for the ultimate struggle
with blameless hearts, true faith and unyielding courage.

**What honor and glory and joy, to do battle
in the presence of God,
and to have Christ approve our victory.**

PRAYER

Lord,
may the loyal suffering of your saints, Pontian and Hippolytus,
fill us with your love,
and make our hearts steadfast in faith.

Grant this through our Lord Jesus Christ, your Son,
who lives and reigns with you and the Holy Spirit,
one God, for ever and ever.

Our Father . . .

August 15

ASSUMPTION
Solemnity

Today the Church celebrates a great privilege granted to Mary,
Mother of God. Her son, Jesus Christ, conquered sin and death,
and she shares in his victory. The solemnity of Mary's Assumption reminds us that one day we too shall be with the Lord in
heaven, provided we do his will here on earth.

READING

A reading from the apostolic constitution on the Assumption by
Pope Pius XII

In their homilies and sermons on this feast the holy fathers and great doctors spoke of the assumption of the Mother of God as something familiar and accepted by the faithful. They gave it greater clarity in their preaching and used more profound arguments in setting out its nature and meaning. Above all, they brought out more clearly the fact that what is commemorated in this feast is not simply the total absence of corruption from the dead body of the Blessed Virgin Mary but also her triumph over death and her glorification in heaven, after the pattern set by her only Son, Jesus Christ.

Hence, the august Mother of God, mysteriously united from all eternity with Jesus Christ, in one and the same decree of predestination, immaculate in her conception, a virgin inviolate in her divine motherhood, the wholehearted companion of the divine Redeemer who won complete victory over sin and its consequences, gained at last the supreme crown of her privileges—to be preserved from the corruption of the tomb, and, like her Son, when death had been conquered, to be carried up body and soul to the exalted glory of heaven, there to sit in splendor at the right hand of her Son, the immortal King of the ages.

RESPONSORY

This is the glorious day,
on which the Virgin Mother of God was taken up to heaven;
let us sing these words in her praise:

Blessed are you among women,
and blessed is the fruit of your womb.

Happy are you, holy Virgin Mary, and most worthy of all praise, from your womb Christ the Sun of Justice has risen.

Blessed are you among women,
and blessed is the fruit of your womb.

All-powerful and ever-living God,
you raised the sinless Virgin Mary,
mother of your Son,
body and soul to the glory of heaven.
May we see heaven as our final goal
and come to share her glory.

We ask this through our Lord Jesus Christ, your Son,
who lives and reigns with you and the Holy Spirit,
one God, for ever and ever.

Our Father . . .

August 16

STEPHEN OF HUNGARY

Saint Stephen was born at Pannonia around the year 969. After his baptism he was crowned king of Hungary in the year 1000. In his relationship with his subjects he was just, peaceful and pious, exactly observing the laws of the Church and ever seeking the welfare of his people. He founded many dioceses and spent great energy in fostering the work of the Church. He died in 1038.

READING

A reading from advice to his son by Saint Stephen

My beloved son, delight of my heart, hope of your posterity, I pray, I command, that at every time and in everything, strengthened by your devotion to me, you may show favor not only to relations and kin, or to the most eminent, be they leaders or rich men or neighbors or fellow-countrymen, but also to foreigners and to all who come to you. By fulfilling your duty in this way you will reach the highest state of happiness. Be merciful to all who are suffering violence, keeping always in your heart the example of the Lord who said: "I desire mercy and not sacrifice." Be patient with everyone, not only with the powerful, but also with the weak.

Finally be strong lest prosperity lift you up too much or adversity cast you down. Be humble in this life, that God may raise you up in the next. Be truly moderate and do not punish or condemn anyone immoderately. Be gentle so that you may never oppose justice. Be honorable so that you may never voluntarily bring disgrace upon anyone. Be chaste so that you may avoid all the foulness of lust like the pangs of death.

All these virtues I have noted above make up the royal crown, and without them no one is fit to rule here on earth or attain to the heavenly kingdom.

RESPONSORY

Give alms in proportion to your means;

if you have many possessions, give generously; if you have little, give some of what you have.

And when you give, give with a cheerful face; give to the Most High as he has given to you.

If you have many possessions, give generously; if you have little, give some of what you have.
Tobit 4:8-9; Sirach 35:11, 12

PRAYER

Almighty Father,
grant that Saint Stephen of Hungary,
who fostered the growth of your Church on earth,
may continue to be our powerful helper in heaven.

We ask this through our Lord Jesus Christ, your Son,

who lives and reigns with you and the Holy Spirit,
one God, for ever and ever.

Our Father . . .

August 19

JOHN EUDES, PRIEST

Saint John Eudes was born in France in the year 1601. After his
ordination to the priesthood he spent several years in giving
missions. Then he founded congregations dedicated to improv-
ing priestly formation and to encouraging women who were
tempted to live immorally to lead Christian lives. He also fostered great devotion to the hearts of Jesus and Mary. He died in
1680.

READING

A reading from a work on the admirable Heart of Jesus by Saint
John Eudes, priest

I ask you to consider that our Lord Jesus Christ is your true head
and that you are a member of his body. He belongs to you as the
head belongs to the body.

He belongs to you, but more than that, he longs to be in you,
living and ruling in you, as the head lives and rules in the body.
He desires that whatever is in him may live and rule in you: his
breath in your breath, his heart in your heart, all the faculties of
his soul in the faculties of your soul, so that these words may be
fulfilled in you: "Glorify God and bear him in your body, that
the life of Jesus may be made manifest in you."

You must receive life from him and be ruled by him. There will
be no true life for you except in him, for he is the one source of
true life. Apart from him you will find only death and destruc-

tion. Let him be the only source of your movements, of the actions and the strength of your life.

Finally, you are one with Jesus as the body is one with the head. You must, then, have one breath with him, one soul, one life, one will, one mind, one heart. And he must be your breath, heart, love, life, your all. These great gifts in the follower of Christ originate from baptism. They are increased and strengthened through confirmation and by making good use of other graces that are given by God. Through the holy eucharist they are brought to perfection.

RESPONSORY

Christ died and rose to life,
that he might be the Lord of the living and the dead.

Whether we live or die, we belong to the Lord.

None of us lives just for himself,
and none of us dies for himself alone.

Whether we live or die, we belong to the Lord.
Romans 14:9, 8, 7

PRAYER

Father,
you chose the priest John Eudes
to preach the infinite riches of Christ.
By his teaching and example
help us to know you better
and live faithfully in the light of the gospel.

Grant this through our Lord Jesus Christ, your Son,
who lives and reigns with you and the Holy Spirit,
one God, for ever and ever.

Our Father . . .

August 20

BERNARD, ABBOT AND DOCTOR
Memorial

Saint Bernard was born in 1090 near Dijon in France. After a religious upbringing, he joined the Cistercians in 1111 and later was chosen abbot of the monastery of Clairvaux. There he directed his companions in the practice of virtue by his own good example. Because of schisms which had arisen in the Church, he traveled all about Europe restoring peace and unity. He wrote many theological and spiritual works. He died in 1153.

READING

A reading from a sermon by Saint Bernard, abbot

Love is sufficient of itself, it gives pleasure by itself and because of itself. It is its own merit, its own reward. Love looks for no cause outside itself, no effect beyond itself. Its profit lies in its practice. Of all the movements, sensations and feelings of the soul, love is the only one in which the creature can respond to the Creator and make some sort of similar return however unequal though it be. For when God loves, all he desires is to be loved in return. The sole purpose of his love is to be loved, in the knowledge that those who love him are made happy by their love of him.

RESPONSORY

Lord, how great are the hidden treasures of your goodness,
which you have stored up for those who fear you.

They are filled with the bounty of your house;
and you give them to drink from the stream of your delights.
Which you have stored up for those who fear you.
Psalm 31:20; 36:9

222

Heavenly Father,
Saint Bernard was filled with zeal for your house
and was a radiant light in your Church.
By his prayers
may we be filled with this spirit of zeal
and walk always as children of light.

We ask this through our Lord Jesus Christ, your Son,
who lives and reigns with you and the Holy Spirit,
one God, for ever and ever.

Our Father . . .

August 21

PIUS X, POPE

Saint Pius was born in 1835 in a village in the province of
Venice. After he became a priest he performed his duties with
distinction. He became bishop of Mantua and patriarch of Venice, and was elected pope in 1903. He took as the motto of his
reign to "renew all things in Christ." He fulfilled this task in the
spirit of simplicity, poverty and courage, arousing the faithful to
a Christian way of life and waging constant warfare against the
errors of his age. He died August 20, 1914.

READING

A reading from the apostolic constitution of Pope Saint Pius X,
on Sacred Scripture

The collection of psalms found in Scripture, composed as it was
under divine inspiration, has, from the very beginnings of the
Church, shown a wonderful power of fostering devotion among
Christians as they offer "to God a continuous sacrifice of praise,
the harvest of lips blessing his name." Following a custom al-

ready established in the Old Law, the psalms have played a conspicuous part in the sacred liturgy itself, and in the divine office. Augustine expresses this well when he says: "God praised himself so that man might give him fitting praise; because God chose to praise himself man found the way in which to bless God."

The psalms have also a wonderful power to awaken in our hearts the desire for every virtue. Athanasius says: "The psalms seem to me to be like a mirror, in which the person using them can see himself, and the stirrings of his own heart; he can recite them against the background of his own emotions." Augustine says in his Confessions: "How I wept when I heard your hymns and canticles, being deeply moved by the sweet singing of your Church. Those voices flowed into my ears, truth filtered into my heart, and from my heart surged waves of devotion."

Indeed, who could fail to be moved by those many passages in the psalms which set forth so profoundly the infinite majesty of God, his omnipotence, his justice and goodness and clemency, too deep for words, and all the other infinite qualities of his that deserve our praise? Who could fail to be roused to the same emotions by the prayers of thanksgiving to God for blessings received by the petitions, so humble and confident, for blessings still awaited, by the cries of a soul in sorrow for sin committed? Who would not be fired with love as he looks on the likeness of Christ, the redeemer, here so lovingly foretold? His was "the voice" Augustine "heard in every psalm, the voice of praise, of suffering, of joyful expectation, of present distress."

RESPONSORY

God has found us worthy to be ministers of his Gospel, and so when we speak,

we strive to please God and not men.

Our preaching does not spring from error, or impure motives, or a desire to deceive.

We strive to please God and not men.
1 Thessalonians 2:4, 3

PRAYER

Father,
to defend the Catholic faith
and to make all things new in Christ,
you filled Saint Pius Tenth
with heavenly wisdom and apostolic courage.
May his example and teaching
lead us to the reward of eternal life.

Grant this through our Lord Jesus Christ, your Son,
who lives and reigns with you and the Holy Spirit,
one God, for ever and ever.

Our Father . . .

August 22

QUEENSHIP OF MARY
Memorial

Jesus Christ, now in glory with the Father and the Holy Spirit in heaven, is that Lord "whose kingdom will have no end." The Church sees this heavenly king as one who so loves and honors his mother Mary, that he has exalted her to be Queen of heaven and earth.

READING

A reading from a homily by Saint Amadeus, bishop

Because of the honor due her Son, it was indeed fitting for the Virgin Mother to have first ruled upon earth and then be raised up to heaven in glory. It was fitting that her fame be spread in

225

this world below, so that she might enter the heights of heaven in overwhelming blessedness. Just as she was borne from virtue to virtue by the Spirit of the Lord, she was transported from earthly renown to heavenly brightness.

The virgin John, rejoicing that the Virgin Mother was entrusted to him at the cross, cared for her with the other apostles here below. The angels rejoiced to see their queen; the apostles rejoiced to see their lady, and both obeyed her with loving devotion.

Able to preserve both flesh and spirit from death she bestowed health-giving salve on bodies and souls. Has anyone ever come away from her troubled or saddened or ignorant of the heavenly mysteries? Who has not returned to everyday life gladdened and joyful because his request had been granted by the Mother of God?

RESPONSORY

A great sign appeared in the heavens:
a woman clothed with the sun,
with the moon under her feet,
and upon her head a crown of twelve stars.

The queen, clothed in cloth of gold, stood on your right hand.
And upon her head a crown of twelve stars.

PRAYER

Father,
you have given us the mother of your Son
to be our queen and mother.
With the support of her prayers
may we come to share the glory of your children
in the kingdom of heaven.

We ask this through our Lord Jesus Christ, your Son,
who lives and reigns with you and the Holy Spirit,
one God, for ever and ever.

Our Father . . .

August 23

ROSE OF LIMA, VIRGIN

Saint Rose was born in Lima, Peru in 1586. She led a virtuous
life at home and, after receiving the habit of the Third Order of
Saint Dominic, she made great progress in a life of penance,
meditation and prayer. She died August 24, 1617.

READING

A reading from the writings of Saint Rose of Lima, virgin

Our Lord and Savior lifted up his voice and said with incomparable majesty: "Let all men know that grace comes after tribulation. Let them know that without the burden of afflictions it is
impossible to reach the height of grace. Let them know that the
gifts of grace increase as the struggles increase. Let men take
care not to stray and be deceived. This is the only true stairway
to paradise, and without the cross they can find no road to climb
to heaven."

When I heard these words, a strong force came upon me and
seemed to place me in the middle of a street, so that I might say
in a loud voice to people of every age, sex and status: "Hear, O
people; hear, O nations. I am warning you about the commandment of Christ by using words that came from his own
lips: We cannot obtain grace unless we suffer afflictions. We
must heap trouble upon trouble to attain a deep participation
in the divine nature, the glory of the sons of God and perfect
happiness of soul."

"If only mortals would learn how great it is to possess divine grace, how beautiful, how noble, how precious. How many riches it hides within itself, how many joys and delights! No one would complain about his cross or about troubles that may happen to him, if he would come to know the scales on which they are weighed when they are distributed to men."

To shame the wise, God chose what the world considers foolish.
God chose those who were nothing at all
to humble those who were everything

so that no one might boast in his presence.

Though the Lord is exalted,
he cares for the lowly,
but the proud he looks down on from afar.

So that no one might boast in his presence.
1 Corinthians 1:28-29; Psalm 138:6

God our Father,
for love of you
Saint Rose gave up everything
to devote herself to a life of penance.
By the help of her prayers
may we imitate her selfless way of life on earth
and enjoy the fullness of your blessings in heaven.

Grant this through our Lord Jesus Christ, your Son,
who lives and reigns with you and the Holy Spirit,
one God, for ever and ever.

Our Father . . .

August 24

BARTHOLOMEW, APOSTLE
Feast

Saint Bartholomew was born at Cana. He was brought to Jesus by the apostle Philip. After the ascension of the Lord, he is said to have preached the Gospel in India where he was rewarded with the crown of martyrdom.

READING

A reading from a homily on the first letter to the Corinthians by Saint John Chrysostom, bishop

It was clear through unlearned men that the cross was persuasive, in fact, it persuaded the whole world.

Paul had this in mind when he said: "The weakness of God is stronger than men." That the preaching of these men was indeed divine is brought home to us in the same way. For how otherwise could twelve uneducated men, who lived on lakes and rivers and wastelands, get the idea for such an immense enterprise? How could men who perhaps had never been in a city or a public square think of setting out to do battle with the whole world? That they were fearful, timid men, the evangelist makes clear; he did not reject the fact or try to hide their weaknesses. Indeed he turned these into a proof of the truth. What did he say of them? That when Christ was arrested, the others fled, despite all the miracles they had seen, while he who was leader of the others denied him!

How then account for the fact that these men, who in Christ's lifetime did not stand up to the attacks by the Jews, set forth to do battle with the whole world once Christ was dead—if, as you claim, Christ did not rise and speak to them and rouse their courage? It is evident, then, that if they had not seen him risen and had proof of his power, they would not have risked so much.

We preach Christ crucified,
a stumbling block to Jews
and an absurdity to Gentiles,
but to those who have heard his call,

Christ is the power of God and the wisdom of God.

We are afflicted in every way possible,
but in all these trials the victory is ours,
because of Christ who loves us.

Christ is the power of God and the wisdom of God.
1 Corinthians 1:23–24; 2 Corinthians 4:8; Romans 8:37

PRAYER

Lord,
sustain within us the faith
which made Saint Bartholomew ever loyal to Christ.
Let your Church be the sign of salvation
for all the nations of the world.

We ask this through our Lord Jesus Christ, your Son,
who lives and reigns with you and the Holy Spirit,
one God, for ever and ever.

Our Father . . .

August 25

LOUIS

Saint Louis was born in 1214 and became king of France when
he was only twenty-two years old. He married and became the
father of eleven children who received from him careful instruction for a Christian life. He spent much of his time in penance
and prayer and in care for the poor. While ruling his kingdom he
had regard not only for peace among peoples and for the tem-

poral good of his subjects, but also for their spiritual welfare. He went on one of the Crusades to recover the tomb of Christ and died near Carthage in 1270.

A reading from a spiritual testament to his son by Saint Louis

My dearest son, my first instruction is that you should love the Lord your God with all your heart and all your strength. Without this there is no salvation. Keep yourself, my son, from everything that you know displeases God, that is to say, from every mortal sin. You should permit yourself to be tormented by every kind of martyrdom before you would allow yourself to commit a mortal sin.

If the Lord has permitted you to have some trial, bear it willingly and with gratitude, considering that it has happened for your good and that perhaps you well deserved it. If the Lord bestows upon you any kind of prosperity, thank him humbly and see that you become no worse for it, either through vain pride or anything else, because you ought not to oppose God or offend him in the matter of his gifts.

Be kindhearted to the poor, the unfortunate and the afflicted. Give them as much help and consolation as you can. Thank God for all the benefits he has bestowed upon you, that you may be worthy to receive greater. Always side with the poor rather than with the rich, until you are certain of the truth.

Be devout and obedient to our mother the Church of Rome and the Supreme Pontiff as your spiritual father.

In conclusion, dearest son, I give you every blessing that a loving father can give a son. May the three Persons of the Holy Trinity and all the saints protect you from every evil. And may the Lord give you the grace to do his will so that he may be served and honored through you, that in the next life we may together come to see him, love him and praise him unceasingly. Amen.

He did what was pleasing in the sight of the Lord;
among all kings none could compare with him.

He was loyal to the Lord and never turned away from him.

The Lord was with him,
because he kept his commandments.

He was loyal to the Lord and never turned away from him.
2 Kings 18:3, 5, 6, 7

PRAYER

Father,
you raised Saint Louis
from the cares of earthly rule
to the glory of your heavenly kingdom.
By the help of his prayers
may we come to your eternal kingdom
by our work here on earth.

Grant this through our Lord Jesus Christ, your Son,
who lives and reigns with you and the Holy Spirit,
one God, for ever and ever.

Our Father . . .

On the same day, August 25

JOSEPH CALASANZ, PRIEST

Saint Joseph Calasanz was born in Spain in 1557. Well educated,
he became a priest and exercised his ministry in his homeland.
Later he dedicated himself to the education of poor boys at
Rome and founded a society pledged to that work. He endured
many trials, especially the slanders of those who were jealous of
his success. He died at Rome in 1648.

A reading from the writings of Saint Joseph Calasanz, priest

Everyone knows the great merit and dignity attached to that holy ministry in which young boys, especially the poor, receive instruction for the purpose of attaining eternal life. This ministry is directed to the well-being of body and soul; at the same time that it shapes behavior it also fosters devotion and Christian doctrine.

Moreover the strongest support is provided not only to protect the young from evil, but also to rouse them and attract them more easily and gently to the performance of good works. Like the twigs of plants the young are easily influenced, as long as someone works to change their souls. But if they are allowed to grow hard, we know well that the possiblity of one day bending them diminishes a great deal and is sometimes utterly lost.

All who undertake to teach must be endowed with deep love, the greatest patience, and, most of all, profound humility. They must perform their work with earnest zeal. Then, through their humble prayers, the Lord will find them worthy to become fellow workers with him in the cause of truth. He will console them in the fulfillment of this most noble duty, and, finally, will enrich them with the gift of heaven.

As Scripture says: "Those who instruct many in justice will shine as stars for all eternity." They will attain this more easily if they make a covenant of perpetual obedience and strive to cling to Christ and please him alone, because, in his words: "What you did to one of the least of my brethren, you did to me."

RESPONSORY

I have longed to give you the Gospel,
and more than that, to give you my very life;

you have become very dear to me.

My little children, I am like a mother giving birth to you,
until Christ is formed in you.

You have become very dear to me.
1 Thessalonians 2:8; Galatians 4:19

PRAYER

Lord,
you blessed Saint Joseph Calasanz
with such charity and patience
that he dedicated himself
to the formation of Christian youth.
As we honor this teacher of wisdom
may we follow his example in working for truth.

We ask this through our Lord Jesus Christ, your Son,
who lives and reigns with you and the Holy Spirit,
one God, for ever and ever.

Our Father . . .

August 27

MONICA
Memorial

Saint Monica was born of a Christian family at Tagaste in Africa
in 331. While still a young maiden she was married to Patricius.
They had children, among whom was Augustine. She poured
forth many tears and prayers to God for his conversion. A
model of a virtuous mother, she nourished the faith by her
prayers and witnessed to it by her deeds. She died at Ostia in
387.

READING

A reading from the Confessions of Saint Augustine, bishop

The day was now approaching when my mother Monica would depart from this life; you knew that day, Lord, though we did not. She and I happened to be standing by ourselves at a window that overlooked the garden in the courtyard of the house. At the time we were in Ostia on the Tiber. And so the two of us, all alone, were enjoying a very pleasant conversation, "forgetting the past and pushing on to what is ahead." We were asking one another in the presence of the Truth—for you are the Truth—what it would be like to share the eternal life enjoyed by the saints, which "eye has not seen, nor ear heard, which has not even entered into the heart of man." We desired with all our hearts to drink from the streams of your heavenly fountain, the fountain of life.

That was the substance of our talk, though not the exact words. But you know, O Lord, that in the course of our conversation that day, the world and its pleasures lost all their attraction for us. My mother said: "Son, as far as I am concerned, nothing in this life now gives me any pleasure. I do not know why I am still here, since I have no further hopes in this world. I did have one reason for wanting to live a little longer: to see you become a Catholic Christian before I died. God has lavished his gifts on me in that respect, for I know that you have even renounced earthly happiness to be his servant. So what am I doing here?"

I do not really remember how I answered her. Shortly, within five days or thereabouts, she fell sick with a fever. Then one day during the course of her illness she became unconscious and for a while she was unaware of her surroundings. My brother and I rushed to her side but she regained consciousness quickly. She looked at us as we stood there and asked in a puzzled voice: "Where was I?"

We were overwhelmed with grief, but she held her gaze steadily upon us and spoke further: "Here you shall bury your mother." I remained silent as I held back my tears. However, my brother haltingly expressed his hope that she might not die in a strange country but in her own land, since her end would be happier there. When she heard this, her face was filled with anxiety, and she reproached him with a glance because he had entertained

235

such earthly thoughts. Then she looked at me and spoke: "Look what he is saying." Thereupon she said to both of us: "Bury my body wherever you will; let not care of it cause you any concern. One thing only I ask you, that you remember me at the altar of the Lord wherever you may be." Once our mother had expressed this desire as best she could, she fell silent as the pain of her illness increased.

RESPONSORY

The time is growing short,
so we must rejoice as though we were not rejoicing;
we must work in the world yet without becoming immersed in
    it,
for the world as we know it is passing away.

We have not adopted the spirit of the world.
For the world as we know it is passing away.
1 Corinthians 7:29, 30, 31; 2:12

PRAYER

God of mercy,
comfort of those in sorrow,
the tears of Saint Monica moved you
to convert her son Saint Augustine to the faith of Christ.
By their prayers, help us to turn from our sins
and to find your loving forgiveness.

Grant this through our Lord Jesus Christ, your Son,
who lives and reigns with you and the Holy Spirit,
one God, for ever and ever.

Our Father . . .

August 28

AUGUSTINE, BISHOP AND DOCTOR
Memorial

Saint Augustine was born at Tagaste in Africa in 354. He was unsettled and restlessly searched for the truth until he was converted to the Faith at Milan and baptized by Ambrose. Returning to his homeland, he embraced an ascetic life and subsequently was elected bishop of Hippo. For thirty-four years he guided his flock, instructing it with sermons and many writings. He fought bravely against the errors of his time and explained the Faith carefully and clearly through his writings. He died in 430.

READING

A reading from the Confessions of Saint Augustine, bishop

O eternal truth, true love and beloved eternity. You are my God. To you do I sigh day and night. When I first came to know you, you drew me to yourself so that I might see that there were things for me to see, but that I myself was not yet ready to see them. Meanwhile you overcame the weakness of my vision, sending forth most strongly the beams of your light, and I trembled at once with love and dread.

I sought a way to gain the strength which I needed to enjoy you. But I did not find it until I embraced "the mediator between God and men, the man Christ Jesus, who is above all, God blessed for ever." He was calling me and saying: "I am the way of truth, I am the life."

Late have I loved you, O Beauty ever ancient, ever new, late have I loved you! You were within me, but I was outside, and it was there that I searched for you. In my unloveliness I plunged into the lovely things which you created. You were with me, but I was not with you. Created things kept me from you; yet if they had not been in you they would not have been at all. You called, you shouted, and you broke through my deafness. You flashed,

you shone, and you dispelled my blindness. You breathed your
fragrance on me; I drew in breath and now I pant for you. I have
tasted you, now I hunger and thirst for more. You touched me,
and I burned for your peace.

RESPONSORY

O Truth, you are the light of my heart.
Let your light speak to me, not my own darkness.
I went astray, but I remembered you

and now I return longing and thirsting for your fountain.

I myself cannot give life.
Of myself I have lived wrongly;
in you I have found life again.

And now I return longing and thirsting for your fountain.

PRAYER

Lord,
renew in your Church
the spirit you gave Saint Augustine.
Filled with this spirit,
may we thirst for you alone as the fountain of wisdom
and seek you as the source of eternal love.

We ask this through our Lord Jesus Christ, your Son,
who lives and reigns with you and the Holy Spirit,
one God, for ever and ever.

Our Father . . .

August 29

BEHEADING OF JOHN THE BAPTIST, MARTYR
Memorial

John the Baptist, the herald of Jesus Christ, was condemned to prison and beheaded by the cruel King Herod, who had been censured by John for the many crimes this wicked ruler had committed.

READING

A reading from a homily by Saint Bede the Venerable, priest

There is no doubt that blessed John suffered imprisonment and chains as a witness to our Redeemer, whose forerunner he was, and gave his life for him. His persecutor had demanded not that he should deny Christ, but only that he should keep silent about the truth. Nevertheless, he died for Christ. Does Christ not say: "I am the truth"? Therefore, because John shed his blood for the truth, he surely died for Christ.

Through his birth, preaching and baptizing, he bore witness to the coming birth, preaching and baptism of Christ, and by his own suffering he showed that Christ also would suffer.

Such was the quality and strength of the man who accepted the end of this present life by shedding his blood after the long imprisonment. He preached the freedom of heavenly peace, yet was thrown into irons by ungodly men. He was locked away in the darkness of prison, though he came bearing witness to the Light of life and deserved to be called a bright and shining lamp by that Light itself, which is Christ.

To endure temporal agonies for the sake of the truth was not a heavy burden for such men as John; rather it was easily borne and even desirable, for he knew eternal joy would be his reward.

Since death was ever near at hand, such men considered it a blessing to embrace it and thus gain the reward of eternal life by acknowledging Christ's name. Hence the apostle Paul rightly says: "You have been granted the privilege not only to believe in Christ but also to suffer for his sake." He tells us why it is Christ's gift that his chosen ones should suffer for him: "The sufferings of this present time are not worthy to be compared with the glory that is to be revealed in us."

RESPONSORY

Herod sent out a band of men to arrest John
and had him chained and imprisoned

on account of his brother Philip's wife, Herodias, whom he had married.

He sent an executioner who beheaded John in prison.

On account of his brother Philip's wife, Herodias, whom he had married.
Mark 6:17, 27

PRAYER

God our Father,
you called John the Baptist
to be the herald of your Son's birth and death.
As he gave his life in witness to truth and justice,
so may we strive to profess our faith in your gospel.

Grant this through our Lord Jesus Christ, your Son,
who lives and reigns with you and the Holy Spirit,
one God, for ever and ever.

Our Father . . .

September 3

GREGORY THE GREAT, POPE AND DOCTOR
Memorial

Saint Gregory was born at Rome around the year 540. He rose through various public offices. He gave them up to enter the monastic life and, once ordained deacon, he discharged the duties of papal representative at Constantinople. On September 3, 590 he was elevated to the Chair of Saint Peter and he proved to be a true shepherd by carrying out his office, helping the poor, spreading and strengthening the faith. He wrote extensively on moral and theological subjects. He died on March 12, 604.

READING

A reading from a sermon by Saint Fulgentius, bishop

The Lord, in his desire to explain the special function of those servants whom he placed over his people, said: "Who do you think is the faithful and wise steward whom his master has set over his household to give them their portion of food at the proper time? That servant is blessed if he is found doing this when his master comes."

And who is the master? None other than Christ, who said to his disciples: "You call me teacher and master, and you are right, for so I am." And who is the master's household? Surely, it is the Church which the Lord redeemed from the power of the adversary, and which he purchased for himself, thereby becoming its master. This household is the holy Catholic Church which is so fruitfully extended far and wide over the world, rejoicing that it has been redeemed by the precious blood of the Lord. Furthermore, he is the Good Shepherd who has laid down his life for his sheep; the Good Shepherd's flock is this household of the Redeemer.

But who is the steward who must be both faithful and wise? The apostle Paul tells us when he says of himself and his companions: "This is how one should regard us, as servants of Christ and stewards of the mysteries of God. Moreover, it is required of stewards that they be found faithful."

But this does not mean that the apostles alone have been appointed our stewards, nor that any of us may give up our duty of spiritual combat, and, as lazy servants, sleep our time away, and be neither faithful nor wise. For the blessed Apostle tell us that the popes and bishops too are stewards. "A bishop," he says, "must be blameless because he is God's steward."

Bishops, then, are the servants of the householder, the stewards of the Master, and have received the portion of food to dispense to you. If we should wonder what that portion of food is, the blessed apostle Paul tells us when he says: "To each according to the measure of faith which God has assigned to him." Hence what Christ calls the portion of food, Paul calls the measure of faith. And we [bishops] give you this portion of food in the Lord's name as often as we teach you in accordance with the rule of the true faith. In turn, you daily receive the portion of food at the hands of the Lord's stewards when you hear the word of truth from the servants of God.

RESPONSORY

He drew his moral and mystical teaching from the source of holy
    Scripture;
through him the life-giving streams of the gospel flowed out to
    all nations.

Though he is dead he still speaks to us today.

As a soaring eagle sees all on earth below,
so he cares for both the great and small with his all-embracing
    charity.

Though he is dead he still speaks to us today.

Father,
you guide your people with kindness
and govern us with love.
By the prayers of Saint Gregory
give the spirit of wisdom
to those you have called to lead your Church.
May the growth of your people in holiness
be the eternal joy of our shepherds.

We ask this through our Lord Jesus Christ, your Son,
who lives and reigns with you and the Holy Spirit,
one God, for ever and ever.

Our Father . . .

September 8

BIRTH OF MARY
Feast

Mary is honored by the Church because of the part she played in the incarnation of her Son. Since the Holy Spirit prepared her to become God's Mother, all the feasts dedicated to her are closely tied in with the mysteries of Christ's life. And so today we honor Jesus, the God-Man, by celebrating the birth of his Mother.

READING

A reading from a discourse by Saint Andrew of Crete, bishop

The radiant and manifest coming of God to men most certainly needed a joyful prelude to introduce the great gift of salvation to us. The present festival, the birth of the Mother of God, is the prelude while the final act is the foreordained union of the Word with flesh. Today the Virgin is born, tended and formed, and prepared for her role as Mother of God, who is the universal King of the ages.

Justly then do we celebrate this mystery since it signifies for us a double grace. We are led toward the truth, and we are led away from our condition of slavery to the letter of the law. How can this be? Darkness yields before the coming of light, and grace exchanges legalism for freedom.

Therefore, let all creation sing and dance and unite to make worthy contribution to the celebration of this day. Let there be one common festival for saints in heaven and men on earth. Let everything, mundane things and those above, join in festive celebration. Today this created world is raised to the dignity of a holy place for him who made all things. The creature is newly prepared to be a divine dwelling place for the Creator.

RESPONSORY

Today let us celebrate with devotion the birth of Mary, the
    ever-virgin Mother of God,

whose splendid life has illumined the Church.

With heart and mind let us sing praise and glory to Christ on this holy feastday of the glorious Virgin Mother of God.
Whose splendid life has illumined the Church.

PRAYER

Father of mercy,
give your people help and strength from heaven.
The birth of the Virgin Mary's Son
was the dawn of our salvation.
May this celebration of her birthday
bring us closer to lasting peace.

Grant this through our Lord Jesus Christ, your Son,
who lives and reigns with you and the Holy Spirit,
one God, for ever and ever.

Our Father . . .

September 9

PETER CLAVER, PRIEST
Memorial

Saint Peter Claver was born in Spain in the year 1580; from 1596 he studied arts and letters at the University of Barcelona. In 1602 he entered the Society of Jesus. With the help especially of Saint Alphonsus Rodriguez, porter of the Jesuit College of Majorca, Peter heard and followed the call to the missions. In 1616 he was ordained to the priesthood in the mission of Colombia. There, until his death, he carried on an apostolate among the black slaves, vowing to be "the slave of the blacks for ever." His strength exhausted, he died at Cartagena, Colombia, on September 8, 1654. He was canonized by Leo XIII in 1888. In 1896 the same Pontiff declared him the special heavenly patron of all missions to the black peoples.

READING

A reading from a letter by Saint Peter Claver, priest

Yesterday, May 30, 1627, on the feast of the Most Holy Trinity, numerous blacks, brought from the rivers of Africa, disembarked from a large ship. Carrying two baskets of oranges, lemons, sweet biscuits, and I know not what else, we hurried toward them. We had to force our way through the crowd until we reached the sick. Large numbers of the sick were lying on the wet ground or rather in puddles of mud. To prevent excessive dampness, someone had thought of building up a mound with a mixture of tiles and broken pieces of bricks. This, then, was their couch, a very uncomfortable one not only for that reason, but especially because they were naked, without any clothing to protect them.

We laid aside our cloaks, therefore, and brought from a warehouse whatever was handy to build a platform. In that way we covered a space to which we at last transferred the sick, by forcing a passage through bands of slaves. Then we divided the sick into two groups: one group my companion approached

245

with an interpreter, while I addressed the other group. There were two blacks, nearer death than life, already cold, whose pulse could scarcely be detected. With the help of a tile we pulled some live coals together and placed them in the middle near the dying men. Into this fire we tossed aromatics. Then, using our own cloaks, for they had nothing of the sort, and to ask the owners for others would have been a waste of words, we provided for them a smoke treatment, by which they seemed to recover their warmth and the breath of life. The joy in their eyes as they looked at us was something to see.

This was how we spoke to them, not with words but with our hands and our actions. And in fact, convinced as they were that they had been brought here to be eaten, any other language would have proved utterly useless. Then we sat, or rather knelt, beside them and bathed their faces and bodies with wine. We made every effort to encourage them with friendly gestures and displayed in their presence the emotions which somehow naturally tend to hearten the sick.

After this we began an elementary instruction about baptism, that is, the wonderful effects of the sacrament on body and soul. When by their answers to our questions they showed they had sufficiently understood this, we went on to a more extensive instruction, namely, about the one God, who rewards and punishes each one according to his merit, and the rest. Finally, when they appeared sufficiently prepared, we told them the mysteries of the Trinity, the Incarnation and the Passion. Showing them Christ fastened to the cross, as he is depicted on the baptismal font on which streams of blood flow down from his wounds, we led them in reciting an act of contrition in their own language.

RESPONSORY

I was hungry and you gave me food;
I was thirsty and you gave me drink;
I was homeless and you took me in.

246

Now I tell you this:
When you did these things for the most neglected of my
    brothers,
you did them for me.

This is what I command:
Love one another as I have loved you.

Now I tell you this:
When you did these things for the most neglected of my
    brothers,
you did them for me.
Matthew 25:35, 40

PRAYER

God of mercy and love,
you offer all peoples
the dignity of sharing in your life.
By the example and prayers of Saint Peter Claver,
strengthen us to overcome all racial hatreds
and to love each other as brothers and sisters.

We ask this through our Lord Jesus Christ, your Son,
who lives and reigns with you and the Holy Spirit,
one God, for ever and ever.

Our Father . . .

September 13

JOHN CHRYSOSTOM, BISHOP AND DOCTOR
Memorial

Saint John Chrysostom was born at Antioch about the year 349.
After an extensive education he was ordained a priest and distinguished himself by his preaching which achieved great
spiritual results among his hearers. He was elected bishop of
Constantinople in 397 and proved himself a capable pastor,
committed to reforming the envy of his enemies. After he had

completed his difficult labors, he died at Comana in Pontus on September 14, 407. His preaching and writing explained Catholic doctrine and presented the ideal Christian life. For this reason he is called Chrysostom, or Golden Mouth.

A reading from a homily by Saint John Chrysostom, bishop

The waters have risen and severe storms are upon us, but we do not fear drowning, for we stand firmly upon a rock. Let the sea rage, it cannot break the rock. Let the waves rise, they cannot sink the boat of Jesus. What are we to fear? Death? "Life to me means Christ, and death is gain." Exile? "The earth and its fullness belong to the Lord." The confiscation of our goods? "We brought nothing into this world, and we shall surely take nothing from it." I have only contempt for the world's threats, I find its blessings laughable. I have no fear of poverty, no desire for wealth. I am not afraid of death nor do I long to live, except for your good.

Do you not hear the Lord saying: "Where two or three are gathered in my name, there am I in their midst"? Will he be absent, then, when so many people united in love are gathered together? Let the world be in upheaval. I hold to his promise and read his message; that is my protecting wall and garrison. What message? "Know that I am with you always, until the end of the world!"

Where I am, there you are too, and where you are, I am. For we are a single body, and the body cannot be separated from the head nor the head from the body. Distance separates us, but love unites us, and death itself cannot divide us. For though my body die, my soul will live and be mindful of my people.

You are my light, sweeter to me than the visible light. The sun's light is useful in my earthly life, but your love is fashioning a crown for me in the life to come.

Because I preach the Gospel, I suffer hardships
even to the point of being thrown into chains like a criminal,
but the word of God is not chained.

I endure all of this for the sake of the chosen.

The Lord is my light and my salvation;
whom should I fear?

I endure all of this for the sake of the chosen.
2 *Timothy 2:9-10; Psalm 27:1*

PRAYER

Father,
the strength of all who trust in you,
you made John Chrysostom
renowned for his eloquence
and heroic in his sufferings.
May we learn from his teaching
and gain courage from his patient endurance.

We ask this through our Lord Jesus Christ, your Son,
who lives and reigns with you and the Holy Spirit,
one God, for ever and ever.

Our Father . . .

September 14

TRIUMPH OF THE CROSS
Feast

Today's feast traces its orgin to the dedication, in 335, of the
church erected by the emperor Constantine on the site of Mount
Calvary. The basilica was said to contain relics of the true cross.

A reading from a discourse by Saint Andrew of Crete, bishop

We are celebrating the feast of the cross which drove away darkness and brought in the light. As we keep this feast, we are lifted up with the crucified Christ, leaving behind us earth and sin so that we may gain the things above. So great and outstanding a possession is the cross that he who wins it has won a treasure. Rightly could I call this treasure the fairest of all fair things and the costliest, in fact as well as in name, for on it and through it and for its sake the riches of salvation that had been lost were restored to us.

Therefore, the cross is something wonderfully great and honorable. It is great because through the cross the many noble acts of Chirst found their consummation—very many indeed, for both his miracles and his sufferings were fully rewarded with victory. The cross is honorable because it is both the sign of God's suffering and the trophy of his victory. It stands for his suffering because on it he freely suffered unto death. But it is also his trophy because it was the means by which the devil was wounded and death conquered; the barred gates of hell were smashed, and the cross became the one common salvation of the whole world. And if you would understand that the cross is Christ's triumph, hear what he himself also said: "When I am lifted up, then I will draw all men to myself." Now you can see that the cross is Christ's glory and triumph.

RESPONSORY

We must glory in the cross of our Lord Jesus Christ;
in him is our salvation, life and resurrection.
Through him we are saved and set free.

Because he suffered death,
he is crowned with glory and honor.
Through him we are saved and set free.
See Galatians 6:14; Hebrews 2:9

God our Father,
in obedience to you
your only Son accepted death on the cross
for the salvation of mankind.
We acknowledge the mystery of the cross on earth.
May we receive the gift of redemption in heaven.

We ask this through our Lord Jesus Christ, your Son,
who lives and reigns with you and the Holy Spirit,
one God, for ever and ever.

Our Father . . .

September 15

OUR LADY OF SORROWS
Memorial

This celebration reminds us that just as Mary suffered along with her Son, so Christ's Church suffers with Christ her Lord through the persecutions and trials that her members must undergo on earth. Through our individual sufferings and trials we can unite ourselves with Mary and her Son.

READING

A reading from a sermon by Saint Bernard, abbot

The martyrdom of the Virgin is set forth both in the prophecy of Simeon and in the actual story of our Lord's passion. The holy old man said of the infant Jesus: "He has been established as a sign which will be contradicted." He went on to say to Mary: "And your own heart will be pierced by a sword."

Truly, O blessed Mother, a sword has pierced your heart. For only by passing through your heart could the sword enter the

251

flesh of your Son. Indeed, after your Jesus—who belongs to everyone, but is especially yours—gave up his life, the cruel spear, which was not withheld from his lifeless body, tore open his side. Clearly it did not touch his soul and could not harm him, but it did pierce your heart. Thus the violence of sorrow has cut through your heart, and we rightly call you more than martyr, since the effect of compassion in you has gone beyond the endurance of physical suffering.

Do not be surprised, brothers, that Mary is said to be a martyr in spirit. Let him be surprised who does not remember the words of Paul, that one of the greatest crimes of the Gentiles was that they were without love. That was far from the heart of Mary; let it be far from her servants.

Perhaps someone will say: "Had she not known before that he would die?" Undoubtedly. "Did she not expect him to rise again at once?" Surely. "And still she grieved over her crucified Son?" Intensely. Who are you and what is the source of your wisdom that you are more surprised at the compassion of Mary than at the passion of Mary's Son? For if he could die in body, could she not die with him in spirit? He died in body through a love greater than anyone had known. She died in spirit through a love unlike any other since his.

RESPONSORY

When they came to the place called Calvary,
they crucified Jesus there.

His mother stood beside the cross.

A sword of sorrow pierced her blameless heart.

His mother stood beside the cross.
Luke 23:33; John 19:25; see Luke 2:35

Father,
as your Son was raised on the cross,
his mother Mary stood by him, sharing his sufferings.
May your Church be united with Christ
in his suffering and death
and so come to share in his rising to new life,
where he lives and reigns with you and the Holy Spirit,
one God, for ever and ever.

Our Father . . .

September 16

CORNELIUS, POPE AND MARTYR, AND CYPRIAN, BISHOP AND MARTYR
Memorial

Saint Cornelius was ordained bishop of the Church of Rome in 251. He fought against the Church's enemies and was driven into exile by the Emperor Gallus. He died in 253 and was buried in the cemetery of Saint Callistus at Rome.

Saint Cyprian was born of pagan parents in Carthage around the year 210. He was converted, ordained, and subsequently made bishop of that city in the year 249. By his writings and his actions Cyprian guided the Church through difficult times. In the persecution of Valerian he was exiled, then martyred on the fourteenth of September, 258.

READING

A reading from the Acts of the martyrdom of Saint Cyprian, bishop

On the morning of the fourteenth of September a great crowd gathered at the Villa Sexti, in accordance with the order of the governor Galerius Maximus. That same day the governor com-

253

manded Bishop Cyprian to be brought before him for trial. After Cyprian was brought in, the governor asked him: "Are you Thascius Cyprian?" and the bishop replied: "Yes, I am." The governor Galerius Maximus said: "You have set yourself up as an enemy of the gods of Rome and our religious practices. You have been discovered as the author and leader of these heinous crimes, and will consequently be held forth as an example for all those who have followed you in your crime. By your blood the law shall be confirmed." Next he read the sentence from a tablet: "It is decided that Cyprian should die by the sword." Cyprian responded: "Thanks be to God!"

After the sentence was passed, a crowd of his fellow Christians said: "We should also be killed with him!" There arose an uproar among the Christians, and a great mob followed after him. Cyprian was then brought out to the grounds of the Villa Sexti, where, taking off his outer cloak and kneeling on the ground, he fell before the Lord in prayer. He removed his dalmatic and gave it to the deacons, and then stood erect while waiting for the executioner. When the executioner arrived Cyprian told his friends to give the man twenty-five gold pieces.

The most blessed martyr Cyprian suffered on the fourteenth of September under the emperors Valerian and Gallienus, in the reign of our true Lord Jesus Christ, to whom belong honor and glory for ever. Amen.

RESPONSORY

We are warriors now, fighting on the battlefield of faith,
and God sees all we do;
the angels watch and so does Christ.

What honor and glory and joy, to have Christ approve our victory.

Let us arm ourselves in full strength
and prepare ourselves for the ultimate struggle
with blameless hearts, true faith and unyielding courage.

**What honor and glory and joy, to have Christ approve our
victory.**

PRAYER

God our Father,
in Saints Cornelius and Cyprian
you have given people an inspiring example
of dedication to the pastoral ministry
and constant witness to Christ in their suffering.
May their prayers and faith give us courage
to work for the unity of your Church.

Grant this through our Lord Jesus Christ, your Son,
who lives and reigns with you and the Holy Spirit,
one God, for ever and ever.

Our Father . . .

September 17

ROBERT BELLARMINE, BISHOP AND DOCTOR

Saint Robert Bellarmine was born in 1542 in the town of Monte
Pulciano in Italy. He entered the Society of Jesus and after ordination to the priesthood distinguished himself brilliantly defending the Catholic faith. He also taught theology in the Roman
College. He became a cardinal and died in Rome in 1621.

READING

A reading from an essay On the Ascent of the Mind to God by
Saint Robert Bellarmine

"Sweet Lord, you are meek and merciful." Who would not give
himself wholeheartedly to your service, if he began to taste even
a little of your fatherly rule? What command, Lord, do you give
your servants? "Take my yoke upon you," you say. And what is

255

this yoke of yours like? "My yoke," you say, "is easy and my burden light." Who would not be glad to bear a yoke that does not press hard but caresses? Who would not be glad for a burden that does not weigh heavy but refreshes? And so you were right to add: "And you will find rest for your souls." And what is this yoke of yours that does not weary, but gives rest? It is, of course, that first and greatest commandment: "You shall love the Lord your God with all your heart." What is easier, sweeter, more pleasant, than to love goodness, beauty and love, the fullness of which you are, O Lord, my God?

Is it not true that you promise those who keep your commandments a reward more desirable than great wealth and sweeter than honey? You promise a most abundant reward, for as your apostle James says: "The Lord has prepared a crown of life for those who love him." What is this crown of life? It is surely a greater good than we can conceive of or desire, as Saint Paul says, quoting Isaiah: "Eye has not seen, ear has not heard, nor has it so much as dawned on man what God has prepared for those who love him."

RESPONSORY

In the midst of the Church he spoke with eloquence;

the Lord filled him with the spirit of wisdom and understanding.

The Lord has rewarded him with joy and gladness.

The Lord filled him with the spirit of wisdom and understanding.

PRAYER

God our Father,
you gave Robert Bellarmine wisdom and goodness
to defend the faith of your Church.
By his prayers
may we always rejoice in the profession of our faith.

We ask this through our Lord Jesus Christ, your son,
who lives and reigns with you and the Holy Spirit,
one God, for ever and ever.

Our Father . . .

September 19

JANUARIUS, BISHOP AND MARTYR

Saint Januarius was a bishop in Italy. Along with his companions he was martyred at Naples. Today he is especially venerated in that city.

Saint Januarius lived the spirit of Saint Paul, as described in
today's reading.

READING

A reading from the first letter of the apostle Paul to the Romans

I consider the sufferings of the present to be as nothing compared with the glory to be revealed in us.

We know that God makes all things work together for the good
of those who have been called according to his decree.

If God is for us, who can be against us? Is it possible that he who
did not spare his own Son but handed him over for the sake of
us all will not grant us all things besides?

Who will separate us from the love of Christ? Trial, or distress,
or persecution, or hunger, or nakedness, or danger or the
sword? Yet in all this we are more than conquerors because of
him who has loved us.

For I am certain that neither death nor life, neither angels nor
principalities, neither the present nor the future, neither height
nor depth nor any other creature, will be able to separate us
from the love of God that comes to us in Christ Jesus, our Lord.

He was a true martyr, who shed his blood for the name of
Christ.

**Fearless of the threats of judges and indifferent to worldly
honors,
he attained the kingdom of heaven.**

The Lord guided the just man on the right path
and showed him God's kingdom.

**Fearless of the threats of judges and indifferent to worldly
honors,
he attained the kingdom of heaven.**

PRAYER

God our Father,
enable us who honor the memory of Saint Januarius
to share with him the joy of eternal life.

Grant this through our Lord Jesus Christ, your Son,
who lives and reigns with you and the Holy Spirit,
one God, for ever and ever.

Our Father . . .

September 21

MATTHEW, APOSTLE AND EVANGELIST
Feast

Born at Capernaum, Saint Matthew was working as a tax collector when he was called by Jesus. He wrote his gospel in Hebrew
and is said to have preached in the East.

A reading from a homily by Saint Bede the Venerable, priest

"Jesus saw a man called Matthew sitting at the tax office, and he said to him: Follow me." Jesus saw Matthew, not merely in the usual sense, but more significantly with his merciful understanding of men.

He saw the tax collector and, because he saw him through the eyes of mercy and chose him, he said to him: "Follow me." This following meant imitating the pattern of his life—not just walking after him. Saint John tells us: "Whoever says he abides in Christ ought to walk in the same way in which he walked."

"And he rose and followed him." There is no reason for surprise that the tax collector abandoned earthly wealth as soon as the Lord commanded him. Nor should one be amazed that neglecting his wealth, he joined a band of men whose leader had, on Matthew's assessment, no riches at all. Our Lord summoned Matthew by speaking to him in words. By an invisible, interior impulse flooding his mind with the light of grace, he instructed him to walk in his footsteps. In this way Matthew could understand that Christ, who was summoning him away from earthly possessions, had incorruptible treasures of heaven in his gift.

Matthew was a talented scribe
and deeply versed in the law of the Lord.
He dedicated all his efforts to the study of God's law
so that with the Lord's guidance he might observe his precepts
    and teach them to others.

The gospel of God's glory is credited to him.
He dedicated all his efforts to the study of God's law
so that with the Lord's guidance he might observe his precepts
    and teach them to others.

259

God of mercy,
you chose a tax collector, Saint Matthew,
to share the dignity of the apostles.
By his example and prayers
help us to follow Christ
and remain faithful in your service.

We ask this through our Lord Jesus Christ, your Son,
who lives and reigns with you and the Holy Spirit,
one God, for ever and ever.

Our Father . . .

September 26

COSMAS AND DAMIAN, MARTYRS

According to ancient documents the tomb of Saints Cosmas and
Damian is in Syria. There a basilica was built in their honor.
Devotion to these martyrs spread to Rome and from there
through the whole Church.

READING

A reading from a sermon by Saint Augustine, bishop

In the glorious deeds of the holy martyrs who everywhere adorn
the Church, we verify the truth of what we have been singing:
"Precious in the sight of the Lord is the death of his saints."
They are precious in our sight and in the sight of him in whose
name it was done. You have heard what Jesus said as he drew
near to his passion, our redemption: "If the grain of wheat does
not fall to the ground and die, it remains barren, but if it dies, it
is very fruitful."

On the cross Christ effected a great exchange. There the purse containing the price to be paid for us was opened. When the soldier's lance cut its way into his side, the price paid for the whole world flowed forth. The martyrs and all the faithful were bought with it, but the faith of the martyrs was also tested: their blood bore witness to their faith. They gave back what had been paid for them and lived up to what Saint John says: "As Christ laid down his life for us, so we should lay down our lives for our brothers." Elsewhere we read: "You have taken your seat at the great table; consider carefully what is set before you, for you must prepare the same in return." The great table is the one at which the Lord of the banquet is himself the food. No one feeds the guests with his very self, yet that is what Christ the Lord does. He invites and he is the food and drink. The martyrs took careful note of what they ate and drank, so that they might return the same.

The Lord of heaven directed their minds and tongues; through them he overcame the devil on earth and crowned them as martyrs in heaven. Happy are they, for their suffering is over, and they have received their honors.

RESPONSORY

These holy men poured out their blood for the Lord;
they loved Christ in life; they followed him in his death.
They have won the glorious crown.

They shared the one Spirit;
they held fast to one faith.
They have won the glorious crown.
See Ephesians 4:4-5

PRAYER

Lord,
we honor the memory of Saints Cosmas and Damian.
Accept our grateful praise

for raising them to eternal glory
and for giving us your fatherly care.

We ask this through our Lord Jesus Christ, your Son,
who lives and reigns with you and the Holy Spirit,
one God, for ever and ever.

Our Father . . .

September 27

VINCENT DE PAUL, PRIEST
Memorial

Saint Vincent de Paul was born in France in 1581. After completing his studies, he was ordained a priest and went to Paris where he served in a parish. He founded the Congregation of the Mission to supervise the formation of priests and to give support to the poor. With the help of Saint Louise de Marillac, he also founded the Congregation of the Daughters of Charity. He died at Paris in 1660.

READING

A reading from a writing of Saint Vincent de Paul, priest

Even though the poor are often rough and unrefined, we must not judge them from external appearances nor from the mental gifts they seem to have received. On the contrary, if you consider the poor in the light of faith, then you will observe that they are taking the place of the Son of God who chose to be poor. Although in his passion he almost lost the appearance of a man and was considered a fool by the Gentiles and a stumbling block by the Jews, he showed them that his mission was to preach to the poor: "He sent me to preach the good news to the poor." We also ought to have this same spirit and imitate Christ's actions, that is, we must take care of the poor, console them, help them, support their cause.

262

Since Christ willed to be born poor, he chose for himself disciples who were poor. He made himself the servant of the poor and shared their poverty. He went so far as to say that he would consider every deed which either helps or harms the poor as done for or against himself. Since God surely loves the poor, he also loves those who love the poor. For when one person holds another dear, he also includes in his affection anyone who loves or serves the one he loves. That is why we hope that God will love us for the sake of the poor. So when we visit the poor and needy, we try to be understanding where they are concerned. We sympathize with them so fully that we can echo Paul's words: "I have become all things to all men." Therefore, we must try to be stirred by our neighbors' worries and distress.

It is our duty to prefer the service of the poor to everything else and to offer such service as quickly as possible. Charity is certainly greater than any rule. Moreover, all rules must lead to charity. With renewed devotion, then, we must serve the poor, especially outcasts and beggars. They have been given to us as our masters and patrons.

RESPONSORY

Though I am not bound to anyone,
I became a slave to all.
To the weak I became weak.

I became all things to all men,
that I might at least save some.

I was eyes for the blind and feet for the lame;
I was father to the poor.

I became all things to all men,
that I might at least save some.
1 Corinthians 9:19, 22; Job 29:15-16

PRAYER

God our Father,

you gave Vincent de Paul
the courage and holiness of an apostle
for the well-being of the poor
and the formation of the clergy.
Help us to be zealous in continuing his work.

Grant this through our Lord Jesus Christ, your Son,
who lives and reigns with you and the Holy Spirit,
one God, for ever and ever.

Our Father . . .

September 28

WENCESLAUS, MARTYR

Saint Wenceslaus was born in Bohemia around the year 907. Brought up as a Christian by his aunt, he began his rule around the year 925. Having experienced many difficulties in ruling over his subjects and in leading them to the faith, he was betrayed by his brother and killed by assassins in 935. He was immediately recognized as a martyr and is venerated as the patron saint of Bohemia.

READING

A reading from the first old Slavic legend

At the death of Vratislaus the people of Bohemia made his son Wenceslaus their king. He was by God's grace a man of utmost faith. He was charitable to the poor, and he would clothe the naked, feed the hungry and offer hospitality to travelers according to the summons of the Gospel. He would not allow widows to be treated unjustly; he loved all his people, both rich and poor; he also provided for the servants of God, and he adorned many churches.

The men of Bohemia, however, became arrogant and prevailed upon Boleslaus, his younger brother. They told him, "Your brother Wenceslaus is conspiring with his mother and his men to kill you."

On the feasts of the dedication of the churches in various cities, Wenceslaus was in the habit of paying them a visit. One Sunday he entered the city of Boleslaus, on the feast of Saints Cosmas and Damian, and after hearing Mass, he planned to return to Prague. But Boleslaus, with his wicked plan in mind, detained him with the words: "Why are you leaving, brother?" The next morning when they rang the bell for matins, Wenceslaus, on hearing the sound, said: "Praise to you, Lord; you have allowed me to live to this morning." And so he rose and went to matins.

Immediately Boleslaus followed him to the church door. Wenceslaus looked back at him and said: "Brother, you were a good subject to me yesterday." But the devil had already blocked the ears of Boleslaus and perverted his heart. Drawing his sword Boleslaus replied: "And now I intend to be a better one!" With these words he struck his brother's head with his sword. But Wenceslaus turned and said, "Brother, what are you trying to do?" And with that he seized Boleslaus and threw him to the ground. But one of Boleslaus' counselors ran up and stabbed Wenceslaus in the hand. With his hand wounded, he let go of his brother and took refuge in the church. But two evil men struck him down at the church door; and then another rushed up and ran him through with a sword. Thereupon Wenceslaus died with the words: "Into your hands, O Lord, I commend my spirit!"

RESPONSORY

The just man shall blossom like the lily;

he shall flourish for ever in the presence of the Lord.

He shall be planted in the house of the Lord,
in the courts of the house of our God.

He shall flourish for ever in the presence of the Lord.
See Hosea 14:6; Psalm 92:13, 14

PRAYER

Lord,
you taught your martyr Wenceslaus
to prefer the kingdom of heaven
to all that the earth has to offer.
May his prayers free us from our self-seeking
and help us to serve you with all our hearts.

We ask this through our Lord Jesus Christ, your Son,
who lives and reigns with you and the Holy Spirit,
one God, for ever and ever.

Our Father . . .

September 29

MICHAEL, GABRIEL AND RAPHAEL, ARCHANGELS
Feast

The angels are spiritual beings created by God. They sometimes
are sent as God's messengers to human beings. They also protect in a mysterious way the Church and the people of God. In
the following reading we shall learn more about the angels and
the archangels whose feast we celebrate today.

READING

A reading from a homily on the gospel by Saint Gregory the
Great, pope

You should be aware that the word "angel" denotes a function
rather than a nature. Those holy spirits of heaven have indeed

always been spirits. They can only be called angels when they deliver some message. Moreover, those who deliver messages of lesser importance are called angels; and those who proclaim messages of supreme importance are called archangels.

And so it was that not merely an angel but the archangel Gabriel was sent to the Virgin Mary. It was only fitting that the highest angel should come to announce the greatest of all messages.

Some angels are given proper names to denote the service they are empowered to perform. Personal names are assigned to some, not because they could not be known without them but rather to denote their ministry when they come among us. Thus, Michael means "Who is like God?"; Gabriel is "The Strength of God"; and Raphael is "God's Remedy."

Whenever some act of wondrous power must be performed, Michael is sent, so that his action and his name may make it clear that no one can do what God does by his superior power.

So too Gabriel, who is called God's strength, was sent to Mary. He came to announce the One who appeared as a humble man to quell the cosmic powers. Thus God's strength announced the coming of the Lord of the heavenly powers, mighty in battle.

Raphael means, as I have said, God's remedy, for when he touched Tobit's eyes in order to cure him, he banished the darkness of his blindness. Thus, since he is to heal, he is rightly called God's remedy.

RESPONSORY

An angel stood by the altar, holding a golden censer;
a large quantity of incense was given to him,

**and clouds of incense rose from the hand of the angel
in the presence of the Lord.**

Thousands upon thousands waited on him,
and myriads upon myriads stood before him.

**And clouds of incense rose from the hand of the angel
in the presence of the Lord.**
See Revelation 8:3, 4; Daniel 7:10

PRAYER

God our Father,
in a wonderful way you guide the work of angels and men.
May those who serve you constantly in heaven
keep our lives safe from all harm on earth.

Grant this through our Lord Jesus Christ, your Son,
who lives and reigns with you and the Holy Spirit,
one God, for ever and ever.

Our Father . . .

September 30

JEROME, PRIEST AND DOCTOR
Memorial

Saint Jerome was born in Dalmatia around the year 340. He
studied the classical authors at Rome, and was baptized there.
He embraced a life of asceticism and went to the East where he
was ordained a priest. Returning to Rome he began to translate
the holy Scriptures into Latin and to promote the monastic life.
Eventually he settled in Bethlehem where he served the needs of
the Church. He wrote many works, especially commentaries on
holy Scripture. He died at Bethlehem in 420.

READING

A reading from a commentary on Isaiah by Saint Jerome, priest

I interpret as I should, following the command of Christ: "Search the Scriptures," and "Seek and you shall find." For if, as Paul says, Christ is the power of God and the wisdom of God, and if the man who does not know Scripture does not know the power and wisdom of God, then ignorance of Scripture is ignorance of Christ.

No one should think that I mean to explain the entire subject matter of this great book of the prophet Isaiah in one brief sermon, since it contains all the mysteries of the lord. It prophesies that Emmanuel is to be born of a virgin and accomplish marvelous works and signs. It predicts his death, burial and resurrection from the dead as the Savior of all men. Whatever is proper to holy Scripture, whatever can be expressed in human language and understood by the human mind, is contained in the book of Isaiah.

RESPONSORY

All Scripture is inspired by God and is valuable
for teaching and for showing the way to holiness,

**so that the man of God might become
fully qualified and equipped for every good work.**

The wise son is one who keeps God's law.

**So that the man of God might become
fully qualified and equipped for every good work.**

See 2 Timothy 3:16-17; Proverbs 28:7

PRAYER

Father,
you gave Saint Jerome delight
in his study of holy scripture.

May your people find in your word
the food of salvation and the fountain of life.

We ask this through our Lord Jesus Christ, your Son,
who lives and reigns with you and the Holy Spirit,
one God, for ever and ever.

Our Father . . .

October 1

THERESA OF THE CHILD JESUS, VIRGIN

Saint Theresa was born in France in 1873. While still a young
girl, she entered the Carmelite monastery at Lisieux. There she
lived a life of humility, evangelical simplicity and trust in God.
By word and example she taught these virtues to the novices of
the community. Offering her life for the salvation of souls and
the growth of the Church, she died September 30, 1897.

READING

A reading from the autobiography of Saint Theresa of the Child
Jesus, virgin

Since my longing for martyrdom was powerful and unsettling, I
turned to the epistles of Saint Paul in the hope of finally finding
an answer. By chance the twelfth and thirteenth chapters of the
first epistle to the Corinthians caught my attention, and in the
first section I read that not everyone can be an apostle, prophet
or teacher, that the Church is composed of a variety of members,
and that the eye cannot be the hand. Even with such an answer
revealed before me, I was not satisfied and did not find peace .

I persevered in the reading and did not let my mind wander
until I found this encouraging theme: "Set your desires on the
greater gifts. And I will now show you the way which surpasses
all others." For the Apostle insists that the greater gifts are noth-

ing at all without love and that this same love is surely the best path leading directly to God. At length I had found peace of mind.

Love appeared to me to be the hinge for my vocation. Indeed I knew that the Church had a body composed of various members, but in this body the necessary and more noble member was not lacking; I knew that the Church had a heart and that such a heart appeared to be aflame with love. I knew that one love drove the members of the Church to action, that if this love were extinguished, the apostles would have proclaimed the Gospel no longer, the martyrs would have shed their blood no more. I saw and realized that love sets off the bounds of all vocations, that love is everything, that this same love embraces every time and every place. In one word, that love is everlasting.

RESPONSORY

From the very beginning, O God, you came to me with your
    love,
which has grown since my childhood.
Its depths I cannot fully grasp.

O Lord, how great is the goodness
you have stored up for those who fear you.
Its depths I cannot fully grasp.
See Psalm 21:4; Job 31:18; Ephesians 3:18; Psalm 31:20

PRAYER

God our Father,
you have promised your kingdom
to those who are willing to become like little children.
Help us to follow the way of Saint Theresa with confidence
so that by her prayers
we may come to know your eternal glory.

Grant this through our Lord Jesus Christ, your Son,

who lives and reigns with you and the Holy Spirit,
one God, for ever and ever.

Our Father . . .

October 2

GUARDIAN ANGELS
Memorial

Angels are mentioned many times in Scripture. They are said to
be very numerous and powerful, and to form a sort of heavenly
court around the throne of God. They owe their being, just as
we humans do, to the Creator. Both they and we are subject to
the rule of Christ, and so they are linked with us in the quest for
the salvation of the world. The Church honors the angels today
as our guardians who help us in our quest.

READING

A reading from a sermon by Saint Bernard, abbot

"He has given his angels charge over you to guard you in all
your ways. Let them thank the Lord for his mercy; his wonderful works are for the children of men." Let them give thanks and
say among the nations, the Lord has done great things for them.
O Lord, what is man that you have made yourself known to
him, or why do you incline your heart to him? And you do
incline your heart to him; you show him your care and your
concern. Finally, you send your only Son and the grace of your
Spirit, and promise him a vision of your countenance. And so,
that nothing in heaven should be wanting in your concern for
us, you send those blessed spirits to serve us, assigning them as
our guardians and our teachers.

"He has given his angels charge over you to guard you in all
your ways." These words should fill you with respect, inspire
devotion and instill confidence; respect for the presence of

272

angels, devotion because of their loving service, and confidence because of their protection. And so the angels are here; they are at your side, they are with you, present on your behalf. They are here to protect you and to serve you. But even if it is God who has given them this charge, we must nonetheless be grateful to them for the great love with which they obey and come to help us in our great need.

So let us be devoted and grateful to such great protectors; let us return their love and honor them as much as we can and should. Yet all our love and honor must go to him, for it is from him that they receive all that makes them worthy of our love and respect.

We should then, my brothers, show our affection for the angels, for one day they will be our coheirs just as here below they are our guardians and trustees appointed and set over us by the Father. We are God's children although it does not seem so, because we are still but small children under guardians and trustees, and for the present little better than slaves.

Even though we are children and have a long, a very long and dangerous way to go, with such protectors what have we to fear? They who keep us in all our ways cannot be overpowered or led astray, much less lead us astray. They are loyal, prudent, powerful. Why then are we afraid? We have only to follow them, stay close to them, and we shall dwell under the protection of God's heaven.

RESPONSORY

God gave his angels charge over you
to protect you in all your ways.

They shall lift you up with their hands,
lest you strike your foot against a stone.

No evil shall harm you,
no plague shall come near your tent.

They shall lift you up with their hands,
lest you strike your foot against a stone.
Psalm 91:11–12, 10

God our Father,
in your loving providence
you send your holy angels to watch over us.
Hear our prayers,
defend us always by their protection
and let us share your life with them for ever.

We ask this through our Lord Jesus Christ, your Son,
who lives and reigns with you and the Holy Spirit,
one God, for ever and ever.

Our Father . . .

October 4

FRANCIS OF ASSISI
Memorial

Saint Francis was born at Assisi in 1182. After a carefree youth, he renounced his paternal wealth and committed himself to God. He led a life of evangelical poverty and preached the love of God to all. He established a rule which a number of his companions followed and which gained the approval of the Holy See. Later, he founded an order of nuns and a society of lay persons who practice penance while living in the world. He died in 1226.

READING

A reading from a letter written to all the faithful by Saint Francis of Assisi

It was through his archangel, Saint Gabriel, that the Father above made known to the holy and glorious Virgin Mary that the worthy, holy and glorious Word of the Father would come from heaven and take from her womb the real flesh of our human frailty. Though he was wealthy beyond reckoning, he still willingly chose to be poor with his blessed mother. And shortly before his passion he celebrated the Passover with his disciples. Then he prayed to his Father saying: "Father, if it be possible, let this cup be taken from me."

Nevertheless, he reposed his will in the will of his Father. The Father willed that his blessed and glorious Son, whom he gave to us and who was born for us, should through his own blood offer himself as a sacrificial victim on the altar of the cross. This was to be done not for himself through whom all things were made, but for our sins. It was intended to leave us an example of how to follow in his footsteps. And he desires all of us to be saved through him, and to receive him with pure heart and chaste body.

Let us also love our neighbors as ourselves. Let us have charity and humility. Let us give alms because these cleanse our souls from the stains of sin. Men lose all the material things they leave behind them in this world, but they carry with them the reward of their charity and the alms they give. For these they will receive from the Lord the reward and recompense they deserve. We must not be wise according to the flesh. Rather we must be simple, humble and pure. We should never desire to be over others. Instead, we ought to be servants who are submissive to every human being for God's sake. The Spirit of the Lord will rest on all who live in this way and persevere in it to the end. He will permanently dwell in them. They will be the Father's children who do his work.

RESPONSORY

Blessed are you who are poor,
for the kingdom of God is yours.

**Blessed are those of gentle spirit;
they shall inherit the land.**

Blessed are you who hunger now;
you shall be satisfied.

Blessed are those of gentle spirit;

they shall inherit the land.
Matthew 5:3-4, 6

PRAYER

Father,
you helped Saint Francis to reflect the image of Christ
through a life of poverty and humility.
May we follow your Son
by walking in the footsteps of Francis of Assisi,
and by imitating his joyful love.

Grant this through our Lord Jesus Christ, your Son,
who lives and reigns with you and the Holy Spirit,
one God, for ever and ever.

Our Father . . .

October 6

BRUNO, PRIEST

Saint Bruno was born at Cologne about the year 1035. He was
educated at Paris and, after ordination to the priesthood, he
taught theology. However, he desired a solitary life and to this
end he founded the first Carthusian monastery. When called
upon by Pope Urban II, he aided the pontiff in meeting the
needs of the Church. He died in 1101.

READING

A reading from a letter to his Carthusian sons by Saint Bruno,
priest

Rejoice, my dearest brothers, because you are blessed and because of the bountiful hand of God's grace upon you. Rejoice,
because you have escaped the various dangers and shipwrecks

of the stormy world. Rejoice because you have reached the quiet
and safe anchorage of a secret harbor. Many wish to come into
this port, and many make great efforts to do so, yet do not
achieve it. Indeed many, after reaching it, have been thrust out,
since it was not granted them from above.

By your work you show what you love and what you know.
When you observe true obedience with prudence and enthusiasm, it is clear that you wisely pick the most delightful and
nourishing fruit of divine Scripture.

RESPONSORY

Had I but wings like a dove
to fly away and find my rest,

**I would flee far away
and encamp in the wilderness.**

The world and all its allurements will pass away,
but whoever does God's will shall live for ever.

**I would flee far away
and encamp in the wilderness.**
Psalm 55:7-8; 1 John 2:17

PRAYER

Father,
you called Saint Bruno to serve you in solitude.
In answer to his prayers
help us to remain faithful to you
amid the changes of this world.

We ask this through our Lord Jesus Christ, your Son,
who lives and reigns with you and the Holy Spirit,
one God, for ever and ever.

Our Father . . .

October 7

OUR LADY OF THE ROSARY
Memorial

This commemorative feast was established by Saint Pius V on the anniversary of the naval victory won by the Christian fleet at Lepanto. The victory was attributed to the help of the holy Mother of God whose aid was invoked through praying the rosary. The celebration of this day invites all to meditate upon the mysteries of Christ, following the example of the Blessed Virgin Mary who was so closely associated with her Son in his incarnation, passion and glorious resurrection.

READING

A reading from a sermon by Saint Bernard, abbot

"The Word was made flesh" and even now "dwells among us." It is by faith that he dwells in our hearts, in our memory, our intellect and penetrates even into our imagination. What concept could man have of God if he did not first fashion an image of him in his heart?

But how, you ask, was this done? Jesus lay in a manger and rested on a virgin's breast, preached on a mountain, and spent the night in prayer. He hung on a cross, grew pale in death, and roamed free among the dead and ruled over those in hell. He rose again on the third day, and showed the apostles the wounds of the nails, the signs of victory; and finally in their presence he ascended to the sanctuary of heaven.

Whatever of all this I consider, it is God I am considering; in all this he is my God. I have said it is wise to meditate on these truths, and I have thought it right to recall the abundant sweetness, given by the fruits of this priestly root; and Mary, drawing abundantly from heaven, has caused this sweetness to overflow for us.

O Virgin Mary, no other daughter of Jerusalem is your equal,
for you are the mother of the King of kings,
you are the Queen of heaven and of angels.

**Blessed are you among women,
and blessed is the fruit of your womb.**

Hail, full of grace; the Lord is with you.

**Blessed are you among women,
and blessed is the fruit of your womb.**

PRAYER

Lord,
fill our hearts with your love,
and as you revealed to us by an angel
the coming of your Son as man,
so lead us through his suffering and death
to the glory of his resurrection,
who lives and reigns with you and the Holy Spirit,
one God, for ever and ever.

Our Father . . .

October 9

DENIS, BISHOP AND MARTYR, AND COMPANIONS, MARTYRS

Saint Gregory of Tours relates that Saint Denis came to France from Rome in the middle of the third century. He became the first bishop of Paris and suffered martyrdom near that city with two members of his clergy.

A reading from a commentary on psalm 118 by Saint Ambrose, bishop

As there are many kinds of persecution, so there are many kinds of martyrdom. Every day you are a witness to Christ. You were tempted by the spirit of fornication, but feared the coming judgment of Christ and did not want your purity of mind and body to be defiled: you are a martyr for Christ. You were tempted by the spirit of avarice to violate the rights of a defenseless widow, but remembered God's law and saw your duty to give help, not act unjustly: you are a witness to Christ. Christ wants witnesses like this to stand ready, as Scripture says: "Do justice for the orphan and defend the widow." You were tempted by the spirit of pride but saw the poor and the needy and looked with loving compassion on them and loved humility rather than arrogance: you are a witness to Christ. What is more, your witness was not in word only but also in deed.

Who can give greater witness than one "who acknowledges that the Lord Jesus has come in the flesh" and keeps the commandments of the Gospel? One who hears but does not act, denies Christ. Even if he acknowledges him by his words, he denies him by his deeds. The true witness is one who bears witness to the commandments of the Lord Jesus and supports that witness by deeds.

In another place we read: "Do not let sin be king in your mortal body." There are as many kings as there are sins and vices; it is before these kings that we are led and before these we stand. These kings have their thrones in many hearts. But if anyone acknowledges Christ, he immediately makes a prisoner of this kind of king and casts him down from the throne of his own heart. How shall the devil maintain his throne in one who builds a throne for Christ in his heart?

These saints of God underwent a great struggle;
passing through fire and water, they were saved

**and received crowns of glory
from the Lord our God.**

They sacrificed their lives to bear witness to God.

**And received crowns of glory
from the Lord our God.**

PRAYER

Father,
you sent Saint Denis and his companions
to preach your glory to the nations,
and you gave them the strength
to be steadfast in their sufferings for Christ.
Grant that we may learn from their example
to reject the power and wealth of this world
and to brave all earthly trials.

We ask this through our Lord Jesus Christ, your Son,
who lives and reigns with you and the Holy Spirit,
one God, for ever and ever.

Our Father . . .

On the same day, October 9

JOHN LEONARDI, PRIEST

Saint John Leonardi was born in Italy in 1541. He studied pharmacy, but he left this profession to become a priest. He preached and taught, seeking especially to instruct boys in Christian doctrine. In 1574 he founded the Order of Clerics Regular of the Mother of God, an undertaking which caused him many hardships. He was also associated with the founding of the first society of priests dedicated to working in foreign missions. Under later popes this small order grew into the Sociey for the Propagation of the Faith, and for this reason John Leonardi is often called the founder of that society. In addition to these efforts, he restored discipline in different religious congregations by his charity and wisdom. He died at Rome in 1609.

READING

A reading from a letter to Pope Paul V by Saint John Leonardi, priest

Those who want to work for moral reform in the world must seek the glory of God before all else. Because he is the source of all good, they must wait for his help, and pray for it in this difficult and necessary undertaking. They must then present themselves to those they seek to reform, as mirrors of every virtue and as lamps on a lampstand. Their upright lives and noble conduct must shine before all who are in the house of God. In this way they will gently entice the members of the Church to reform instead of forcing them, lest, in the words of the Council of Trent, they demand of the body what is not found in the head, and thus upset the whole order of the Lord's household.

They will be like skilled physicians taking great pains to dispose of all the diseases that afflict the Church and require a cure. They will ready themselves to provide suitable remedies for each illness.

As far as remedies applicable to the whole Church are concerned, reform must begin with high and low alike, with superiors and inferiors. Yet the reformers must look first to those who are set over the rest, so that reform can begin at the point from which it may spread to the others.

Be especially concerned with cardinals, patriarchs, archbishops, bishops and priests, whose particular duty is the care of souls, and make them men to whom guidance of the Lord's flock can

282

be safely entrusted. So let us work down from the highest to the lowest, from superiors to inferiors. Those men who must initiate ecclesiastical reform must not be looked down upon.

Nothing should be left untried that can train children from early childhood in good morals and in the earnest practice of Christianity. To this end nothing is more effective than pious instructions in Christian doctrine. Children should be entrusted only to good and God-fearing teachers.

These are the thoughts,most holy Father, that the Lord has chosen to inspire in me for the present on this most important matter. If at first glance they appear difficult, compare them with the magnitude of the situation. Then they will seem very easy indeed. Great works are accomplished only by great men, and great men should be involved in great works.

RESPONSORY

This holy man accomplished everything God asked of him, and God said to him:

**Of all the peoples of this world,
you alone I have found just in my sight.
Enter into my resting place.**

He renounced earthly joys,
and so gained the kingdom of heaven.

**Of all the peoples of this world,
you alone I have found just in my sight.
Enter into my resting place.**

PRAYER

Father,
giver of all good things,
you proclaimed the good news to countless people
through the ministry of Saint John Leonardi.
By the help of his prayers
may the true faith continue to grow.

Grant this through our Lord Jesus Christ, your Son,
who lives and reigns with you and the Holy Spirit,
one God, for ever and ever.

Our Father . . .

October 14

CALLISTUS I, POPE AND MARTYR

Saint Callistus is reputed to have been a slave. Once he obtained
his liberty, he was ordained a deacon by Pope Zephyrinus and
succeeded him in the Chair of Saint Peter. He was crowned with
martyrdom in 222 and was buried on the Aurelian Way.

READING

A reading from a treatise to Fortunatus by Saint Cyprian, bishop
and martyr

"The sufferings of this present time are not to be compared with
the glory that is to be revealed in us." Who would not strive
wholeheartedly to attain to such glory, to become a friend of
God and straightway rejoice with Christ, receiving heavenly
rewards after earth's torment and suffering? Soldiers of this
world take pride in returning to their home country in triumph
after they have defeated the enemy. How much greater is the
glory in returning triumphantly to heaven after conquering the
devil. The bold deceiver is laid low, the trophies of victory are
restored to the place from which Adam was cast out for his sin.
We offer to the Lord a most acceptable gift, our incorrupt faith,
the unshaken courage of our spirit and the glorious pride of our
dedication.

The spirit of a strong and stable character strengthened by meditation endures. This unshaken spirit, which is strengthened by a
certain and solid faith in the future will be enlivened against
all the terrors of the devil and threats of this world. During

persecution the earth is closed off from us, but heaven lies open; the Antichrist threatens, but Christ protects us; death is brought on, but eternal life follows. What an honor, what happiness to depart joyfully from this world, to go forth in glory from the anguish and pain, in one moment to close the eyes that looked on the world of men and in the next to open them at once to look on God and Christ! You are suddenly withdrawn from earth to find yourself in the kingdom of heaven.

These are the thoughts you must grasp with your heart and mind and reflect on day and night. In time of persecution the battle wins the crown, but in peace it is the testimony of a good conscience.

RESPONSORY

The just are the friends of God.
They live with him forever.

The just are the friends of God.
They live with him forever.

God himself is their reward.
Glory to the Father . . .

The just are the friends of God.
They live with him forever.

PRAYER

God of mercy,
hear the prayers of your people
that we may be helped by Saint Callistus,
whose martyrdom we celebrate with joy.

We ask this through our Lord Jesus Christ, your Son,
who lives and reigns with you and the Holy Spirit,
one God, for ever and ever.

Our Father . . .

October 15

TERESA OF AVILA, VIRGIN AND DOCTOR
Memorial

Saint Teresa was born at Avila in Spain in 1515. She joined the Carmelite Order, made great progress in the way of perfection and enjoyed mystical revelations. When she reformed the Order, she met with much resistance, but she succeeded with undaunted courage. She also wrote books filled with sublime doctrine, the fruit of her own spiritual life. She died at Alba in 1582.

READING

A reading from a work by Saint Teresa of Avila, virgin

If Christ Jesus dwells in a man as his friend and noble leader, that man can endure all things, for Christ helps and strengthens us and never abandons us. He is a true friend. And I clearly see that if we expect to please him and receive an abundance of his graces, God desires that these graces must come to us from the hands of Christ, through his most sacred humanity, in which God takes delight.

All blessings come to us through our Lord. He will teach us, for in beholding his life we find that he is the best example.

What more do we desire from such a good friend at our side? Unlike our friends in the world, he will never abandon us when we are troubled or distressed. Blessed is the one who truly loves him and always keeps him near.

Whenever we think of Christ we should recall the love that led him to bestow on us so many graces and favors, and also the great love God showed in giving us in Christ a pledge of his love; for love calls for love in return. Let us strive to keep this always before our eyes and to rouse ourselves to love him. For if at some time the Lord should grant us the grace of impressing his love on our hearts, all will become easy for us and we shall accomplish great things quickly and without effort.

Those who turn their backs on you will perish.

What joy to be near my God,
to place all my trust in the Lord.

Whoever is united to the Lord
becomes one spirit with him.

What joy to be near my God,
to place all my trust in the Lord.
Psalm 73:27, 28; 1 Corinthians 6:17

PRAYER

Father,
by your Spirit you raised up Saint Teresa of Avila
to show your Church the way to perfection.
May her inspired teaching
awaken in us a longing for true holiness.

Grant this through our Lord Jesus Christ, your Son,
who lives and reigns with you and the Holy Spirit,
one God, for ever and ever.

Our Father . . .

October 16

HEDWIG, RELIGIOUS

Saint Hedwig was born in Bavaria around the year 1174. She
married a prince and they had seven children. She led a most
devoted life, looking after the poor and the sick, and founding
hospitals for them. When her husband died, she entered the
monastery of Trebnitz and died there in 1243.

A reading from the life of Saint Hedwig

Hedwig knew that those living stones that were to be placed in the building of the heavenly Jerusalem had to be smoothed out by buffetings and pressures in this world, and that many tribulations would be needed before she could cross over into her heavenly homeland. Because of such great daily fasts and abstinences she grew so thin that many wondered how such a feeble and delicate woman could endure these torments. The more attentively she kept watch, the more she grew in the strength of the spirit and in grace, and the more the fire of devotion and divine love blazed within her.

Just as her devotion made her always seek after God, so her generous piety turned her toward her neighbor, and she bountifully bestowed alms on the needy. She gave aid to colleges and to religious persons dwelling within or outside monasteries, to widows and orphans, to the weak and the feeble, to lepers and those bound in chains or imprisoned, to travelers and needy women nursing infants. She allowed no one who came to her for help to go away uncomforted.

And because this servant of God never neglected the practice of all good works, God also conferred on her such grace that when she lacked human means to do good, and her own powers failed, through divine favor of the sufferings of Christ she had the power to relieve the bodily and spiritual troubles of all who sought her help.

RESPONSORY

She set herself to work with courage;
she put forth all her strength;
therefore her lamp will never go out.

She had discovered how good it is
to work for the God of wisdom.

Therefore her lamp will never go out.
See Proverbs 31:17, 18

PRAYER

All powerful God,
may the prayers of Saint Hedwig bring us your help
and may her life of remarkable humility
be an example to us all.

We ask this through our Lord Jesus Christ, your Son,
who lives and reigns with you and the Holy Spirit,
one God, for ever and ever.

Our Father . . .

On the same day, October 16

MARGARET MARY ALACOQUE, VIRGIN

Saint Margaret Mary was born in 1647 in France. She joined the
Sisters of the Visitation at Paray-le-Monial where she lived such
a holy life that she was favored with heavenly visions. She was
especially devoted to the Sacred Heart of Jesus and was responsible for spreading that devotion throughout the Church. She
died on October 17, 1690.

READING

A reading from a letter by Saint Margaret Mary, virgin

The sacred heart [of Christ] is an inexhaustible fountain and its
sole desire is to pour itself out into the hearts of the humble so as
to free them and prepare them to lead lives according to his
good pleasure.

From this divine heart three streams flow endlessly. The first is
the stream of mercy for sinners; it pours into their hearts senti-

289

ments of contrition and repentance. The second is the stream of charity which helps all in need and especially aids those seeking perfection in order to find the means of surmounting their difficulties. From the third stream flow love and light for the benefit of his friends who have attained perfection; these he wishes to unite to himself so that they may share his knowledge and commandments and, in their individual ways, devote themselves wholly to advancing his glory.

This divine heart is an abyss filled with all blessings, and into it the poor should submerge all their needs. It is an abyss of joy in which all of us can immerse our sorrows. It is an abyss of lowliness to counteract our foolishness, an abyss of mercy for the wretched, an abyss of love to meet our every need.

Are you making no progress in prayer? Then you need only offer God the prayers which the Savior has poured out for us in the sacrament of the altar. Offer God his fervent love in reparation for your sluggishness. In the course of every activity pray as follows: "My God, I do this or I endure that in the heart of your Son and according to his holy counsels. I offer it to you in reparation for anything blameworthy or imperfect in my actions." Continue to do this in every circumstance of life.

But above all preserve peace of heart. This is more valuable than any treasure. In order to preserve it there is nothing more useful than renouncing your own will and substituting for it the will of the divine heart. In this way his will can carry out for us whatever contributes to his glory, and we will be happy to be his subjects and to trust entirely in him.

RESPONSORY

I thank you, Father, Lord of heaven and earth,
for hiding these things from the learned and clever,
and revealing them to little children.

Yes, Father, this is what you have willed.

The God of my heart is my portion for ever.

Yes, Father, this is what you have willed.
Matthew 11:25-26; Psalm 73:26

Lord,
pour out on us the riches of the Spirit
which you bestowed on Saint Margaret Mary.
May we come to know the love of Christ,
which surpasses all human understanding,
and be filled with the fullness of God.

Grant this through our Lord Jesus Christ, your Son,
who lives and reigns with you and the Holy Spirit,
one God, for ever and ever.

Our Father . . .

October 17

IGNATIUS OF ANTIOCH, BISHOP AND MARTYR
Memorial

Saint Ignatius was a successor of Saint Peter as bishop of Antioch. Condemned to death by being thrown to wild animals, he was brought to Rome for execution and was martyred there under the Emperor Trajan in 107. On the journey to Rome he wrote seven letters to different churches. In these he discussed Christ, the structure of the Church, and the Christian life in a manner at once wise and learned. At Antioch, this day was observed in his memory as early as the fourth century.

READING

A reading from a letter to the Romans by Saint Ignatius, bishop and martyr

I am writing to all the churches to let it be known that I will gladly die for God if only you do not stand in my way. I plead with you: show me no untimely kindness. Let me be food for the wild beasts, for they are my way to God. I am God's wheat and shall be ground by their teeth so that I may become Christ's pure bread. Pray to Christ for me that the animals will be the means of making me a sacrificial victim for God.

No earthly pleasures, no kingdoms of this world can benefit me in any way. I prefer death in Christ Jesus to power over the farthest limits of the earth. He who died in place of us is the one object of my quest. He who rose for our sakes is my one desire.

The prince of this world is determined to lay hold of me and to undermine my will which is intent on God. Let none of you here help him; instead show yourselves on my side, which is also God's side. Believe instead what I am now writing to you. For though I am alive as I write to you, still my real desire is to die. My love of this life has been crucified, and there is no yearning in me for any earthly thing. Rather within me is the living water which says deep inside me: "Come to the Father." I no longer take pleasure in perishable food or in the delights of this world. I want only God's bread, which is the flesh of Jesus Christ, formed from the seed of David, and for drink I crave his blood, which is love that cannot perish.

Pray for me that I may obtain my desire. I have not written to you as a mere man would, but as one who knows the mind of God.

RESPONSORY

Nothing will be hidden from you
if you have perfect faith and love for Jesus Christ,
since these are the beginning and end of life.

Faith, indeed, is the beginning and love is the end.

Clothe yourself with gentleness,
and be renewed in faith,

which is the flesh of the Lord,
and in love, which is the blood of Jesus Christ.

Faith, indeed, is the beginning and love is the end.

PRAYER

All-powerful and ever-living God,
you ennoble your Church
with the heroic witness of all
who give their lives for Christ.
Grant that the victory of Saint Ignatius of Antioch
may bring us your constant help
as it brought him eternal glory.

We ask this through our Lord Jesus Christ, your Son,
who lives and reigns with you and the Holy Spirit,
one God, for ever and ever.

Our Father . . .

October 18

LUKE, EVANGELIST

Feast

Saint Luke was born of a pagan family. Converted to the faith,
he became a fellow-worker of the apostle Paul. From Saint
Paul's preaching he compiled one of the gospels. He handed
down an account of the beginnings of the Church in another
work, the "Acts of the Apostles," which tells of events up to the
time of Saint Paul's first sojourn in Rome.

Our reading for today reflects, in the words of Saint Paul, the
way of life he taught and which Saint Luke followed.

A reading from the letter of the apostle Paul to the Romans

Your love must be sincere. Detest what is evil, cling to what is good. Love one another with the affection of brothers. Anticipate each other in showing respect. Do not grow slack but be fervent in spirit; he whom you serve is the Lord. Rejoice in hope, be patient under trial, persevere in prayer. Look on the need of the saints as your own; be generous in offering hospitality.

Bless your persecutors; bless and do not curse them. Rejoice with those who rejoice, weep with those who weep. Have the same attitude toward all. Put away ambitious thoughts and associate with those who are lowly. Do not be wise in your own estimation. Never repay injury with injury. See that your conduct is honorable in the eyes of all.

If possible, live peaceably with everyone. Beloved, do not avenge yourselves; leave that to God's wrath, for it is written: "'Vengeance is mine; I will repay,' says the Lord." But "if your enemy is hungry, feed him; if he is thirsty, give him something to drink; by doing this you will heap burning coals upon his head." Do not be conquered by evil but conquer evil with good.

RESPONSORY

He carefully traced the whole story from the beginning
and wrote his gospel,

**so that we might understand
the truth of the teaching we had received.**

He gave us a record concerning all that Jesus did and taught.

**So that we might understand
the truth of the teaching we had received.**
See Luke 1:3, 4; Acts 1:1

Father,
you chose Luke the evangelist to reveal
by preaching and writing
the mystery of your love for the poor.
Unite in heart and spirit
all who glory in your name,
and let all nations come to see your salvation.

Grant this through our Lord Jesus Christ, your Son,
who lives and reigns with you and the Holy Spirit,
one God, for ever and ever.

Our Father . . .

October 19

ISAAC JOGUES AND JOHN DE BREBEUF, PRIESTS AND MARTYRS, AND COMPANIONS, MARTYRS

Between the years 1642 and 1649 eight members of the Society of Jesus were killed in North America, after fearful torture by members of the Huron and Iroquois tribes. These men had worked hard to bring the natives of that region to the true faith. Saint Isaac Jogues died on October 18, 1647, and Saint John de Brebeuf on March 16, 1648.

READING

A reading from the spiritual diaries by Saint John de Brebeuf, priest and martyr

For two days now I have experienced a great desire to be a martyr and to endure all the torments the martyrs suffered.

Jesus, my Lord and Savior, what can I give you in return for all

295

the favors you have first conferred on me? I "will take" from your hand "the cup" of your sufferings and "call on your name." I vow before your eternal Father and the Holy Spirit, before your most holy Mother and her most chaste spouse, before the angels, apostles and martyrs, before my blessed fathers Saint Ignatius and Saint Francis Xavier—in truth I vow to you, Jesus my Savior, that as far as I have the strength I will never fail to accept the grace of martyrdom, if some day you in your infinite mercy should offer it to me, your most unworthy servant.

For this reason, my beloved Jesus, and because of the surging joy which moves me, here and now I offer my blood and body and life. May I die only for you, if you will grant me this grace, since you willingly died for me. Let me so live that you may grant me the gift of such a happy death. In this way, my God and Savior, "I will take" from your hand "the cup" of your sufferings and "call on your name": Jesus, Jesus, Jesus!

My God, it grieves me greatly that you are not known, that in this savage wilderness all have not been converted to you, that sin has not been driven from it. My God, even if all the brutal tortures which prisoners in this region must endure should fall on me, I offer myself most willingly to them and I alone shall suffer them all.

RESPONSORY

Through faith the saints conquered kingdoms and did what was
    just.
They secured promises and were strong in battle.

All of them have won approval for their witness to the faith.

God tried them, and found them worthy of himself.

All of them have won approval for their witness to the faith.
Hebrews 11:33, 34, 39; Wisdom 3:5

Father,
you consecrated the first beginnings
of the faith in North America
by the preaching and martyrdom
of Saints John and Isaac and their companions.
By the help of their prayers
may the Christian faith continue to grow
throughout the world.

We ask this through our Lord Jesus Christ, your Son,
who lives and reigns with you and the Holy Spirit,
one God, for ever and ever.

Our Father . . .

On the same day, October 19

PAUL OF THE CROSS, PRIEST

Saint Paul of the Cross was born in Italy in 1694. As a young man he helped his father who was a merchant. However, aspiring to a life of perfection, he left all behind and brought together a group of associates who joined with him in caring for the poor and the sick. After he became a priest, he worked even more earnestly for the salvation of souls by founding homes, preaching, and afflicting himself with harsh penances. He died at Rome on October 18, 1775.

READING

A reading from a letter by Saint Paul of the Cross, priest

It is very good and holy to consider the passion of our Lord and to meditate on it, for by this sacred path we reach union with God. In this most holy school we learn true wisdom, for it was there that all the saints learned it.

Therefore, be constant in practicing every virtue, and especially in imitating the patience of our dear Jesus, for this is the summit of pure love. Live in such a way that all may know that you bear outwardly as well as inwardly the image of Christ crucified, the model of all gentleness and mercy. For if a man is united inwardly with the Son of the living God, he also bears his likeness outwardly by his continual practice of heroic goodness, and especially through a patience reinforced by courage, which does not complain either secretly or in public. Conceal yourselves in Jesus crucified, and hope for nothing except that all men be thoroughly converted to his will.

RESPONSORY

God forbid that I should boast
except in the cross of our Lord Jesus Christ.

**Through it the world has been crucified to me,
and I to the world.**

I will rejoice in the Lord,
I will exult in God, my Savior.

**Through it the world has been crucified to me,
and I to the world.**
Galatians 6:14; Habakkuk 3:18

PRAYER

Father,
you gave your priest Saint Paul
a special love for the cross of Christ.
May his example inspire us
to embrace our own cross with courage.

Grant this through our Lord Jesus Christ, your Son,
who lives and reigns with you and the Holy Spirit,
one God, for ever and ever.

Our Father . . .

October 23

JOHN OF CAPISTRANO, PRIEST

Saint John was born in Capistrano in Italy in 1386. He studied law at Perugia and for a time was governor of that city. He entered the Order of Friars Minor and, after ordination to the priesthood, he led an untiring apostolic life preaching throughout Europe both to strengthen Christian life and to refute heresy. He died in Austria in 1456.

READING

A reading from the treatise Mirror of the Clergy by Saint John of Capistrano, priest

Those who are called to the table of the Lord must glow with the brightness that comes from the good example of a praiseworthy and blameless life. They must completely remove from their lives the filth and uncleanness of vice. Their upright lives must make them like the salt of the earth for themselves and for the rest of mankind. The brightness of their wisdom must make them like the light of the world that brings light to others. They must learn from their eminent teacher, Jesus Christ, what he declared not only to his apostles and disciples, but also to all the priests and clerics who were to succeed them, when he said: "You are the salt of the earth. But what if salt goes flat? How can you restore its flavor? Then it is good for nothing but to be thrown out and trampled underfoot."

[Jesus also said:] "You are the light of the world." Now a light does not illumine itself, but instead it diffuses its rays and shines all around upon everything that comes into its view. So it must be with the glowing lives of upright and holy clerics. By the brightness of their holiness they must bring light and serenity to all who gaze upon them. They have been placed here to care for others. Their own lives should be an example to others, showing how they must live in the house of the Lord.

Speak out when the time is right;
do not hide your wisdom,

for speech makes wisdom known,
and all a man has learned appears in his words.

Preach the word, persevere in the task,
both when convenient and inconvenient;
correct, reprove, summon to obedience,
but do all with patience and sound doctrine.

For speech makes wisdom known,
and all a man has learned appears in his words.
Sirach 4:23-24; 2 Timothy 4:2

PRAYER

Lord,
you raised up Saint John of Capistrano
to give your people comfort in their trials.
May your Church enjoy unending peace
and be secure in your protection.

We ask this through our Lord Jesus Christ, your Son,
who lives and reigns with you and the Holy Spirit,
one God, for ever and ever.

Our Father . . .

October 24

ANTHONY CLARET, BISHOP

Saint Anthony Claret was born in Spain in 1807. After being
ordained priest he traveled many years through Catalonia
preaching to the people. He founded a society of missionaries
and, after being named a bishop in Cuba, he won renown for his

pastoral zeal. After returning to Spain, he continued to work for the Church. He died in France in 1870.

A reading from a work by Saint Anthony Mary Claret, bishop

Driven by the fire of the Holy Spirit, the holy apostles traveled throughout the earth. Inflamed with the same fire, apostolic missionaries have reached, are now reaching and will continue to reach the ends of the earth, from one pole to the other, in order to proclaim the word of God. They are deservedly able to apply to themselves those words of the apostle Paul: "The love of Christ drives us on."

The love of Christ arouses us, urges us to run, and to fly, lifted on the wings of holy zeal. The zealous man desires and achieves all great things and he labors strenuously so that God may always be better known, loved and served in this world and in the life to come, for this holy love is without end.

Because he is concerned also for his neighbor, the man of zeal works to fulfill his desire that all men be content on this earth and happy and blessed in their heavenly homeland, that all may be saved, and that no one may perish for ever, or offend God, or remain even for a moment in sin. Such are the concerns we observe in the holy apostles and in all who are driven by the apostolic spirit.

For myself, I say this to you: The man who burns with the fire of divine love is a son of the Immaculate Heart of Mary, and wherever he goes, he enkindles that flame; he desires and works with all his strength to inflame all men with the fire of God's love. Nothing deters him: he rejoices in poverty; he labors strenuously; he welcomes hardships; he laughs off false accusations; he rejoices in anguish. He thinks only of how he might follow Jesus Christ and imitate him by his prayers, his labors, his sufferings, and by caring always and only for the glory of God and the salvation of souls.

I have longed to give you the Gospel,
and more than that, to give you my very life;

you have become very dear to me.

My little children, I am like a mother giving birth to you,
until Christ is formed in you.

You have become very dear to me.

1 Thessalonians 2:8; Galatians 4:19

PRAYER

Father,
you endowed Anthony Claret
with the strength of love and patience
to preach the gospel to many nations.
By the help of his prayers
may we work generously for your kingdom
and gain our brothers and sisters for Christ,
who lives and reigns with you and the Holy Spirit,
one God, for ever and ever.

Our Father . . .

October 28

SIMON AND JUDE, APOSTLES
Feast

The name of Saint Simon usually appears eleventh in the list of
the apostles. Nothing is known of him except that he was born
at Cana and is surnamed "The Zealot."

Saint Jude, also called Thaddeus, was the apostle who asked the
Lord at the Last Supper why he had manifested himself only to
his disciples and not to the whole world (John 14:22).

A reading from a commentary on the gospel of John by Saint
Cyril of Alexandria, bishop

Our Lord Jesus Christ has appointed certain men to be guides
and teachers of the world and stewards of his divine mysteries.
Now he bids them to shine out like lamps and to cast out their
light over every country under the sun and over people scattered in all directions and settled in distant lands.

These holy men became the "pillar and mainstay of the truth,"
and Jesus said that he was sending them just as the Father had
sent him.

Once Jesus said: "I have come to call not the righteous but
sinners to repentance." And then at another time he said: "I
have come down from heaven, not to do my own will, but the
will of him who sent me. For God sent his Son into the world,
not to condemn the world, but that the world might be saved
through him."

By these words he is making clear the dignity of the apostolate
and the incomparable glory of the power given to them, but he
is also, it would seem, giving them a hint about the methods
they are to adopt in their apostolic mission. Accordingly, in
affirming that they are sent by him just as he was sent by the
Father, Christ sums up in a few words the approach they themselves should take to their ministry. From what he said they
would gather that it was their vocation to call sinners to repentance, to heal those who were sick whether in body or spirit, to
seek in all their dealings never to do their own will but the will of
him who sent them, and as far as possible to save the word by
their teaching.

You did not choose me, but I chose you
to go forth and bear fruit

that will last for ever.

My Father is glorified when you bring forth fruit in abundance.
That will last for ever.
John 15:16, 8

Father,
you revealed yourself to us
through the preaching of your apostles Simon and Jude.
By their prayers,
give your Church continued growth
and increase the number of those who believe in you.

Grant this through our Lord Jesus Christ, your Son,
who lives and reigns with you and the Holy Spirit,
one God, for ever and ever.

Our Father . .

November 1

ALL SAINTS
Solemnity

The Church has formally declared that certain heroically holy
people are in heaven. Such people are said to be "canonized."

Today the Church honors all those who have died in the love of
Christ and are now in heaven with him even though most of
them are not known to the Church at large. Thus, one's own
relatives and friends and all others who have lived good lives
and are now with God in heaven, are among the saints.

READING

A reading from a sermon by Saint Bernard, abbot

Why should our praise and glorification, or even the celebration of this feastday mean anything to the saints? What do they care about earthly honors when their heavenly Father honors them by fulfilling the faithful promise of the Son? The saints have no need of honor from us; neither does our devotion add the slightest thing to what is theirs. Clearly, if we venerate their memory, it serves us, not them. But I tell you, when I think of them, I feel myself inflamed by tremendous yearning.

Calling the saints to mind arouses in us, above all else, a longing to enjoy their company, so desirable in itself. In short, we long to be united in happiness with all the saints. But our dispositions change. The Church of all the first followers of Christ awaits us, but we do nothing about it. The saints want us to be with them, and we are indifferent. The souls of the just await us, and we ignore them.

Come, brothers, let us at length spur ourselves on. We must rise again with Christ, we must seek the world which is above and set our mind on the things of heaven. Let us long for those who are longing for us, hasten to those who are waiting for us, and ask those who look for our coming to intercede for us. We should not only want to be with the saints, we should also hope to possess their happiness. While we desire to be in their company, we must also earnestly seek to share in their glory. Do not imagine that there is anything harmful in such an ambition as this; there is no danger in setting our hearts on such glory.

Therefore, we should aim at attaining this glory with a wholehearted and prudent desire. That we may rightly hope and strive for such blessedness, we must above all seek the prayers of the saints. Thus, what is beyond our own powers to obtain will be granted through their intercession.

RESPONSORY

Praise God, all you who serve him, both great and small,

for the Lord God Almighty has begun his reign.

Sing for joy, God's chosen ones,
let all the saints give him fitting praise.

For the Lord God Almighty has begun his reign.
Revelation 19:5, 6; Psalm 33:1

Father, all-powerful and ever-living God,
today we rejoice in the holy men and women
of every time and place.
May their prayers bring us your forgiveness and love.

We ask this through our Lord Jesus Christ, your Son,
who lives and reigns with you and the Holy Spirit,
one God, for ever and ever.

Our Father . . .

November 2

ALL SOULS

Today we remember in our prayers all those who have died in
Christ's love, but who have not yet become completely and
utterly selfless and totally devoted to God's will. The Church
prays that these people will, with God's grace, soon be made
ready to enter heaven.

READING

A reading from a book on the death of his brother by Saint
Ambrose, bishop

We see that death is gain, life is loss. Paul says: "For me life is
Christ, and death a gain." What does "Christ" mean but to die
in the body, and receive the breath of life? Let us then die with
Christ, to live with Christ.

It was by the death of one man that the world was redeemed. Christ did not need to die if he did not want to, but he did not look on death as something to be despised, something to be avoided, and he could have found no better means to save us than by dying. Thus his death is life for all. We are sealed with the sign of his death; when we pray we preach his death, when we offer sacrifice we proclaim his death. His death is victory; his death is a sacred sign; each year his death is celebrated with solemnity by the whole world.

What more should we say about his death since we use this divine example to prove that it was death alone that won freedom from death, and death itself was its own redeemer? Death is then no cause for mourning, for it is the cause of mankind's salvation. Death is not something to be avoided, for the Son of God did not think it beneath his dignity, nor did he seek to escape it.

Death was not part of nature, it became part of nature. God did not decree death from the beginning; he prescribed it as a remedy. Human life was condemned because of sin to unremitting labor and unbearable sorrow and so began to experience the burden of wretchedness. There had to be a limit to its evils; death had to restore what life had forfeited. Without the assistance of grace, immortality is more of a burden than a blessing.

The soul has to turn away from the aimless paths of this life, from the defilement of an earthly body; it must reach out to those assemblies in heaven (though it is given only to the saints to be admitted to them) to sing the praises of God.

RESPONSORY

There are some who have died a godly death;

they shall receive the splendid reward which awaits them.

Then the just will shine like the sun in the kingdom of their Father.

They shall receive the splendid reward which awaits them.
See 2 Maccabees 12:45; Matthew 13:43

Merciful Father,
hear our prayers and console us.
As we renew our faith in your Son,
whom you raised from the dead,
strengthen our hope that all our departed brothers and sisters
will share in his resurrection,
who lives and reigns with you and the Holy Spirit,
one God, for ever and ever.

Our Father . . .

November 3

MARTIN DE PORRES, RELIGIOUS

Saint Martin de Porres was born at Lima, Peru, of a Spanish father and a Negro mother in 1579. As a boy he studied medicine which later, as a member of the Dominican Order, he put to good use in helping the poor. He led a humble and disciplined life and was devoted to the holy eucharist. He died in 1639.

READING

A reading from a homily at the Canonization of Saint Martin de Porres by Pope John XXIII

The example of Martin's life is ample evidence that we can strive for holiness and salvation as Christ Jesus has shown us: first, by loving God "with all your heart, with all your soul, and with all your mind; and second, by loving your neighbor as yourself."

When Martin had come to realize that Christ Jesus "suffered for us and that he carried our sins on his body to the cross," he would meditate with remarkable ardor and affection about Christ on the cross. He had an exceptional love for the great sacrament of the eucharist and often spent long hours in prayer before the blessed sacrament. His desire was to receive the sacrament in communion as often as he could.

Saint Martin, always obedient and inspired by his divine teacher, dealt with his brothers with that profound love which comes from pure faith and humility of spirit. He loved men because he honestly looked on them as God's children and as his own brothers and sisters. Such was his humility that he loved them even more than himself and considered them to be better and more righteous than he was.

He did not blame others for their shortcomings. Certain that he deserved more severe punishment for his sins than others did, he would overlook their worst offenses. He was tireless in his efforts to reform the criminal, and he would sit up with the sick to bring them comfort. For the poor he would provide food, clothing and medicine. He did all he could to care for poor farmhands, blacks and mulattoes who were looked down upon as slaves, the dregs of society in their time. Common people responded by calling him "Martin the charitable."

It is remarkable how even today his influence can still move us toward the things of heaven. Sad to say, not all of us understand these spiritual values as well as we should, nor do we give them a proper place in our lives. Many of us, in fact, strongly attracted by sin, may look upon these values as of little moment, even something of a nuisance, or we ignore them altogether. It is deeply rewarding for men striving for salvation to follow in Christ's footsteps and to obey God's commandments. If only everyone could learn this lesson from the example that Martin gave us.

RESPONSORY

Blessed is the man who is found without fault,
who does not make gold his life's object,
who does not put his trust in wealth.

His future will be secure in the Lord.

Who is this man that we may praise him,
for he has done wonders in his life?

His future will be secure in the Lord.
Sirach 31:8, 11, 9

PRAYER

Lord,
you led Martin de Porres by a life of humility
to eternal glory.
May we follow his example
and be exalted with him in the kingdom of heaven.

Grant this through our Lord Jesus Christ, your Son,
who lives and reigns with you and the Holy Spirit,
one God, for ever and ever.

Our Father . . .

November 4

CHARLES BORROMEO, BISHOP
Memorial

Saint Charles Borromeo was born in Lombardy in the year 1538.
After having taken honors in both civil and canon law, he was
made cardinal and bishop of Milan by his uncle, Pope Pius IV.
As a true pastor of his flock he tirelessly promoted Christian life
by the reform of his diocese, the convocation of synods, and the
promulgation of regulations intended to foster the Church's
mission. He died on November 3, 1584.

READING

A reading from a sermon given during the last synod he attended, by Saint Charles, bishop

310

I admit that we are all weak, but if we want help, the Lord God has given us the means to find it easily. Would you like me to teach you how to grow from virtue to virtue and how, if you are already recollected at prayer, you can be even more attentive next time, and so give God more pleasing worship? Listen, and I will tell you. If a tiny spark of God's love already burns within you, do not expose it to the wind, for it may get blown out. Keep the stove tightly shut so that it will not lose its heat and grow cold. In other words, avoid distractions as well as you can. Stay quiet with God. Do not spend your time in useless chatter.

If teaching and preaching is your job, then study diligently and apply yourself to whatever is necessary for doing the job well. Be sure that you first preach by the way you live. If you do not, people will notice that you say one thing, but live otherwise, and your words will bring only cynical laughter and a derisive shake of the head.

We must meditate before, during and after everything we do. The prophet says: "I will pray, and then I will understand."

This is the way we can easily overcome the countless difficulties we have to face day after day, which, after all, are part of our work. In meditation we find the strength to bring Christ to birth in ourselves and in other men.

RESPONSORY

Seek after integrity and holiness, faith and love, patience and
    gentleness.

**These are the things you must command and teach;
be an example to all who believe.**

If you give them this advice,
you will be a good servant of Christ Jesus.

**These are the things you must command and teach;
be an example to all who believe.**
1 *Timothy 6:11, 4:11, 12, 6*

Father,
keep in your people the spirit
which filled Charles Borromeo.
Let your Church be continually renewed
and show the image of Christ to the world
by being conformed to his likeness,
who lives and reigns with you and the Holy Spirit,
one God, for ever and ever.

Our Father . . .

November 9

DEDICATION OF SAINT JOHN LATERAN
Feast

The anniversary of the dedication of the Lateran Basilica, which
was erected by the Emperor Constantine, has been observed on
this day since the twelfth century. This feast was at first observed only in Rome but later in honor of the basilica, which is
called the mother church of Christendom, the celebration was
extended to the whole Latin Church. This action was taken as a
sign of devotion to and of unity with the Chair of Peter which, as
Saint Ignatius of Antioch wrote, "presides over the whole assembly of charity."

READING

A reading from a sermon by Saint Caesarius of Arles

My fellow Christians, today is the birthday of this church, an occasion for celebration and rejoicing. We, however, ought to be the true and living temple of God. Nevertheless, Christians rightly commemorate this feast of the church, their mother, for they know that through her they were reborn in the spirit. At our first birth, we were vessels of God's wrath; reborn, we became vessels of his mercy. Our first birth brought death to us, but our second restored us to life.

If we think more carefully about the meaning of our salvation, we shall realize that we are indeed living and true temples of God. "God does not dwell only in structures fashioned by human hands," in homes of wood and stone, but rather he dwells principally in the soul made according to his own image and fashioned by his own hand. Therefore, the apostle Paul says: "The temple of God is holy, and you are that temple."

When Christ came, he banished the devil from our hearts, in order to build in them a temple for himself. Let us therefore do what we can with his help, so that our evil deeds will not deface that temple. For whoever does evil, does injury to Christ. As I said earlier, before Christ redeemed us, we were the house of the devil, but afterward, we merited the privilege of being the house of God. God himself in his loving mercy saw fit to make of us his own home.

My fellow Christians, do we wish to celebrate joyfully the birth of this temple? Then let us not destroy the living temples of God in ourselves by works of evil. Whenever we come to church, we must prepare our hearts to be as beautiful as we expect this church to be. Do you wish to find this basilica immaculately clean? Then do not soil your soul with the filth of sins. Do you wish this basilica to be full of light? God too wishes that your souls be not in darkness, but that the light of good works shine in us, so that he who dwells in the heavens will be glorified. Just as you enter this church building, so God wishes to enter into your soul, for he promised: "I shall live in them and I shall walk the corridors of their hearts."

I saw water flowing eastward from beneath the threshold of the
temple, alleluia.
Wherever the river flowed everything became alive;

those who were saved by it cried out:
Alleluia, alleluia.

When the temple was dedicated,
the people sang songs of praise and beautiful hymns.

Those who were saved by it cried out:
Alleluia, alleluia.

See Ezekiel 47:1, 9

PRAYER

Father,
you called your people to be your Church.
As we gather together in your name,
may we love, honor, and follow you
to eternal life in the kingdom you promise.

Grant this through our Lord Jesus Christ, your Son,
who lives and reigns with you and the Holy Spirit,
one God, for ever and ever.

Our Father . . .

November 10

LEO THE GREAT, POPE AND DOCTOR
Memorial

Saint Leo was probably born in Rome and was raised to the See
of Peter in 440. He was a true pastor and father of souls. He
labored strenuously to safeguard the purity of the faith and
vigorously defended the unity of the Church. He pushed back
or at least softened the onrush of the barbarians. He has then

deservedly won the title "the Great." He died in 461.

A reading from a sermon by Saint Leo the Great, pope

Although the universal Church of God is constituted of distinct orders of members, still, in spite of the many parts of its holy body, the Church subsists as an integral whole, just as the Apostle says: "We are all one in Christ," nor is anyone separated from the office of another in such a way that a lower group has no connection with the head. In the unity of faith and baptism, our community is then undivided. There is a common dignity as the apostle Peter says in these words: "And you are built up as living stones into spiritual houses, a holy priesthood, offering spiritual sacrifices which are acceptable to God through Jesus Christ." And again: "But you are a chosen people, a royal priesthood, a holy nation, a people of election."

For all, regenerated in Christ, are made kings by the sign of the cross. They are consecrated priests by the oil of the Holy Spirit, so that beyond the special service of our ministry as priests, all spiritual and mature Christians know that they are a royal race and are sharers in the office of the priesthood. For what is more king-like than to find yourself ruler over your body after having surrendered your soul to God? And what is more priestly than to promise the Lord a pure conscience and to offer him in love unblemished victims on the altar of one's heart?

Jesus said to Simon: I tell you most solemnly that you are Peter, and I will build my Church upon this rock foundation,

and the powers of hell will never overcome it.

For all eternity, God's Church stands firm.

And the powers of hell will never overcome it.
Matthew 16:18, Psalm 48:9

God our Father,
you will never allow the power of hell
to prevail against your Church,
founded on the rock of the apostle Peter.
Let the prayers of Pope Leo the Great
keep us faithful to your truth
and secure in your peace.

We ask this through our Lord Jesus Christ, your Son,
who lives and reigns with you and the Holy Spirit,
one God, for ever and ever.

Our Father . . .

November 11

MARTIN OF TOURS, BISHOP
Memorial

Saint Martin of Tours was born of pagan parents around the
year 316. He gave up military life and was baptized. Soon after,
he founded a monastery in France where he led a monastic life
under the direction of Saint Hilary. He was ordained a priest
and chosen bishop of Tours. He provided an example of the
ideal good pastor, founding other monasteries, educating the
clergy, and preaching the Gospel to the poor. He died in 397.

READING

A reading from a letter by Sulpicius Severus

Martin knew long in advance the time of his death and he told
his brethren that it was near. Meanwhile, he found himself

obliged to make a visitation of the parish of Candes. The clergy of that church were quarreling, and he wished to reconcile them.

Although he knew that his days on earth were few, he did not refuse to undertake the journey for such a purpose, for he believed that he would bring his virtuous life to a good end if by his efforts peace was restored in the church.

He spent some time in Candes, or rather in its church, where he stayed. Peace was restored, and he was planning to return to his monastery when suddenly he began to lose his strength. He summoned his brethren and told them he was dying. All who heard this were overcome with grief. In their sorrow they cried to him with one voice: "Father, why are you deserting us? Who will care for us when you are gone? Savage wolves will attack your flock, and who will save us from their bite when our shepherd is struck down? We know you long to be with Christ, but your reward is certain and will not be any less for being delayed. You will do better to show pity for us, rather than forsake us."

Thereupon he broke into tears, for he was a man in whom the compassion of our Lord was continually revealed. Turning to our Lord, he made this reply to their pleading: "Lord, if your people still need me, I am ready for the task; your will be done."

Here was a man words cannot describe. Death could not defeat him nor toil dismay him. He was quite without a preference of his own; he neither feared to die nor refused to live. With eyes and hands always raised to heaven he never withdrew his unconquered spirit from prayer. It happened that some priests who had gathered at his bedside suggested that he should give his poor body some relief by lying on his other side. He answered: "Allow me, brothers, to look toward heaven rather than at the earth, so that my spirit may set on the right course when the time comes for me to go on my journey to the Lord."

Happy this man who did not deceive, nor judge, nor condemn
    anyone.

He spoke only of Christ, of his peace and his mercy.

Here is a man whom words cannot describe.
Death could not defeat him nor toil dismay him.
He neither feared to die nor refused to live.

He spoke only of Christ, of his peace and his mercy.

PRAYER

Father,
by his life and death
Martin of Tours offered you worship and praise.
Renew in our hearts the power of your love,
so that neither death nor life may separate us from you.

Grant this through our Lord Jesus Christ, your Son,
who lives and reigns with you and the Holy Spirit,
one God, for ever and ever.

Our Father . . .

November 12

JOSAPHAT, BISHOP AND MARTYR
Memorial

Saint Josaphat was born in the Ukraine of Orthodox parents
about the year 1580. Embracing the Catholic faith, he became a
Basilian monk. Ordained to the priesthood and chosen bishop of
Polock, he worked faithfully for the unity of the Church.
Enemies plotted his death, and he was martyred in 1623.

A reading from the Encyclical Letter Ecclesiam Dei by Pope Pius XI

In designing his Church God worked with such skill that in the fullness of time it would resemble a single great family embracing all men. It can be identified, as we know, by certain distinctive characteristics, notably its universality and unity.

Christ the Lord passed on to his apostles the task he had received from the Father: "I have been given all authority in heaven and on earth. Go, therefore, and make disciples of all nations." He wanted the apostles as a body to be intimately bound together, first by the inner tie of the same faith and love "which flows into our hearts through the Holy Spirit," and, second, by the external tie of authority exercised by Peter, the source and visible basis of their unity for all time. So that the unity and agreement among them would endure, God wisely stamped them, one might say, with the marks of holiness and martyrdom.

Both these distinctions fell to Josaphat, archbishop of Polock of the Slavonic rite of the Eastern Church. He is rightly looked upon as the great glory and strength of the Eastern Rite Slavs. Few have brought them greater honor or contributed more to their spiritual welfare than Josaphat, their pastor and apostle, especially when he gave his life as a martyr for the unity of the Church. He felt, in fact, that God had inspired him to restore worldwide unity to the Church and he realized that his greatest chance of success lay in preserving the Slavonic rite and Saint Basil's rule of monastic life within the one universal Church.

Concerned mainly with seeing his own people reunited to the See of Peter, he sought out every available argument which would foster and maintain Church unity.

Jesus said: Holy Father, protect those you have given me with the power of your name,

that they may be perfectly one;
then the world will know that it was you who sent me.

The glory which you gave me,
I have given to them.

That they may be perfectly one;
then the world will know that it was you who sent me.
John 17:11, 23, 22

PRAYER

Lord,
fill your Church with the Spirit
that gave Saint Josaphat courage
to lay down his life for his people.
By his prayers
may your Spirit make us strong
and willing to offer our lives
for our brothers and sisters.

We ask this through our Lord Jesus Christ, your Son,
who lives and reigns with you and the Holy Spirit,
one God, for ever and ever.

Our Father . . .

November 13

FRANCES XAVIER CABRINI, VIRGIN
Memorial

Saint Frances Xavier Cabrini was born in Lombardy, Italy, in
1850. In the diocese of Lodi, she founded the Missionary Sisters
of the Sacred Heart in 1880. In 1887 she established many
schools, hospitals and orphanages. With the encouragement of
Pope Leo XIII, she set out for the United States in 1889, where,
for the next twenty-eight years, she established many schools,

hospitals and orphanages. Her missionary zeal also led her to South America where she founded schools in Argentina, Brazil and Nicaragua. Mother Cabrini died in Chicago on December 22, 1917, and on July 7, 1946 she became the first United States citizen to be canonized.

READING

A reading from a homily at the Canonization of Saint Frances Xavier Cabrini by Pope Pius XII

Inspired by the grace of God, we join the saints in honoring the holy virgin Frances Xavier Cabrini. She was a humble woman who became outstanding not because she was famous, or rich or powerful, but because she lived a virtuous life. From the tender years of her youth, she kept her innocence as white as a lily and preserved it carefully with the thorns of penitence; as the years progressed, she was moved by a certain instinct and super-natural zeal to dedicate her whole life to the service and greater glory of God.

She welcomed delinquent youths into safe homes and taught them to live upright and holy lives. She consoled those who were in prison and recalled to them the hope of eternal life. She encouraged prisoners to reform themselves and to live honest lives.

She comforted the sick and the infirm in the hospitals and dili-gently cared for them. She extended a friendly and helping hand especially to immigrants and offered them necessary shel-ter and relief, for having left their homeland behind, they were wandering about in a foreign land with no place to turn for help. Because of their condition she saw that they were in danger of deserting the practice of Christian virtues and their Catholic faith.

Undoubtedly she accomplished all this through the faith which was always so vibrant and alive in her heart; through the divine love which burned within her; and, finally, through constant

321

prayer by which she was so closely united with God from whom she humbly asked and obtained whatever her human weakness could not obtain.

I was hungry and you gave me food;
I was thirsty and you gave me drink;
I was homeless and you took me in.

Now I tell you this:
When you did these things for the most neglected of my
brothers,
you did them for me.

This is what I command:
Love one another as I have loved you.

Now I tell you this:
When you did these things for the most neglected of my
brothers,
you did them for me.
Matthew 25:35, 40

God our Father,
you called Frances Xavier Cabrini from Italy
to serve the immigrants of America.
By her example teach us concern for the stranger,
the sick, and the frustrated.
By her prayers help us to see Christ
in all the men and women we meet.

Grant this through our Lord Jesus Christ, your Son,
who lives and reigns with you and the Holy Spirit,

one God, for ever and ever.

Our Father . . .

November 15

ALBERT THE GREAT, BISHOP AND DOCTOR

Saint Albert was born at a town along the Danube River about the year 1206. Having studied at Padua and Paris, he entered the Order of Preachers and excelled as a teacher. Ordained bishop of Ratisbon, he strove earnestly to establish peace among peoples and between cities. He wrote brilliantly on many subjects to the advantage of sacred and secular sciences alike. He died at Cologne in 1280.

In the following reading we can see some of Saint Albert's teachings on the Blessed Sacrament.

READING

A reading from a commentary on the gospel of Luke by Saint Albert the Great, bishop

"Do this in remembrance of me." Two things should be noted here. The first is the command that we should use this sacrament, which is indicated when Jesus says: "Do this." The second is that this sacrament commemorates the Lord's going to death for our sake.

This sacrament is profitable because it grants remission of sins; it is most useful because it bestows the fullness of grace on us in this life. "The Father of spirits instructs us in what is useful for our sanctification." And his sanctification is in Christ's sacrifice, that is, when he offers himself in this sacrament to the Father for our redemption, to us for our use.

Christ could not have commanded anything more beneficial, for this sacrament is the fruit of the tree of life. Anyone who receives this sacrament with the devotion of sincere faith will never taste death. "It is a tree of life for those who grasp it, and blessed is he who holds it fast. The man who feeds on me shall live on account of me."

Nor could he have commanded anything more lovable, for this sacrament produces love and union. It is characteristic of the greatest love to give itself as food. "Had not the men of my tent exclaimed: Who will feed us with his flesh to satisfy our hunger?" as if to say: I have loved them and they have loved me so much that I desire to be within them, and they wish to receive me so that they may become my members. There is no more intimate or more natural means for them to be united to me, and I to them.

Nor could he have commanded anything which is more like eternal life. Eternal life flows from this sacrament because God with all sweetness pours himself out upon the blessed.

RESPONSORY

Just as the Father handed a kingdom over to me,
I now hand one over to you.
In my kingdom you will eat and drink at my table.

I chose you and appointed you to go forth and bear fruit.

In my kingdom you will eat and drink at my table.
Luke 22:29; John 15:16

PRAYER

God our Father,
you endowed Saint Albert with the talent
of combining human wisdom with divine faith.
Keep us true to his teachings
that the advance of human knowledge
may deepen our knowledge and love of you.

Grant this through our Lord Jesus Christ, your Son,
who lives and reigns with you and the Holy Spirit,
one God, for ever and ever.

Our Father . . .

November 16

MARGARET OF SCOTLAND

Saint Margaret was born around the year 1046 in Hungary
where her father was exiled. She was married to King Malcolm
III of Scotland and gave birth to eight children. The ideal mother
and queen, she died at Edinburgh in 1093.

The following reading reflects the true spirit of marriage and
parenthood, a spirit of which Saint Margaret is a notable example.

READING

A reading from the pastoral constitution on the Church in the
modern world of the Second Vatican Council

Husband and wife, by the covenant of marriage, are no longer
two, but one flesh. By their intimate union of persons and of
actions they give mutual help and service to each other, experience the meaning of their unity, and gain an ever deeper understanding of it day by day.

This intimate union in the mutual self-giving of two persons, as
well as the good of the children, demands full fidelity from both,
and an indissoluble unity between them.

Christ the Lord has abundantly blessed this richly complex love,
which springs from the divine source of love and is founded on
the model of his union with the Church.

325

In earlier times God met his people in a covenant of love and fidelity. So now the Savior of mankind, the Bridegroom of the Church, meets Christian husbands and wives in the sacrament of matrimony. Further, he remains with them in order that, as he loved the Church and gave himself up for her, so husband and wife may, in mutual self-giving, love each other with perpetual fidelity.

True married love is caught up into God's love; it is guided and enriched by the redeeming power of Christ and the saving action of the Church, in order that the partners may be effectively led to God and receive help and strength in the sublime responsibility of parenthood.

Christian partners are therefore strengthened, and as it were consecrated, by a special sacrament for the duties and the dignity of their state. By the power of this sacrament they fulfill their obligations to each other and to their family and are filled with the spirit of Christ.

Children, as active members of the family, contribute in their own way to the holiness of their parents. With the love of grateful hearts, with loving respect and trust, they will return the generosity of their parents and will stand by them as true sons and daughters when they meet with hardship and the loneliness of old age.

RESPONSORY

The woman who fears the Lord is to be praised.
She is clothed with strength and dignity.

Give her the reward of her deeds;
they will proclaim her as she enters the gates.
She is clothed with strength and dignity.
Proverbs 31:30, 25, 31

Lord,
you gave Saint Margaret of Scotland
a special love for the poor.
Let her example and prayers
help us to become a living sign of your goodness.

We ask this through our Lord Jesus Christ, your Son,
who lives and reigns with you and the Holy Spirit,
one God, for ever and ever.

Our Father . . .

On the same day, November 16

GERTRUDE, VIRGIN

Saint Gertrude was born in Germany in 1256. As a young girl
she was received into the Cistercian nuns at Helfta and applied
herself to her studies, concentrating on literature and philosophy. Devoting her life to God, she dedicated herself to the pursuit of perfection, and gave herself over to prayer and contemplation. She died November 17, 1301.

READING

A reading from the Revelations by Saint Gertrude, virgin

May my soul bless you, O Lord God my Creator, may my soul
bless you. From the very core of my being may all your merciful
gifts sing your praise. Your generous care for your daughter has
been rich in mercy; indeed it has been immeasureable, and as far
as I am able I give you thanks. I praise and glorify your great
patience which bore with me even though, from my infancy and
childhood, adolescence and early womanhood, until I was
nearly twenty-six, I was always so blindly irresponsible. Looking back I see that but for your protecting hand I would have

been quite without conscience in thought, word or deed. But you came to my aid by giving me a natural dislike of evil and a natural delight in what is good, and provided me with necessary correction from those among whom I lived.

To make amends for the way I previously lived, I offer you, most loving Father, all the sufferings of your beloved Son, from that first infant cry as he lay on the hay in the manger, until that final moment when, bowing his head, with a mighty voice, Christ gave up his spirit. I think, as I make this offering, of all that he underwent, his needs as a baby, his dependence as a young child, the hardships of youth and the trials of early manhood.

To atone for all my neglect I offer, most loving Father, all that your only-begotten Son did during his life, whether in thought, word or deed.

And now, as an act of thanksgiving, I praise and worship you, Father, in deepest humility for your most loving kindness and mercy. Though I was hurrying to my eternal loss, your thoughts of me were thoughts of peace and not of affliction, and you lifted me up with so many great favors.

Finally, you drew me to yourself by your faithful promises of the good things you would give me from the hour of my death. So great are these promises that for their sake alone, even if you had given me nothing besides, my heart would sigh for you always and be filled with a lively hope.

RESPONSORY

The Lord loved Gertrude with an everlasting love;

**from her childhood, he drew her to himself
and led her into the wilderness.
There he spoke tenderly to her.**

He espoused her to himself for ever
in faith and in love.

From her childhood, he drew her to himself
and led her into the wilderness.
There he spoke tenderly to her.

See Jeremiah 31:3; Hosea 2:14, 21

Father,
you filled the heart of Saint Gertrude
with the presence of your love.
Bring light into our darkness
and let us experience the joy of your presence
and the power of your grace.

Grant this through our Lord Jesus Christ, your Son,
who lives and reigns with you and the Holy Spirit,
one God, for ever and ever.

Our Father . . .

November 17

ELIZABETH OF HUNGARY
Memorial

Saint Elizabeth, born in 1207, was the daughter of Andrew, king
of Hungary. While still a young girl she was married to Louis,
the ruler of Thuringia, and gave birth to three children. She
devoted herself to prayer and meditation. After her husband's
death, she embraced a life of poverty, erecting a hospital in
which she herself served the sick. She died at Marburg in 1231.

READING

A reading from a letter by Conrad of Marburg, spiritual director
of Saint Elizabeth

Elizabeth was a lifelong friend of the poor and gave herself entirely to relieving the hungry. She ordered that one of her castles should be converted into a hospital in which she gathered many of the weak and feeble. She generously gave alms to all who were in need, not only in that place but in all the territories of her husband's empire. She spent all her own revenue from her husband's four principalities, and finally she sold her luxurious possessions and rich clothes for the sake of the poor.

Twice a day, in the morning and in the evening, Elizabeth went to visit the sick. She personally cared for those who were particularly repulsive; to some she gave food, to others clothing; some she carried on her own shoulders, and performed many other kindly services. Her husband, of happy memory, gladly approved of these charitable works. Finally, when her husband died, she sought the highest perfection; filled with tears, she implored me to let her beg for alms from door to door.

On Good Friday of that year, when the altars had been stripped, she laid her hands on the altar in a chapel in her own town, where she had established the Friars Minor, and before witnesses she voluntarily renounced all worldly display and everything that our Savior in the gospel advises us to abandon. Even then she saw that she could still be distracted by the cares and worldly glory which had surrounded her while her husband was alive. Against my will she followed me to Marburg. Here in the town she built a hospice where she gathered together the weak and the feeble. There she attended the most wretched and contemptible at her own table.

Apart from those active good works, I declare before God that I have seldom seen a more contemplative woman.

Before her death I heard her confession. When I asked what should be done about her goods and possessions, she replied that anything which seemed to be hers belonged to the poor. She asked me to distribute everything except one worn-out dress in which she wished to be buried. When all this had been decided, she received the body of our Lord. Afterward, until vespers, she spoke often of the holiest things she had heard in sermons. Then, she devoutly commended to God all who were sitting near her, and as if falling into a gentle sleep, she died.

RESPONSORY

You acted bravely, and your heart has been strengthened because you loved chastity.

Your name will be praised for ever.

Your prayers and generosity have been accepted in God's sight, and because of them he has remembered you.

Your name will be praised for ever.
Judith 15:11; Acts 10:4

PRAYER

Father,
you helped Elizabeth of Hungary
to recognize and honor Christ
in the poor of this world.
Let her prayers help us to serve our brothers and sisters
in time of trouble and need.

We ask this through our Lord Jesus Christ, your Son,
who lives and reigns with you and the Holy Spirit,
one God, for ever and ever.

Our Father . . .

November 18

DEDICATION OF THE CHURCHES OF PETER AND PAUL, APOSTLES

Anniversaries of dedication were celebrated in the Vatican Basilica of Saint Peter and the Basilica of Saint Paul on the Ostian Way as early as the twelfth century. The two basilicas had been completed in the fourth century. More recently this commemoration was extended to the entire Latin Rite. Just as the Maternity of the Virgin Mother of God is celebrated on the anniversary of the Basilica of Saint Mary Major (August 5), so on this day we honor the two princes of Christ's apostles.

Today's reading speaks of the virtues of Peter and Paul and of other early Christian martyrs.

READING

A reading from a sermon by Saint Leo the Great, pope

"Precious in the eyes of the Lord is the death of his holy ones." No type of cruelty can tear down the religion established by the mystery of Christ's cross. The Church is not diminished by persecutions, but rather increased. The field of the Lord is always being enriched with a more abundant harvest, while the seeds which are sown one by one yield a manifold return.

On the commemoration of all the saints it is right for us to rejoice in his heavenly band, fashioned by God as models of patience and a support for our faith. But we must glory and exult even more in the eminence of these two forebears [Peter and Paul], whom the grace of God raised to so high a summit among all the members of the Church, and established like two eyes that bring light to the body whose head is Christ.

As to their merits and virtues, we should not think of any difference or distinction between them; their calling was the same, their labors were similar, theirs was a common death.

332

Our experience has shown, as our predecessors have proved, that we may believe and hope that in all the labors of the present life, by the mercy of God, we shall always be helped by the prayers of our special patrons. Just as we are humbled by our own sins, so we shall be raised up by the merits of these apostles.

RESPONSORY

In life the holy apostles served Christ with a generous spirit, and they founded the Church upon the witness of their blood.

They drank the blood of the Lord
and were made the friends of God.

Just as love united them in this life,
so death could not separate them.

They drank the blood of the Lord
and were made the friends of God.

PRAYER

Lord,
give your Church the protection of the apostles.
From them it first received the faith of Christ.
May they help your Church to grow in your grace
until the end of time.

Grant this through our Lord Jesus Christ, your Son,
who lives and reigns with you and the Holy Spirit,
one God, for ever and ever.

Our Father . . .

November 21

PRESENTATION OF MARY
Memorial

This feast commemorates the dedication of the church of Saint Mary which was built in Jerusalem near the site of the Temple. With Christians of the East, the Latin Church also recalls on this day the tradition according to which Mary as a small child was presented to the Lord by her parents in the Temple.

READING

A reading from a sermon by Saint Augustine, bishop

Stretching out his hand over his disciples, the Lord Christ declared: "Here are my mother and my brothers; anyone who does the will of my Father who sent me is my brother and my sister and my mother." I would urge you to ponder these words. Did the Virgin Mary, who believed by faith and conceived by faith, who was the chosen one from whom our Savior was born among men, who was created by Christ before Christ was created in her—did she not do the will of the Father? Indeed the blessed Mary certainly did the Father's will, and so it was for her a greater thing to have been Christ's disciple than to have been his mother, and she was more blessed in her discipleship than in her motherhood. Hers was the happiness of first bearing in her womb him whom she would obey as her master.

Now listen and see if the words of Scripture do not agree with what I have said. The Lord was passing by and crowds were following him. His miracles gave proof of divine power, and a woman cried out: "Happy is the womb that bore you, blessed is that womb!" But the Lord, not wishing people to seek happiness in a purely physical relationship, replied: "More blessed are those who hear the word of God and keep it." Mary heard God's word and kept it, and so she is blessed. She kept God's truth in her mind, a nobler thing than carrying his body in her womb. The truth and the body were both Christ. He was kept in Mary's mind insofar as he is truth; he was carried in her womb

334

insofar as he is man. But what is kept in the mind is of a higher order than what is carried in the womb.

The Virgin Mary is both holy and blessed, and yet the Church is greater than she. Mary is part of the Church, a member of the Church, a holy, an eminent—the most eminent—member, but still only a member of the entire body. The body undoubtedly is greater than she, one of its members. This body has the Lord for its head, and head and body together make up the whole Christ. In other words, our head is divine—our head is God.

Now, beloved, give me your whole attention, for you also are members of Christ; you also are the body of Christ. Consider how you yourselves can be among those of whom the Lord said: "Here are my mother and my brothers." As for our being the brothers and sisters of Christ, we can understand this because although there is only one inheritance and Christ is the only Son, his mercy would not allow him to remain alone. It was his wish that we too should be heirs of the Father, and coheirs with himself.

Now having said that all of you are brothers of Christ, shall I not dare to call you his mother? Much less would I dare to deny his own words. Tell me how Mary became the mother of Christ, if it was not by giving birth to the members of Christ? You, to whom I am speaking, are the members of Christ. Of whom were you born? "Of Mother Church," I hear the reply of your hearts. You became sons of this mother at your baptism, you came to birth then as members of Christ. Now you in your turn must draw to the font of baptism as many as you possibly can. You became sons when you were born there yourselves, and now by bringing others to birth in the same way, you have it in your power to become the mothers of Christ.

RESPONSORY

I will cry out with joy to the Lord;
my soul will rejoice in my God,

for he has clothed me with the robe of salvation,

like a bride adorned with her jewels.

My soul proclaims the greatness of the Lord,
my spirit rejoices in God my Savior.

**For he has clothed me with the robe of salvation,
like a bride adorned with her jewels.**
Isaiah 61:10; Luke 1:46-47

PRAYER

Eternal Father,
we honor the holiness and glory of the Virgin Mary.
May her prayers bring us
the fullness of your life and love.

We ask this through our Lord Jesus Christ, your Son,
who lives and reigns with you and the Holy Spirit,
one God, for ever and ever.

Our Father . . .

November 22

CECILIA, VIRGIN AND MARTYR
Memorial

In the fifth century a basilica dedicated to Saint Cecilia was
erected at Rome. From that time devotion to her spread, largely
owing to accounts of her sufferings. She is praised as the most
perfect model of the Christian woman because of her virginity
and the martyrdom which she suffered for love of Christ. Saint
Cecilia has been the traditional patroness of music and musicians, and so it is quite appropriate that the Chruch has selected
the following reading about singing to the Lord a new song.

A reading from a discourse on the psalms by Saint Augustine, bishop

"Praise the Lord with the lyre, make melody to him with the harp of ten strings! Sing to him a new song." Rid yourself of what is old and worn out, for you know a new song. A new man, a new covenant—a new song. Let us sing a new song not with our lips but with our lives.

"Sing to him a new song, sing to him with joyful melody." Every one of us tries to discover how to sing to God. You must sing to him, but you must sing well. He does not want your voice to come harshly to his ears, so sing well, brothers.

If you were asked, "Sing to please this musician," you would not like to do so without having taken some instruction in music, because you would not like to offend an expert in the art. An untrained listener does not notice the faults a musician would point out to you. Who, then, will offer to sing well for God, the great artist whose discrimination is faultless, whose attention is on the minutest detail, whose ear nothing escapes? When will you be able to offer him a perfect performance that you will in no way displease such a supremely discerning listener?

See how he himself provides you with a way of singing. Do not search for words, as if you could find a lyric which would give God pleasure. Sing to him "with songs of joy." This is singing well to God, just singing with songs of joy.

But how is this done? You must first understand that words cannot express the things that are sung by the heart. Take the case of people singing while harvesting in the fields or in the vineyards or when any other strenuous work is in progress. Although they begin by giving expression to their happiness in sung words, yet shortly there is a change. As if so happy that words can no longer express what they feel, they discard the restricting syllables. They burst out into a simple sound of joy,

337

of jubilation. Such a cry of joy is a sound signifying that the heart is bringing to birth what it cannot utter in words.

Now, who is more worthy of such a cry of jubilation than God himself, whom all words fail to describe? If words will not serve, and yet you must not remain silent, what else can you do but cry out for joy? Your heart must rejoice beyond words, soaring into an immensity of gladness, unrestrained by syllabic bonds. "Sing to him with songs of joy."

RESPONSORY

My mouth will be filled with your praise.
I will sing of your greatness all the day long.

My lips will shout for joy when I sing to you.

In you I will rejoice and be glad;
I will sing to your name, Most High.

My lips will shout for joy when I sing to you.
Psalm 71:8, 23; 9:3

PRAYER

Lord of mercy,
be close to those who call upon you.
With Saint Cecilia to help us,
hear and answer our prayers.

Grant this through our Lord Jesus Christ, your Son,
who lives and reigns with you and the Holy Spirit,
one God, for ever and ever.

Our Father . . .

November 23

CLEMENT I, POPE AND MARTYR

Saint Clement, the third pope to rule the Roman Church after Saint Peter, reigned toward the end of the first century. He wrote a famous epistle to the Corinthians to strengthen and encourage peace and unity among them.

READING

A reading from a letter to the Corinthians by Saint Clement, pope

Beloved, how blessed and wonderful are God's gifts! There is life everlasting, joy in righteousness, truth in freedom, faith, confidence, and self-control in holiness. And these are the gifts that we can comprehend; what of all the others that are being prepared for those who look to him. Only the Creator, the Father of the ages, the all holy, knows their grandeur and their loveliness. And so we should strive to be found among those who wait for him so that we may share in these promised gifts. And how is this to be, beloved brothers? It will come about if by our faith our minds remain fixed on God; if we aim at what is pleasing and acceptable to him, if we accomplish what is in harmony with his faultless will and follow the path of truth, rejecting all injustice, viciousness, covetousness, quarrels, malice and deceit.

This is the path, beloved, by which we find our salvation, Jesus Christ, the high priest of our sacrifices, the defender and ally in our helplessness.

Let us then serve in his army, brothers, following his blameless commands with all our might. The great cannot exist without the small, nor the small without the great; they blend together to their mutual advantage. Take the body, for example. The head is nothing without the feet, just as the feet are nothing without the head. The smallest parts of our body are necessary and valuable to the whole. All work together for the preservation of the whole body.

339

Our entire body, then, will be preserved in Christ Jesus, and each of us should be subject to his neighbor in accordance with the grace given to each. The stronger should care for the weak, and the weak should respect the stronger. The wealthy should give to the poor, and the poor man should thank God that he has sent him someone to supply his needs. The wise should manifest their wisdom not in words but in good deeds. The humble should not talk about their own humility but allow others to bear witness to it. Since, therefore, we have all this from him, we ought to thank him for it all. Glory to him for ever. Amen.

RESPONSORY

This wise man built his house upon rock.
No deceit was found in his mouth.

God chose him as his priest.

Behold a great priest, who in his days pleased God
and was found just.

God chose him as his priest.
See Matthew 7:24; 1 Peter 2:22; 1 Samuel 2:28

PRAYER

All-powerful and ever-living God,
we praise your power and glory
revealed to us in the lives of all your saints.
Give us joy on this feast of Saint Clement,
the priest and martyr
who bore witness with his blood to the love he proclaimed
and the gospel he preached.

We ask this through our Lord Jesus Christ, your Son,
who lives and reigns with you and the Holy Spirit,
one God, for ever and ever.

Our Father . . .

On the same day, November 23

COLUMBAN, ABBOT

Saint Columban was born in Ireland before the middle of the sixth century. He was well trained in the classics and theology. After entering the monastic life, he went to France and founded many monasteries which he ruled with strict discipline. After being forced into exile, he went to Italy and founded the monastery of Bobbio. He died in 615.

READING

A reading from an instruction by Saint Columban, abbot

Moses wrote in the law: "God made man in his image and likeness." Consider, I ask you, the dignity of these words. God is all-powerful. We cannot see or understand him, describe or assess him. Yet he fashioned man from clay and endowed him with the nobility of his own image. What has man in common with God? Or earth with spirit?— for "God is a spirit." It is a glorious privilege that God should grant man his eternal image and the likeness of his character. Man's likeness to God, if he preserves it, imparts high dignity.

True love is shown not merely "in word, but in deed and in truth." So we must turn back our image undefiled and holy to our God and Father, for he is holy; in the words of Scripture: "Be holy, for I am holy." We must restore his image with love, for he is love; in John's words: "God is love." We must restore it with loyalty and truth, for he is loyal and truthful. The image we depict must not be that of one who is unlike God; for one who is harsh and irascible and proud would display the image of a despot.

Let us not imprint on ourselves the image of a despot, but let Christ paint his image in us with his words: "My peace I give you, my peace I leave with you." But the knowledge that peace is good is of no benefit to us if we do not practice it. Men like nothing better than discussing and minding the business of others, passing comments at random and criticizing people behind their backs. So those who cannot say: "The Lord has given me a discerning tongue, that I may with a word support him who is weary" should keep silent, or if they do say anything it should promote peace.

Anyone who comes to me
and listens to my words and acts on them,
I will show you what he is like.

**He is like a man who while building his house
dug deeply and laid his foundation on rock.**

Happy is the man who fears the Lord.
Who is his equal?
Who can compare with him?

**He is like a man who while building his house
dug deeply and laid his foundation on rock.**
Luke 6:47, 48; Sirach 25:15

PRAYER

Lord,
you called Saint Columban to live the monastic life
and to preach the gospel with zeal.
May his prayers and example
help us to seek you above all things
and to work with all our hearts
for the spread of the faith.

Grant this through our Lord Jesus Christ, your Son,
who lives and reigns with you and the Holy Spirit,
one God, for ever and ever.

Our Father . . .

November 30

ANDREW, APOSTLE
Feast

Saint Andrew, born at Bethsaida, was a disciple of John the Baptist before he became a follower of Christ, to whom he also brought his brother Peter. With Philip he presented the Gentiles to Christ and, before the miracle in the desert, he pointed out to Christ the boy carrying the loaves and fishes. After Pentecost he preached the Gospel in many lands and was put to death by crucifixion.

READING

A reading from a homily on the Gospel of John by Saint John Chrysostom, bishop

After Andrew had stayed with Jesus and had learned much from him, he did not keep this treasure to himself, but hastened to share it with his brother [Peter]. Notice what Andrew said to him: "We have found the Messiah, that is to say, the Christ." Notice how his words reveal what he has learned in so short a time. They show the power of the master who has convinced them of this truth. Andrew's words reveal a soul waiting with the utmost longing for the coming of the Messiah, looking forward to his appearing from heaven, rejoicing when he does appear, and hastening to announce so great an event to others. To support one another in the things of the spirit is the true sign of good will between brothers, loving kinship and sincere affection.

Notice, too, how, even from the beginning, Peter is docile and receptive in spirit. He hastens to Jesus without delay. Saint John does not say that Peter believed immediately, but that "he [Andrew] brought him to Jesus." Andrew was to hand him over to Jesus, to learn everything for himself. There was also another disciple present, and he hastened with them for the same purpose.

When John the Baptist said: "This is the Lamb," and "he baptizes in the Spirit," he left the deeper understanding of these things to be received from Christ. All the more so would Andrew act in the same way, since he did not think himself able to give a complete explanation. He brought his brother to the very source of light, and Peter was so joyful and eager that he would not delay even for a moment.

RESPONSORY

As soon as Andrew heard the Lord preaching,
he left the nets which were his livelihood and way of life,

and followed the Lord who gives eternal life.

This is the man who endured suffering for the love of Christ and
   for his law.
And followed the Lord who gives eternal life.

PRAYER

Lord,
in your kindness hear our petitions.
You called Andrew the apostle
to preach the Gospel and guide your Church in faith.
May he always be our friend in your presence
to help us with his prayers.

We ask this through our Lord Jesus Christ, your Son,
who lives and reigns with you and the Holy Spirit,
one God, for ever and ever.

Our Father . . .

December 3

FRANCIS XAVIER, PRIEST
Memorial

Francis Xavier was born in Spain in 1506. While studying the liberal arts at Paris, he became a follower of Ignatius Loyola. In 1537 he was ordained at Rome and there devoted himself to works of charity. Francis went to the Orient in 1541 where for ten years he tirelessly proclaimed the Gospel in India and Japan, and through his preaching brought many to believe. He died in 1552 near the China coast on the island of Sancian.

READING

A reading from the letters to Saint Ignatius by Saint Francis Xavier, priest

We have visited the villages of the new converts who accepted the Christian religion a few years ago. The country is so utterly barren and poor. The native Christians have no priests. They know only that they *are* Christians. There is nobody to say Mass for them; nobody to teach them the Creed, the Our Father, the Hail Mary and the Commandments of God's Law.

I have not stopped since the day I arrived. I conscientiously made the rounds of the villages. I bathed in the sacred waters all the children who had not yet been baptized. This means that I have purified a very large number of children so young that, as the saying goes, they could not tell their right hand from their left. The older children would not let me say my Office or eat or sleep until I taught them one prayer or another. Then I began to understand: "The kingdom of heaven belongs to such as these."

I could not refuse so devout a request without failing in devotion myself. I taught them, first the confession of faith in the Father, the Son and the Holy Spirit; then the Apostles' Creed, the Our Father and Hail Mary. I noticed among them persons of great intelligence. If only someone could educate them in the Christian way of life, I have no doubt that they would make excellent Christians.

Many, many people hereabouts are not becoming Christians for one reason only: there is nobody to make them Christians.

I wish they [university students] would work as hard at converting these people as they do at their books, and so settle their account with God for their learning and the talents entrusted to them.

This thought would certainly stir most of them to meditate on spiritual realities, to listen actively to what God is saying to them. They would forget their own desires, their human affairs, and give themselves over entirely to God's will and his choice.

They would cry out with all their heart: "Lord, I am here! What do you want me to do?" Send me anywhere you like—even to India!

RESPONSORY

So great a harvest, and so few to gather it in;

pray to the Lord of the harvest,
beg him to send out laborers for his harvest.

You will receive power when the Holy Spirit comes upon you, and you will be my witness to the ends of the earth.

Pray to the Lord of the harvest,
beg him to send out laborers for his harvest.
Luke 10:2; Acts 1:8

PRAYER

God our Father,
by the preaching of Francis Xavier
you brought many nations to yourself.
Give his zeal for the faith to all who believe in you,
that your Church may rejoice in continued growth
throughout the world.

Grant this through our Lord Jesus Christ, your Son,
who lives and reigns with you and the Holy Spirit,
one God, for ever and ever.

Our Father . . .

December 4

JOHN DAMASCENE, PRIEST AND DOCTOR

John Damascene was born of a Christian family in Damascus in
the latter part of the seventh century. Learned in philosophy, he
became a monk in the monastery of Saint Sabbas near Jerusalem
and was then ordained a priest. He wrote many doctrinal works,
particularly against iconoclasts. He died in the middle of the
eighth century.

READING

A reading from The Statement of Faith by Saint John Damascene, priest

O Lord, by the blessing of the Holy Spirit, you prepared my
creation and my existence, not because man willed it or flesh
desired it, but by your ineffable grace. You sent me forth into
the light by adopting me as your son and you enrolled me
among the children of your holy and spotless Church.

You nursed me with the spiritual milk of your divine utterances.
You kept me alive with the solid food of the body of Jesus
Christ, your only-begotten Son and our God, and you let me
drink from the chalice of his life-giving blood, poured out to
save the whole world.

You loved us, O Lord, and gave up your only-begotten Son for
our redemption. And he undertook the task willingly and did
not shrink from it. Indeed, he applied himself to it as though
destined for sacrifice, like an innocent lamb. Although he was

347

God, he became man, and in his human will, became obedient to you, God his Father, "unto death, even death on a cross."

In this way you have humbled yourself, Christ my God, so that you might carry me, your stray sheep, on your shoulders. You let me graze in green pastures, refreshing me with the waters of orthodox teaching the hands of your shepherds. Now you have called me, Lord, by the hand of your bishop to minister to your people. I do not know why you have done so, for you alone know that. Lord, lighten the heavy burden of the sins through which I have seriously transgressed. Purify my mind and heart. Like a shining lamp, lead me along the straight path. When I open my mouth, tell me what I should say. By the fiery tongue of your Spirit make my own tongue ready. Stay with me always and keep me in your sight.

Lead me to pastures, Lord. Do not let my heart lean either to the right or to the left, but let your good Spirit guide me along the straight path. Whatever I do, let it be in accordance with your will, now until the end.

RESPONSORY

True teaching was in his mouth;
no evil was ever found on his lips.

He walked with me in goodness and in peace.

My hand will be a steady help to him,
my arm will give him strength.

He walked with me in goodness and in peace.
Malachi 2:6; Psalm 89:22

PRAYER

Lord,
may the prayers of Saint John Damascene help us,
and may the true faith he taught so well
always be our light and our strength.

We ask this through our Lord Jesus Christ, your Son,
who lives and reigns with you and the Holy Spirit,
one God, for ever and ever.

Our Father . . .

December 6

NICHOLAS, BISHOP

Nicholas was the bishop of Myra in Lycia (now part of Turkey).
He died in the middle of the fourth century and, particularly
since the tenth century, has been honored by the whole Church.

In today's reading Saint Augustine gives us a picture of what a
good bishop should be as well as a picture of our own duty of
teaching others by our own good example.

READING

A reading from a treatise on John by Saint Augustine, bishop

When the Lord asks Peter if he loves him, he is asking something he already knows. Yet he does not ask only once, but a
second and third time. Each time Peter's answer is the same:
"You know I love you." Each time the Lord gives him the same
command: "Tend my sheep."

"Do you love me? Tend my sheep." Surely this means: "If you
love me, your thoughts must focus on taking care of my sheep,
not taking care of yourself. You must tend them as mine, not as
yours; seek in them my glory, not yours. Seek my gain, not
yours. Otherwise you will find yourself among those who belong to the times of peril, "those who are guilty of self-love and
the other sins that go with that beginning of evils."

So the shepherds of Christ's flock must never indulge in self-
love; if they do they will be tending the sheep not as Christ's but
as their own.

The love of Christ ought to reach such a spiritual pitch in his shepherds that it overcomes the natural fear of death which makes us shrink from the thought of dying even though we desire to live with Christ. However distressful death may be, the strength of love ought to master the distress. I mean the love we have for Christ who, although he is our life, consented to suffer death for our sake.

RESPONSORY

The Lord glorified him in the sight of kings,
and gave him commandments for his people.

God revealed to him his glory.

The Lord chose him to be his servant,
a shepherd of his own Israel.

God revealed to him his glory.
Sirach 45:3; Psalm 78:70, 71

PRAYER

Father,
hear our prayers for mercy,
and by the help of Saint Nicholas
keep us safe from all danger,
and guide us on the way of salvation.

Grant this through our Lord Jesus Christ, your Son,
who lives and reigns with you and the Holy Spirit,
one God, for ever and ever.

Our Father . . .

December 7

AMBROSE, BISHOP AND DOCTOR

Memorial

Ambrose was born of a Roman family who lived in the provincial city of Trier about the year 340. He studied at Rome and served in the imperial government at Sirmium. In 374, while living in Milan, he was elected bishop of the city by popular acclaim and ordained on December 7. He devotedly carried out his duties and especially distinguished himself by his service to the poor and as an effective pastor and teacher of the faithful. He strenuously guarded the laws of the Church and defended orthodox teaching by writings and actions against heretics. He died on Holy Saturday, April 4, 397.

READING

A reading from a letter by Saint Ambrose, bishop

The Church of the Lord is built upon the rock of the apostles among so many dangers in the world; it therefore remains unmoved. The Church's foundation is unshakable and firm against assaults of the raging sea. Waves lash at the Church but do not shatter it. Although the elements of this world constantly beat upon the Church with crashing sounds, the Church possesses the safest harbor of salvation for all in distress.

There is a stream which flows down on God's saints like a torrent. There is also a rushing river giving joy to the heart that is at peace and makes for peace.

He who reads much and understands much, receives his fill. He who is full, refreshes others. So Scripture says: "If the clouds are full, they will pour rain upon the earth."

Therefore, let your words be rivers, clean and limpid, so that you may charm the ears of people. And by the grace of your words win them over to follow your leadership. Solomon says: "The weapons of the understanding are the lips of the wise";

and in another place he says: "Let your lips be bound with wisdom." That is, let the meaning of your words shine forth, let understanding blaze out. Let no word escape your lips in vain or be uttered without depth of meaning.

RESPONSORY

Proclaim the message, in season and out of season;

refute falsehood, correct error, call to obedience.

Who is able to boast as you can?
You have anointed kings as champions of righteousness.

Refute falsehood, correct error, call to obedience.
2 Timothy 4:2; Sirach 48:4, 8

PRAYER

Lord,
you made Saint Ambrose
an outstanding teacher of the Catholic faith
and gave him the courage of an apostle.
Raise up in your Church more leaders after your own heart,
to guide us with courage and wisdom.

We ask this through our Lord Jesus Christ, your Son,
who lives and reigns with you and the Holy Spirit,
one God, for ever and ever.

Our Father . . .

December 8

IMMACULATE CONCEPTION
Solemnity

Today the Church honors Mary as the only merely human being

who has never been touched by sin. As the mother of God, she shares with her Son in his works of re-creating this fallen world. Saint Anselm, in today's reading speaks beautifully about this great privilege of Mary.

READING

A reading from a sermon by Saint Anselm, bishop

Blessed Lady, sky and stars, earth and rivers, day and night—everything that is subject to the power or use of man—rejoice that through you they are in some sense restored to their lost beauty and are endowed with inexpressible new grace.

The universe rejoices with new and indefinable loveliness. Not only does it feel the unseen presence of God himself, its Creator, it sees him openly, working and making it holy. These great blessings spring from the blessed fruit of Mary's womb.

To Mary God gave his only-begotten Son, whom he loved as himself. The whole universe was created by God, and God was born of Mary. God created all things, and Mary gave birth to God. The God who made all things gave himself form through Mary, and thus he made his own creation. He who could create all things from nothing would not remake his ruined creation without Mary.

God, then, is the Father of the created world and Mary the mother of the re-created world. God is the Father by whom all things were given life, and Mary the mother through whom all things were given new life. Without God's Son, nothing could exist; without Mary's Son, nothing could be redeemed.

Proclaim with me the glory of the Lord,

for great is his merciful love for me.

From this day all generations will call me blessed.
For great is his merciful love for me.
Psalm 34:4; 86:13; Luke 1:48

PRAYER

Father,
you prepared the Virgin Mary
to be the worthy mother of your Son.
You let her share beforehand
in the salvation Christ would bring by his death,
and kept her sinless from the first moment of her conception.
Help us by her prayers
to live in your presence without sin.

We ask this through our Lord Jesus Christ, your Son,
who lives and reigns with you and the Holy Spirit,
one God, for ever and ever.

Our Father . . .

December 11

DAMASUS I, POPE

Damasus was born in Spain around the year 305. He was admitted to the Roman clergy and in 366, during a period of upheaval in the Church, was ordained bishop of Rome. He summoned synods to work against schismatics and heretics and widely promoted the cult of martyrs whose burial places he honored with sacred verse. He died in 384.

At this celebration of Saint Damasus, who loved and honored the holy martyrs, the reading from Saint Augustine will help us, too, to honor and love the martyrs.

A reading from a treatise against the heretic Faustus by Saint Augustine, bishop

We, the Christian community, assemble to celebrate the memory of the martyrs with ritual solemnity because we want to be inspired to follow their example, share in their merits, and be helped by their prayers. Yet we erect no altars to any of the martyrs, even in the martyrs' burial chapels themselves.

No bishop, when celebrating at an altar where these holy bodies rest, has ever said, "Peter, we make this offering to you," or "Paul, to you," or "Cyprian, to you." No, what is offered is offered always to God, who crowned the martyrs. We offer in the chapels where the bodies of those he crowned rest, so the memories that cling to those places will stir our emotions and encourage us to greater love both for the martyrs whom we can imitate and for God whose grace enables us to do so.

So we venerate the martyrs with the same veneration of love and fellowship that we give to the holy men of God still with us. We sense that the hearts of these latter are just as ready to suffer death for the sake of the Gospel, and yet we feel more devotion toward those who have already emerged victorious from the struggle. We honor those who are fighting on the battlefield of this life here below, but we honor more confidently those who have already achieved the victor's crown and live in heaven.

But the veneration strictly called "worship," that is, the special homage belonging only to the divinity, is something we give and teach others to give to God alone. The offering of a sacrifice belongs to worship in this sense (that is why those who sacrifice to idols are called idol-worshipers), and we neither make nor tell others to make any such offering to any martyr, any holy soul, or any angel.

Precious in the sight of the Lord is the death of his faithful ones;

**their very bones are dear to him,
not one of them shall be broken.**

The Lord clothes them with gladness.

**Their very bones are dear to him,
not one of them shall be broken.**
Psalm 116:15; 34:21; see Judith 10:3

PRAYER

Father,
as Saint Damasus loved and honored your martyrs,
so may we continue to celebrate their witness for Christ,
who lives and reigns with you and the Holy Spirit,
one God, for ever and ever.

Our Father . . .

December 12

JANE FRANCES DE CHANTAL, RELIGIOUS

Jane Frances was born in Dijon, France, in 1572. She was married to the nobleman de Chantal, and had six sons to whom she carefully taught the Christian faith. When her husband died, she wholeheartedly embraced the religious life under the guidance of Saint Francis de Sales and performed works of charity especially for the poor and sick. She founded the Visitation Order which she directed wisely until her death in 1641.

READING

A reading from the Memoirs by the secretary of Saint Jane Frances de Chantal

One day Saint Jane spoke the following eloquent words, which listeners took down exactly as spoken: "My dear daughters, many of our holy fathers in the faith, men who were pillars of the Church, did not die martyrs. Why do you think this was?" Each one present offered an answer; then their mother continued. "Well, I myself think it was because there is another martyrdom: the martyrdom of love. Here God keeps his servants and handmaids in this present life so that they may labor for him, and he makes of them both martyrs and confessors. I know," she added, "that the Daughters of the Visitation are meant to be martyrs of this kind and that, by the favor of God, some of them, more fortunate than others in that their desire has been granted, will actually suffer such a martyrdom."

One sister asked what form this martyrdom took. The saint answered: "Yield yourself fully to God, and you will find out! Divine love takes its sword to the hidden recesses of our inmost soul and divides us from ourselves. I know one person whom love cut off from all that was dearest to her, just as completely and effectively as if a tyrant's blade had severed spirit from body."

We realized that she was speaking of herself. When another sister asked how long the martyrdom would continue, the saint replied: "From the moment when we commit ourselves unreservedly to God, until our last breath. I am speaking, of course, of great-souled individuals who keep nothing back for themselves, but instead are faithful in love. Our Lord does not intend this martyrdom for those who are weak in love and perseverance. Such people he lets continue on their mediocre way, so that they will not be lost to him; he never does violence to our free will."

Finally, the saint was asked whether this martyrdom of love could be put on the same level as martyrdom of the body. She answered: "We should not worry about equality. I do think, however, that the martyrdom of love cannot be relegated to a second place, for 'love is as strong as death.' For the martyrs of love suffer infinitely more in remaining in this life so as to serve God, than if they died a thousand times over in testimony to their faith and love and fidelity."

There are many things that are true, honorable and just, many that are pure, worthy of love and deserving of praise: these you must do.

And the God of peace will be with you.

If there is anything virtuous, anything worthy of admiration, think of these things above all else.

And the God of peace will be with you.
See Philippians 4:8-9

PRAYER

Lord,
you chose Saint Jane Frances to serve you
both in marriage and in religious life.
By her prayers
help us to be faithful in our vocation
and always to be the light of the world.

We ask this through our Lord Jesus Christ, your Son,
who lives and reigns with you and the Holy Spirit,
one God, for ever and ever.

Our Father . . .

On the same day, December 12

OUR LADY OF GUADALUPE
Memorial

The shrine of Our Lady of Guadalupe, near Mexico City, is one of the most celebrated places of pilgrimages in North America. On December 9, 1531, the Blessed Virgin Mary appeared to an Indian convert, Juan Diego, and left with him a picture of herself impressed upon his cloak. Devotion to Mary under this title has continually increased, and today she is the Patroness of the Americas. Because of the close link between the Church in Mexico and the Church in the United States this feast was also celebrated in the United States and then placed on the calendar for the dioceses of the United States.

READING

A reading from a sermon by Saint Sophronius, bishop

"Hail, full of grace, the Lord is with you." What joy could surpass this, O Virgin Mother? What grace can excel that which God has granted to you alone?

Truly, "you are blessed among women." For you have changed Eve's curse into a blessing; and Adam, who hitherto lay under a curse, has been blessed because of you.

Truly, you are blessed among women. Through you the Father's blessing has shone forth on mankind, setting them free of their ancient curse.

Truly, you are blessed among women, because, though a woman by nature, you will become, in reality, God's mother. If he whom you are to bear is truly God made flesh, then rightly do we call you God's mother. For you have truly given birth to God.

RESPONSORY

How blessed are you, Virgin Mary,
for you carried within you the Lord, the Creator of the world.
Mother of your Maker, you remain a virgin for ever.

Hail Mary, full of grace, the Lord is with you.
Mother of your Maker, you remain a virgin for ever.

God of power and mercy,
you blessed the Americas at Tepeyac
with the presence of the Virgin Mary at Guadalupe.
May her prayers help all men and women
to accept each other as brothers and sisters.
Through your justice present in our hearts
may your peace reign in the world.

We ask this through our Lord Jesus Christ, your Son,
who lives and reigns with you and the Holy Spirit,
one God, for ever and ever.

Our Father . . .

December 13

LUCY, VIRGIN AND MARTYR
Memorial

Lucy died at Syracuse, probably during the persecution of
Diocletian. From antiquity her cult spread throughout the
Church, and her name was therefore introduced into the Roman
Canon.

READING

A reading from the book On Virginity by Saint Ambrose, bishop

You are one of God's people, of God's family, a virgin among
virgins; you light up your grace of body with your splendor of
soul. The Word of God moves swiftly; he is not won by the
lukewarm, nor held fast by the negligent. Let your soul be attentive to his word; follow carefully the path God tells you to take,
for he is swift in his passing.

How do we hold him fast? Not by restraining chains or knotted ropes but by bonds of love, by spiritual reins, by the longing of the soul.

Whoever seeks Christ in this way, finds him. Whoever seeks Christ in this way, whoever prays to Christ in this way, is not abandoned by him; on the contrary, Christ comes again and again to visit such a person, for he is with us until the end of the world.

RESPONSORY

The grace of the Lord gave her strength in the battle,
and she was glorified before God and man.
In the presence of the prince she spoke with wisdom,
and therefore the Lord of heaven and earth has loved her.

She is the virgin
who prepared a joyful home for God in her heart.
And therefore the Lord of heaven and earth has loved her.

PRAYER

Lord,
give us courage through the prayers of Saint Lucy.
As we celebrate her entrance into eternal glory,
we ask to share her happiness in the life to come.

Grant this through our Lord Jesus Christ, your Son,
who lives and reigns with you and the Holy Spirit,
one God, for ever and ever.

Our Father . . .

December 14

JOHN OF THE CROSS, PRIEST AND DOCTOR
Memorial

John of the Cross was born at Fontiveros in Spain around 1542. After a number of years as a Carmelite, he was persuaded by Saint Teresa of Avila in 1568 to lead a reform movement among the brothers which brought a new energy to the Carmelite Order. Renowned for his wisdom and sanctity, he died at Ubeda in 1591. His spiritual writings remain a fitting testimony to his life.

READING

A reading from a spiritual Canticle by Saint John of the Cross, priest

Though holy doctors have uncovered many mysteries and wonders, and devout souls have understood them in this earthly condition of ours, yet the greater part still remains to be unfolded by them, and even to be understood by them.

We must then dig deeply in Christ. He is like a rich mine with many pockets containing treasures: however deep we dig we will never find their end or their limit. Indeed, in every pocket new seams of fresh riches are discovered on all sides.

For this reason the apostle Paul said of Christ: "In him are hidden all the treasures of the wisdom and knowledge of God." The soul cannot enter into these treasures, nor attain them, unless it first crosses into and enters the thicket of suffering, enduring interior and exterior labors, and unless it first receives from God very many blessings in the intellect and in the senses, and has undergone long spiritual training.

The gate that gives entry into these riches of his wisdom is the cross; because it is a narrow gate, while many seek the joys that can be gained through it, it is given to few to desire to pass through it.

362

No eye can see, no ear can hear, no heart can imagine
the marvels that God has prepared for those who love him.

Yet God has revealed them to us through his Spirit.
The marvels that God has prepared for those who love him.
1 Corinthians 2:9-10

PRAYER

Father,
you endowed John of the Cross with a spirit of self-denial
and a love of the cross.
By following his example,
may we come to the eternal vision of your glory.

We ask this through our Lord Jesus Christ, your Son,
who lives and reigns with you and the Holy Spirit,
one God, for ever and ever.

Our Father . . .

December 21

PETER CANISIUS, PRIEST AND DOCTOR
Commemoration

Peter Canisius was born in Nijmegen, Holland, in 1521. He
studied at Cologne, entered the Society of Jesus, and was ordained a priest in 1546. Sent to Germany, he worked strenuously for many years by his writings and teachings to safeguard
and confirm the Catholic faith. Of his numerous books, the
Catechism is most renowned. Saint Peter died at Fribourg,
Switzerland, in 1597.

A reading from the writings by Saint Peter Canisius, priest

Before he set out for Germany—he is rightly called the second apostle of that country—Saint Peter Canisius received the apostolic blessing, and underwent a profound spiritual experience. He describes it in these words.

"It was as if you opened to me the heart in your most sacred body: I seemed to see it directly before my eyes. You told me to drink from this fountain, inviting me, that is, to draw the waters of my salvation from your wellsprings, my Savior. I was most eager that streams of faith, hope and love should flow into me from that source. I was thirsting for poverty, chastity, obedience. I asked to be made wholly clean by you, to be clothed by you, to be made resplendent by you.

"So, after daring to approach your most loving heart and to plunge my thirst in it, I received a promise from you of a garment made of three parts: these were to cover my soul in its nakedness, and to belong especially to my religious profession. They were peace, love and perseverance. Protected by this garment of salvation, I was confident that I would lack nothing but all would succeed and give you glory."

When a teacher of the law becomes a disciple of the kingdom of
    heaven,
he is like the head of a household
who is able to take from his storeroom treasures new and old.

Wisdom makes its home in a discerning heart,
and it can even teach those who are foolish.
He is like the head of a household
who is able to take from his storeroom treasures new and old.
Matthew 13:52; see Proverbs 14:33

Lord,
you gave Saint Peter Canisius
wisdom and courage to defend the Catholic faith.
By the help of his prayers
may all who seek the truth rejoice in finding you
and may all who believe in you
be loyal in professing their faith.

Grant this through our Lord Jesus Christ, your Son,
who lives and reigns with you and the Holy Spirit,
one God, for ever and ever.

Our Father . . .

December 23

JOHN OF KANTY, PRIEST
Commemoration

John was born at Kanty in the diocese of Krakow in 1390. After
his ordination to the priesthood, he taught for many years at the
academy in Krakow and then became pastor of the parish at
Olkusz. He distinguished himself as an orthodox teacher of the
faith, and by his piety and love of neighbor gave Christian
example to his colleagues and students. He died in 1473.

READING

A reading from a letter by Pope Clement XIII

Saint John of Kanty deserves a high place among the great saints
and scholars who practice what they preach and defend the true
faith against those who attack it. When heresy and schism were
gaining ground in neighboring territories, his teaching at the
University of Krakow was untainted by any error. At the pulpit
he fought to raise the standard of holiness among the faithful.

His preaching was reinforced by his humility, his chastity, his compassion, his bodily penance and the other qualities of a dedicated priest and apostle.

With the sense of worship that he brought to his teaching of the sacred sciences he combined humility. He never put himself above another, but treated himself as of no account, even though he was acknowledged by all as their master. So far was he from pretenses that he even wished to be an object of contempt in the eyes of all who underestimated his worth. He could take their insults and cutting remarks in stride.

With his humility went a rare and childlike simplicity. The thoughts of his heart were revealed in his words and actions. If he suspected that someone had taken offense at speaking the truth, before going to the altar he would ask forgiveness for what was not so much his own sin as the other person's misunderstanding. Every day after his round of duties he would go straight from the lecture room to church. There he would spend long hours in contemplation and prayer before the hidden Christ of the eucharist. The God in his heart and the God on his lips were one and the same God.

RESPONSORY

Share your bread with the hungry,
and take the poor and homeless into your own house.

**Then your light will break forth like the dawn,
and your holiness will go before you.**

When you see a man who is naked, clothe him,
and do not scorn your brother.

**Then your light will break forth like the dawn,
and your holiness will go before you.**
Isaiah 58:7-8

Almighty Father,
through the example of John of Kanty
may we grow in the wisdom of the saints.
As we show understanding and kindness to others,
may we receive your forgiveness.

We ask this through our Lord Jesus Christ, your Son,
who lives and reigns with you and the Holy Spirit,
one God, for ever and ever.

Our Father . . .

December 25

CHRISTMAS
Solemnity

Today's solemnity has been a celebration of the birth of Christ since about 330, beginning in Rome. No one knows the date of Christ's birth, but this day was chosen by the Church to replace a pagan holiday celebrating the re-birth of the sun-god. Christians see in the Lord's birth the coming into the world of Christ, the true light of the World.

READING

A reading from a sermon by Saint Leo the Great, pope

Dearly beloved, today our Savior is born; let us rejoice. Sadness should have no place on the birthday of life. The fear of death has been swallowed up; life brings us joy with the promise of eternal happiness.

No one is shut out from this joy; all share the same reason for rejoicing. Our Lord, victor over sin and death, finding no man free from sin, came to free us all.

In the fullness of time, chosen in the unfathomable depths of God's wisdom, the Son of God took for himself our common humanity in order to reconcile it with its creator. He came to overthrow the devil, the origin of death, in that very nature by which he had overthrown mankind.

Let us throw off our old nature and all its ways and, as we have come to birth in Christ, let us renounce the works of the flesh.

Christian, remember your dignity, and now that you share in God's own nature, do not return by sin to your former base condition. Bear in mind who is your head and of whose body you are a member. Do not forget that you have been rescued from the power of darkness and brought into the light of God's kingdom.

Through the sacrament of baptism you have become a temple of the Holy Spirit. Do not drive away so great a guest by evil conduct and become again a slave to the devil, for your liberty was bought by the blood of Christ.

RESPONSORY

Today true peace came down to us from heaven.

Today the whole earth was filled with heaven's sweetness.

Today a new day dawns,
the day of our redemption, prepared by God from ages past,
the beginning of our never ending gladness.

Today the whole earth was filled with heaven's sweetness.

PRAYER

God of love, Father of all,
the darkness that covered the earth
has given way to the bright dawn of your Word
made flesh.

Make us a people of this light.
Make us faithful to your Word,
that we may bring your life to the waiting world.

Grant this through Christ our Lord.

Our Father . . .

December 26

STEPHEN, FIRST MARTYR
Feast

Stephen, we are told, in the Acts of the Apostles, "was a man
filled with grace and power, who worked great wonders and
signs among the people." He spoke out fearlessly against
Christ's enemies, who had him stoned to death. Saul, who later
was converted and became Paul, was at the scene, and "con-
curred in the act of killing."

READING

A reading from a sermon by Saint Fulgentius of Ruspe, bishop

Yesterday we celebrated the birth in time of our eternal King.
Today we celebrate the triumphant suffering of his soldier. Yesterday our king, clothed in his robe of flesh, left his place in the
virgin's womb and graciously visited the world. Today his soldier leaves the tabernacle of his body and goes triumphantly to
heaven.

Our king, despite his exalted majesty, came in humility for our
sake; yet he did not come empty-handed. He gave of his
bounty, yet without any loss to himself. In a marvelous way he
changed into wealth the poverty of his faithful followers while
remaining in full possession of his own inexhaustible riches.

And so the love that brought Christ from heaven to earth raised Stephen from earth to heaven; shown first in the king, it later shone forth in his soldier. His love of God kept him from yielding to the ferocious mob; his love for his neighbor made him pray for those who were stoning him. Love inspired him to reprove those who erred, to make them amend; love led him to pray for those who stoned him, to save them from punishment.

Love, indeed, is the source of all good things; it is an impregnable defense, and the way that leads to heaven. He who walks in love can neither go astray nor be afraid: love guides him, protects him, and brings him to his journey's end.

My brothers, Christ made love the stairway that would enable all Christians to climb to heaven. Hold fast to it, therefore, in all sincerity, give one another practical proof of it, and by your progress in it, make your ascent together.

RESPONSORY

Yesterday the Lord was born on earth that Stephen might be
    born in heaven;

the Lord entered into our world that Stephen might enter into
    heaven.

Yesterday our King, clothed in our flesh,
came forth from the virgin's womb to dwell among us.

The Lord entered into our world that Stephen might enter into
    heaven.

PRAYER

Lord,
today we celebrate the entrance of Saint Stephen
into eternal glory.
He died praying for those who killed him.
Help us to imitate his goodness
and to love our enemies.

We ask this through our Lord Jesus Christ, your Son,
who lives and reigns with you and the Holy Spirit,
one God, for ever and ever.

Our Father . . .

December 27

JOHN, APOSTLE AND EVANGELIST
Feast

John became a disciple of Jesus and became one of the
evangelists, as well as a writer of letters to the Christians of his
time. Our reading for today quotes from one of these letters and
gives a good idea of John's love and trust in the Lord.

READING

A reading from the first letter of the apostle John

Here then, is the message
we have heard from [Jesus Christ]
and announce to you:
that God is light;
in him there is no darkness.
If we say, "We have fellowship with him,"
while continuing to walk in darkness,
we are liars and do not act in truth.
But if we walk in light,
as he is in the light,
we have fellowship with one another,
and the blood of his Son Jesus cleanses us from all sin.

If we say, "We are free of the guilt of sin,"
we deceive ourselves; the truth is not to be found in us.
But if we acknowledge our sins,
he who is just can be trusted

to forgive our sins
and cleanse us from every wrong.
If we say, "We have never sinned,"
we make him a liar
and his word finds no place in us.
My little ones,
I am writing this to keep you from sin.
But if anyone should sin,
we have, in the presence of the Father,
Jesus Christ, an intercessor who is just.
He is an offering for our sins,
and not for our sins only,
but for those of the whole world.

The way we can be sure of our knowledge of him
is to keep his commandments.

RESPONSORY

We proclaim to you the eternal life
which was with the Father and has been revealed to us.
We write of this that you may rejoice,

and that your joy may be full.

These things have been written,
that you may believe that Jesus is the Christ, the Son of God,
and believing you may have life in his name.

And that your joy may be full.
1 John 1:2, 4; John 20:31

PRAYER

God our Father,
you have revealed the mysteries of your Word
through John the apostle.
By prayer and reflection
may we come to understand the wisdom he taught.

Grant this through our Lord Jesus Christ, your Son,
who lives and reigns with you and the Holy Spirit,
one God, for ever and ever.

Our Father . . .

December 28

HOLY INNOCENTS, MARTYRS

Feast

The gospel of Matthew tells of the slaughter of the innocent
children by King Herod in the hope that he might have been
able to destroy the Christ Child among their number.

READING

A reading from a sermon by Saint Quodvultdeus, bishop

A tiny child is born, who is a great king. Wise men are led to him
from afar. They come to adore one who lies in a manger and yet
reigns in heaven and on earth. When they tell of one who is
born a king, Herod is disturbed. To save his kingdom he re-
solves to kill him, though if he would have faith in the child, he
himself would reign in peace in this life and for ever in the life to
come.

Why are you afraid, Herod, when you hear of the birth of a
king? He does not come to drive you out, but to conquer the
devil. But because you do not understand this you are disturbed
and in a rage. To destroy one child whom you seek, you show
your cruelty in the death of so many children.

You are not restrained by the love of weeping mothers or fathers
mourning the deaths of their sons, nor by the cries and sobs of
the children. You destroy those who are tiny in body because
fear is destroying your heart. You imagine that if you accom-

plish your desire you can prolong your own life, though you are seeking to kill Life himself.

The children die for Christ, though they do not know it. The parents mourn for the death of martyrs. The [Christ] child makes of those as yet unable to speak fit witnesses to himself. But you, Herod, do not know this and are disturbed and furious. While you vent your fury against the child, you are already paying him homage, and do not know it.

To what merits of their own do the children owe this kind of victory? They cannot speak, yet they bear witness to Christ. They cannot use their limbs to engage in battle, yet already they bear off the palm of victory.

RESPONSORY

They worshiped him who lives for ever and ever;

they laid their crowns before the throne of the Lord their God.

They fell on their faces before his throne,
and gave praise to him who lives for ever and ever.

They laid their crowns before the throne of the Lord their God.
Revelation 5:14; 4:10; 7:11

PRAYER

Father,
the Holy Innocents offered you praise
by the death they suffered for Christ.
May our lives bear witness
to the faith we profess with our lips.

We ask this through our Lord Jesus Christ, your Son,
who lives and reigns with you and the Holy Spirit,
one God, for ever and ever.

Our Father . . .

December 29

THOMAS BECKET, BISHOP AND MARTYR
Commemoration

Thomas Becket was born in London in 1118. A cleric of the diocese of Canterbury, he first became chancellor to the king and then in 1162 was chosen bishop. His tireless defense of the rights of the Church against Henry II prompted the king to exile Becket to France for six years. After returning to his homeland, he endured many trials and in 1170 was murdered by agents of the king.

READING

A reading from a letter by Saint Thomas Becket, bishop

For our sake [Christ] offered himself to the Father upon the altar of the cross. He now looks down from heaven on our actions and secret thoughts, and one day he will give each of us the reward his deeds deserve.

It must therefore be our endeavor to destroy the reign of sin and death, and by nurturing faith and uprightness of life, to build up the Church of Christ into a holy temple of the Lord.

The harvest is good and one reaper or even several would not suffice to gather all of it into the granary of the Lord. Yet the Roman Church remains the head of all the churches and the source of Catholic teaching. Of this there can be no doubt. Everyone knows that the keys of the kingdom of heaven were given to Peter. Upon his faith and teaching the whole fabric of the Church will continue to be built until we all reach full maturity in Christ and attain to unity in faith and knowledge of the Son of God.

Of course many are needed to plant and many to water now that the faith has spread so far and the population become so great. Nevertheless, no matter who plants or waters, God gives no harvest unless what he plants is the faith of Peter, and unless he himself assents to Peter's teaching. All important questions that arise among God's people are referred to the judgment of Peter in the person of the Roman Pontiff. Under him the ministers of Mother Church exercise the powers committed to them, each in his own sphere of responsibility.

Remember then how our fathers worked out their salvation; remember the sufferings through which the Church has grown, and the storms the ship of Peter has weathered because it has Christ on board. Remember how the crown was attained by those whose sufferings gave new radiance to their faith. The whole company of saints bears witness to the unfailing truth that without real effort no one wins the crown.

RESPONSORY

The Lord crowned you with holiness;

he clothed you in glory.
God, the Holy One of Israel, dwells in you.

You have fought the good fight,
you have run the race to the finish;
now a crown of holiness awaits you.

He clothed you in glory.
God, the Holy One of Israel, dwells in you.

PRAYER

Almighty God,
you granted the martyr Thomas
the grace to give his life for the cause of justice.
By his prayers make us willing to renounce for Christ
our life in this world
so that we may find it in heaven.

We ask this through our Lord Jesus Christ, your Son,

who lives and reigns with you and the Holy Spirit,
one God, for ever and ever.

Our Father . . .

December 31

SYLVESTER I, POPE
Commemoration

Sylvester was ordained bishop of Rome in 314. He ruled the
Church during the reign of Constantine the Great when heresy
and schism had provoked great discord. He died in 335 and is
buried in the cemetery of Priscilla on the Salarian Way.

The following reading shows that the Church today is animated
by the same spirit of bringing salvation to all people as was the
Church of Saint Sylvester's day.

READING

A reading from the decree on the missionary activity of the
Church of the Second Vatican Council

The Lord Jesus, from the very beginning, "called to himself
those whom he wanted; he arranged for twelve to be with him,
and to be sent by him to preach." Thus the apostles were the
first beginnings of the new Israel, and at the same time the
origin of the sacred hierarchy.

Afterward, when he had once for all, by his death and resurrection, brought to completion in his own person the mysteries of
our salvation and of the renewal of all things, the Lord, having
received all power in heaven and on earth, before he was taken
up into heaven, founded his Church as the sacrament of salvation, and sent the apostles into the whole world, just as he
himself had been sent to the Father. He commanded them: "Go

then and teach all nations, baptizing them in the name of the
Father and of the Son and of the Holy Spirit, teaching them to
observe all things that I have commanded you."

From then onward there is a duty laid on the Church of spreading the faith and the salvation that come from Christ. This duty
is in virtue of the express command inherited from the apostles
by the college of bishops, assisted by the priests, in communion
with Peter's successor, the chief shepherd of the Church. It is in
virtue also of the life that Christ causes to flow into his members.

The mission of the Church is therefore fullfilled by that activity
by which the Church in obedience to Christ's command and
under the impulse of the grace and love of the Holy Spirit,
becomes fully and actively present to all men and to all peoples.

RESPONSORY

Let the peace of Christ reign in your hearts;
as members of one body you have been called to that peace;
be thankful.

All of you are one in Christ Jesus.

Sing to the Lord a new song,
let the assembly of the faithful sing his praise.

All of you are one in Christ Jesus.
Colossians 3:15; Galatians 3:28; Psalm 149:1

PRAYER

Lord,
help and sustain your people
by the prayers of Pope Sylvester.
Guide us always in this present life
and bring us to the joy that never ends.

We ask this through our Lord Jesus Christ, your Son,

378

who lives and reigns with you and the Holy Spirit,
one God, for ever and ever.

Our Father . . .

INDEX OF CELEBRATIONS